GW01367848

Truth Recovery and Justice after Conflict

This book considers the problem of managing the unfinished business of a violent past in societies moving out of political violence. Truth Commissions are increasingly used to unearth the acts committed by the various protagonists and to acknowledge the suffering of their victims. This book uniquely focuses on the conditions which predispose – or prevent – embarkation on a truth recovery process, and the rationale for that process. There is, it argues, no magic moment of 'readiness' for truth recovery: the conditions are constructed by political 'willingness' rather than spontaneously occurring.

Much of the literature on Northern Ireland's past provides historical analyses of the conflict – Republican, state or Loyalist violence – and is often (implicitly or explicitly) associated with one or other of the partisans in the conflict. This book focuses on the dynamic between the protagonists and how each of their positions, in this case on truth recovery, combine to produce the overall political status quo in Northern Ireland. As the society struggles to move forward, Marie Breen Smyth considers whether the entrenched positions of some, and the failure to understand the views of others, can be shifted by a societal revisiting and re-evaluation of the past.

Truth Recovery and Justice after Conflict arises from a decade's writing and research with both victims and those close to the armed groups in Northern Ireland. It is also informed by the author's work in South Africa, West Africa, Israel and the Occupied Palestinian Territories. It will be of great interest to students and researchers in politics, international relations, peace studies and law.

Marie Breen Smyth is Reader in the Department of International Politics, University of Wales, Aberystwyth; and Director of the Centre for the Study of Radicalisation and Contemporary Political Violence. She has edited five volumes and written a number of books, including *Northern Ireland's Troubles: The Human Costs* (with Mike Morrissey).

Routledge Studies in Peace and Conflict Resolution
Series Editors: Tom Woodhouse and Oliver Ramsbotham
University of Bradford

Peace and Security in the Postmodern World
The OSCE and conflict resolution
Dennis J.D. Sandole

Truth Recovery and Justice after Conflict
Managing violent pasts
Marie Breen Smyth

Peace and International Relations
A new agenda
Oliver Richmond

Memory and Conflict Resolution
Rhys Kelly

Truth Recovery and Justice after Conflict

Managing violent pasts

Marie Breen Smyth

Routledge
Taylor & Francis Group

LONDON AND NEW YORK

First published 2007
by Routledge
2 Park Square, Milton Park, Abingdon, Oxon OX14 4RN

Simultaneously published in the USA and Canada
by Routledge
270 Madison Ave, New York, NY 10016

*Routledge is an imprint of the Taylor & Francis Group,
an informa business*

© 2007 Marie Breen Smyth

Typeset in Times New Roman by
Newgen Imaging Systems (P) Ltd, Chennai, India
Printed and bound in Great Britain by
the MPG Books Group

All rights reserved. No part of this book may be reprinted
or reproduced or utilised in any form or by any electronic,
mechanical, or other means, now known or hereafter
invented, including photocopying and recording, or in any
information storage or retrieval system, without permission in
writing from the publishers.

British Library Cataloguing in Publication Data
A catalogue record for this book is available
from the British Library

Library of Congress Cataloging in Publication Data
Smyth, Marie, 1953–
    Truth recovery and justice after conflict : managing violent pasts /
    Marie Breen Smyth.
        p. cm. – (Routledge studies in peace and conflict resolution)
    Includes bibliographical references.
        1. Truth commissions. 2. Truth commissions – Northern Ireland.
    3. Peace-building. 4. Peace-building – Northern Ireland. I. Title.
JC580.S59 2007
303.6'9–dc22   2007014221

ISBN: 978–0–415–43398–3 (hbk)
ISBN: 978–0–203–93422–7 (ebk)

In memory of my beloved husband
Alan Johnston Breen
16 February 1948–7 July 2005

Contents

Acknowledgements viii
List of abbreviations ix

1 Introduction 1
2 The function of truth recovery in transitional societies 6
3 Truth and cultures of organised and normalised lying 22
4 Shame, honour and cultures of violence and peace 40
5 Victims, healing, forgiveness and truth 67
6 Framing the grievances of the past: Northern Ireland since the Belfast Agreement 91
7 Readiness for truth: the Northern Ireland Affairs Committee Inquiry 108
8 Is Northern Ireland ready for truth? 143
9 Conclusions 174

Notes 182
Bibliography 192
Index 203

Acknowledgements

Phillip Appleman, 'Waiting for the Fire' from New and Selected Poems 1956–1996. Copyright © 1997 by Phillip Appleman. Reprinted with the permission of the University of Arkansas Press, www.uapress.com. I also wish to acknowledge the help of my colleagues in Healing Through Remembering who provided me with invaluable opportunities to learn from them about truth recovery and its various dimensions, and without them this book would not have been written. Thanks also to my colleagues in the University of Wales, Aberystwyth, especially Professor Andrew Linklater who patiently read and commented on earlier drafts, to Professor Jenny Edkins for pointing me towards Levi, to Elaine Lowe who prepared the final manuscript and Dr Jeroen Gunning for collegial empathy. Patricia Campbell in Northern Ireland undertook some of the analysis and Mike Morrissey contributed his comments and usual incisive insights. In Pontrhydfendigaid, thanks to Sue, Alan and Beth Davies for their friendship and taking me for regular walks. The help and support of my parents, brothers, parents-in-law and sister and brother-in-law and my neighbours in Clady, my friends in Ireland, Wales, United States and South Africa was essential in these last years of illness and sudden widowhood. I owe special thanks to Gwyn Evans for his support, to Margaret Ames for her friendship and especially to Ken Sparks who made all the difference.

Abbreviations

ABCNY	Association of the Bar of the City of New York
APLA	Azanian People's Liberation Army, South Africa
AZAPO	Azanian People's Organisation, South Africa
CEH	Comisión de Esclarectimiento Histórico, the Guatemalan Truth Commission
CFNI	Community Foundation for Northern Ireland
CLMC	Combined Loyalist Military Command, Northern Ireland
Coiste na n-Iarchimi	A Republican ex-prisoners organisation in Northern Ireland (Ex-Prisoners' Committee)
DUP	Democratic Unionist Party
ECHR	European Court of Human Rights
EPIC	Ex-Prisoners' Interpretative Centre, UVF-aligned ex-prisoners' organisation in Northern Ireland
FACT	Families Achieving Change Together (victims group in Northern Ireland)
FAIR	Families Acting for Innocent Relatives (victims group based in Unionist community)
FEAR	Victims' group in the Unionist community in Northern Ireland
Firinne	(Truth) group of victims of state violence in Northern Ireland
HET	Historic Enquiries Team, police team dedicated to examining unresolved killings in Northern Ireland
HTR	Healing Through Remembering, a voluntary group concerned with managing Northern Ireland's past
INLA	Irish National Liberation Army
IRA	Irish Republican Army
LTTE	Liberation Tigers of Tamil Ealam
MK	Umkhonto We Sizwe (armed wing of the African National Congress, South Africa)
NIAC	Northern Ireland Affairs Committee, Westminster
NIHE	Northern Ireland Housing Executive, public housing authority
NIHRC	Northern Ireland Human Rights Commission
NILT	Northern Ireland Life and Times (a continuous social attitudes survey of Northern Ireland)

NIO	Northern Ireland Office
NIVA	Northern Ireland Veterans' Association (for ex-British soldiers)
RFJ	Relatives for Justice – victims' group in Northern Ireland's Nationalist community
RTLM	Radio Télévision Libre des Mille Collines, radio station in Rwanda
SADF	South African Defence Force
SAVER/NAVER	Victims group based in North and South Armagh and Mid-Ulster, Northern Ireland
SDLP	Social Democratic and Labour Party, Northern Ireland
TRC	Truth and Reconciliation Commission, South Africa
UDA	Ulster Defence Association (Loyalist paramilitary group)
UDR	Ulster Defence Regiment (now defunct regiment of the British army, amalgamated in 1992 into the Royal Irish Rangers to form the Royal Irish Regiment)
UFF	Ulster Freedom Fighters, a sub-grouping within the UDA
UNHRC	United Nations Human Rights Committee
UUP	Ulster Unionist Party
UVF	Ulster Volunteer Force, Loyalist paramilitary group
VOICE	West Tyrone-based victims group in Northern Ireland
WAVE	A cross-community victims' group in Northern Ireland

1 Introduction

> If we ever thought of the wreckage
> of our unnatural acts,
> we would never sleep again
> without dreaming a rain of fire:
> somewhere God is bargaining for Sodom,
> a few good men could save the city; but
> in that dirty corner of the mind
> we call the soul
> the only wash that purifies is tears,
> and after all our body counts,
> our rape, our mutilations,
> nobody here is crying; people who would weep
> at the death of a dog
> stroll these unburned streets dry-eyed.
> But forgetfulness will never walk
> with innocence; we save our faces
> at the risk of our lives, needing
> the wisdom of our losses, the gift of despair,
> or we could kill again.
>
> Phillip Appleman[1]

Much of the literature on transitional justice, whether located within the field of law or international relations, adopts a legal, retributive justice focus, and is often generated by lawyers. Increasingly, those interested in conflict resolution and peace-building, victimology and contemporary history, from outside the legal profession have become interested in the challenges and paradoxes presented by the management of the violent past of newly pacified regions. This book is an attempt to move beyond what is posited as that rather narrow legalistic framework, and to consider transitional justice in general and truth recovery in particular as contextualised not only in the world of victims and perpetrators, but also in the world of politicians, civil society actors, silent majorities and interested third parties. The project of this book is to move not only beyond rather thin conceptualisations of truth and justice in times of transition, and the perception of this as primarily or simply the concern of victims, perpetrators, their legal representatives and truth commissions towards a re-conceptualisation of truth and justice, but also beyond perceiving even victimhood and responsibility as matters not merely of elite agreement and negotiation, but of popular contestation and interest.

Even within the legal framework, an exclusive focus on retributive forms of justice with its emphasis on punitive outcomes, at the expense of more restorative forms which emphasise the establishment or restoration of relationship between the victim and victimiser is problematic. Arguably, the retributive form relies on the knowledge and expertise of elite legal authorities who define and determine the meanings, processes and outcomes of quests for truth and justice in the transition out of political violence. Similarly, human rights discourses, not only seem unable to establish in international and local law victims' formal rights to justice, and punishment of perpetrators or reparation, but also tend to favour punitive rather than restorative judgements for perpetrators, especially in the international domain. Together these attributes create conditions in which (re)negotiation of concepts such as truth and justice is restricted to a qualified (rather than an elite) community of victims, perpetrators, their proxies and legal representatives, leaving civil society, the media and other societal institutions in the role of bystanders and commentators, as if they did not have a substantial stake in such (re)negotiation.

This book is a preliminary attempt to imagine how truth and responsibility might be re-imagined in broader ways, within contexts where such redefinition is crucial to the creation and sustenance of a more secure and connected sense of societal solidarity, which supersedes, at least to some extent, the societal fractures of the past. These are societies in which citizens (and state agents) have killed and harmed each other systematically across fault-lines or ethnic, racial or national difference. The book is not only a scholarly work; it arises out of the attempt to apply such an imagination to the daily life of the author in a personal life conducted in Northern Ireland and South Africa.

The book leaves largely uninterrogated the idea of a 'peace process' which occurs periodically throughout. It is possible to see peace processes as entirely constructed by the imposition of certain frameworks of meaning on an armed conflict by powerful external and internal political actors. This imposition results in certain political events and developments being interpreted within the framework of a peace process and emphasising events which fit easily into such a frame, whilst sidelining events which provide evidence of moves away from peace. The asserted existence of a peace process is perhaps more evidence of active engagement of internal and external actors and the exertion of political will to find resolution and settlement, rather than any diminution of levels of hostility. Certainly, efforts will be directed at achieving cessations or at least reductions in levels of violence, but the existence or even resurgence of violence does not necessarily negate a peace process. Therefore it is argued that a peace process is primarily the framework of meaning applied to the situation, rather than any material alteration or empirical summary of the political conditions within the conflict itself. That peace processes fail may well be as much a product of the waning strategic and other interests of powerful third parties, or their distraction from the management of the peace process by other more pressing political demands, as it is a product of the tractability or otherwise of the conflicts themselves.

This is, however, a subject for another day. In this book, the term peace process is used largely uncritically. Here the focus is more narrowly on certain aspects of those political conditions, specifically, truth, responsibility, victims, shame and prospects for building new societal solidarities.

The book arises out of writing and research with both victims and those close to the armed groups in Northern Ireland, and the author's participation there in Healing Through Remembering, a voluntary initiative concerned with formulating proposals on the management of Northern Ireland's past. The book is also informed by the author's work in South Africa, West Africa and Israel and the Occupied Palestinian Territories. Much of the literature on truth recovery is composed of edited works concerned with international comparative evaluations of the functions and outcomes of truth commissions and tribunals, or detailed consideration of particular processes, most popularly the South African Truth and Reconciliation Commission.

Since 1973, more than twenty truth commissions have been established in post-conflict societies, the majority of which have been comprehensive and state-sponsored. Other methods of managing the past, such as memorialisation, documentation, storytelling have been deployed largely operated by civil society organisations. These approaches, however, do not offer the official recognition afforded by a state-sponsored, official process. Such processes offer, *inter alia*, the possibility of reconstructing the history of conflict, and of drawing a line between the past and the future of the society. Yet there is often resistance to the establishment of state-sponsored truth recovery mechanisms. Factors such as a sense of collective guilt about the past have led to a bilateral agreement to avoid close inquiry into the past. Where no sense of collective responsibility has developed, resistance to any comprehensive inquiry into the past is to be expected.

The primary concern of the book is with the contribution that processes of truth recovery may make to the project of consolidating new societal solidarities after conflict is ended, rather than with the more narrow concerns with ending impunity, obtaining justice or prosecuting the guilty. Truth recovery is cast more broadly than the usual conceptualisation as a formal legal process with prosecutory dimensions. Here, we are concerned with the conditions which predispose or prevent embarkation on a truth recovery process and the rationale for that process. Using a detailed case study of Northern Ireland, the book argues that there is no magic moment of 'readiness' for truth recovery, but rather that the conditions are constructed rather than spontaneously occurring. The role of the state and the concept of political 'willingness' are placed at the centre of the analysis. This book takes as its focus the dynamic between the protagonists and how each of their positions, in this case on truth recovery, combine to produce the overall political status quo. As a society struggles to move forward, the book considers if the entrenched positions of some, and the failure of others to understand and recognise the positions of others can be shifted by a societal revisiting and re-evaluation of the past.

In Chapter 2, the book aims to examine the function of truth recovery in transitional societies, what claims are made for formal processes of truth recovery, and how might they act on societies in transition. It enumerates the main claims made for truth recovery in societies coming out of violence. This chapter reviews the purpose and expectations of truth recovery in societies coming out of political violence, in terms of their value to victims, their challenge to perpetrators and their potential contribution to putting the past to rest, to transforming antagonistic relationships and writing a more inclusive history of the conflict.

In Chapter 3, the book then moves on to consider the problems surrounding the notion of 'truth', and points to particular complexities in the definition of truth, and the conditions within violently divided societies in which truth is subsumed by cultures of organised or normalised lying. The chapter then examines the implication of this more complex conceptualisation for truth recovery.

The concept of shame is examined in Chapter 4, and the idea of shame as a regulating agent is discussed in the light of the work of Norbert Elias and Primo Levi's accounts of life in Auschwitz. The alteration brought about to patterns of shame during conditions of armed conflict is seen in the light of cultures of warrior honour, and their role in supporting political violence. The use of shame as a deterrent to violence and the development of shame as part of a 're-civilising process' in the post-conflict period is also examined.

The concept of victimhood is interrogated in Chapter 5, and simple dualistic definitions of victims and perpetrators are questioned, and a more complex conceptualisation of victimhood proposed. Common assumptions about the role of victims in post-conflict truth recovery are also critically examined.

The book then moves on to consider the issue of readiness of a society coming out of a conflict by considering a detailed case study of the Northern Ireland peace process. A brief background to the study is provided in Chapter 6, with a focus on developments since the Belfast Agreement. This chapter sets the context of contemporary political deadlock in Northern Ireland and the reasons for it, the waning of international interest and the failure to establish a devolved government. The patterns of violence and responsibility for violence during the conflict are set out, and a survey of the major unresolved grievances and puzzles of the past is provided.

In Chapter 7, a detailed analysis of the deliberations of the Northern Ireland Affairs Committee (NIAC) at Westminster, which was charged with the responsibility into inquiring into the feasibility of a truth recovery process for Northern Ireland is undertaken. The NIAC held a comprehensive inquiry into ways of dealing with Northern Ireland's past and heard a large volume of evidence from a range of sources before concluding that Northern Ireland was 'not ready' for truth recovery. The evidence not only provides a cross section of the range of opinion within Northern Ireland on the issue of truth recovery, but the manner of its evaluation by the committee affords insight into how the British government formed its view.

This chapter examines the evidence to the inquiry in some detail, and raises questions about the way the committee weighed the evidence and the basis for its conclusion that Northern Ireland was not ready for truth recovery. The chapter concludes by raising questions about the impartiality of this government committee's deliberations on the issue.

Chapter 8 considers the state of readiness of Northern Ireland for a truth recovery process in the light of the political impasse and considers the potential value of truth recovery in destabilising a deadlocked political status quo. An analysis of the resistance to truth recovery, and the disposition towards truth recovery of the various groupings of protagonists in Northern Ireland, Republicans, Loyalists and including the state is provided. The chapter also critiques the notion of 'readiness' for truth recovery and considers the official conclusion, that Northern Ireland is not ready for truth recovery. Using Zartman's concept of 'ripeness' (usually applied to armed conflicts amenable to transformation through negotiation), it is argued that 'readiness' cannot be judged except in hindsight, and the more useful concept of 'willingness' is advocated.

Chapter 9 examines the fears lying behind resistance to truth recovery, namely of destabilising the society. The initiation of truth recovery implies that the 'war is over' and reconciliation is a priority. The continuation of the 'war by other means' reinforces the respective protagonists' reliance on their bifurcated 'narratives' about the past, and ensures that the war continues. The potential impact of any truth recovery process on these narratives and on political stability is examined, in the context of the desirability of 'destabilising' the current deadlocked political status quo. The chapter also briefly considers the models of official truth recovery available and the chances of Northern Ireland embarking on an official truth recovery process, in the light of waning international attention and the lack of relatively disinterested third parties to champion such a process. The book draws conclusions about the potential impact of truth recovery on relationships within Northern Ireland, the stability of peace processes and the prospects for truth recovery and political progress.

2 The function of truth recovery in transitional societies

Truth commissions or official bodies of various kinds established to shed light on human rights abuses or violations of international law during a previous defined period of time have come to be regarded as part of the process of societal transitions out of political violence. A growing scholarship on the varieties, role, function and effectiveness of truth processes from 1974 onward (e.g. Hayner, 1994, 2001; Hamber, 1998; Barahona De Brito *et al.*, 2001; Biggar, 2001; Cairns and Roe, 2003) has pointed to the varieties of form, various functions and limitations of such initiatives. The wide variety of such bodies, and their diverse remits and levels of impact is knowledge available to those who consider the dilemmas associated with the challenge of managing the past.

Several lessons and principles about the operation of such bodies emerge from the literature. The need to examine comprehensively all aspects of the conflict, including the role of the state; the importance of independence and international involvement; the significance of state sponsorship; the dilemmas associated with providing incentives in the form of amnesties for perpetrators in return for their testimony thus pre-empting criminal proceedings; the quality and completeness of evidence; securing and maintaining cooperation from former parties to the conflict; the psychological impact of public truth processes on victims; methods of addressing corporate and institutional complicity and involvement in violations; and the role of truth processes in public education are all issues explored comparatively across a number of contexts.

The work of uncovering the past and providing a mechanism for listening to victims' voices in societies divided by and in the transition out of violent conflict can potentially fulfil a number of functions. These have been dealt with at greater length elsewhere[1] and will be dealt with only briefly here.

The potential for ending denial

Appleman's poem argues that 'forgetfulness will never walk with innocence; we save our faces at the risk of our lives, needing the wisdom of our losses, the gift of despair, or we could kill again....' The human consequences of conflict are depicted not only in the work of truth commissions, but in that of journalists, international humanitarian organisations, human rights organisations and in a wide variety of creative endeavours. Truth recovery mechanisms, particularly state-sponsored attempts to comprehensively survey the damage done, can raise public consciousness, and focus on the human consequences which are not always prominent in public discourses, and certainly not during the period of conflict.

Normatively, various mechanisms, such as denial, stoicism, indifference, pleasure at the suffering of enemies and emotional numbing have emerged as methods of dealing with the ubiquitous violence of the past, and this compounded the effects of jingoism, censorship and propaganda to facilitate the toleration of violence. Processes such as denial serve a purpose during armed conflict, and facilitate psychological survival. Indeed, some, such as Cohen, argue that all societies are built on such denial (Cohen, 2001: p. 294). Denial and objectification of the 'enemy' are psychological devices universally deployed by armed groups and their civilian supporters to facilitate the practice of violence.

In peacetime, however, such devices are dangerous because of the role they can play in the facilitation of violence. The return to violence is a political risk alongside the risk of the proliferation of more domestic forms of violence during peace processes (Darby and McGinty, 2000).

Truth recovery mechanisms can potentially facilitate the initiation of processes characteristic of more-peaceful societies, processes that support the new peaceful dispensation. Elias' concept of 'the civilising process' may be of service here; Elias explicates the link between the processes of change in social relations and the change in the psychic structure through shifts in standards of behavioural expectations (etiquette) and the shift in behaviour towards higher levels of self-restraint. Elias described 'the continuous correspondence between the social structure and the structure of the personality'.[2] These 'civilising processes' are methods of ensuring that people can find ways of satisfying their basic needs without 'destroying, frustrating, demeaning or in other ways harming each other....' According to Elias, increased thresholds of shame and repugnance are the processes through which such behaviour regulation is achieved. The significance (and the potential value of) shame in the Northern Ireland context will be dealt with at length in Chapter 4.

Modernity, according to Elias,[3] led to a shift in the view of the social universe, from the previous egocentric view to a perspective where people were able to see themselves 'from a distance' – as others saw them, achieving a more-detached view of themselves. Certainly, a public truth recovery process offers the opportunity for such perspectives of the conflict to be manifest and engaged with 'from a distance'.

Societies coming out of conflict could benefit from shifts in individual behaviour towards the new etiquette of a peaceful society. The ability to acknowledge aspects of the past without recourse to denial and, to feel compassion for fellow citizens and those who previously were considered to be enemies, are examples of this behavioural shift. The psychic landscape that facilitates killing and other forms of violence is one in which compassion, particularly compassion for our enemies, is largely absent. Yet this landscape does not automatically vanish when the conflict ends. Rituals, rites of transition and formal processes such as truth commissions, inquiries, tribunals and public hearings create the conditions where old enmities, grievances associated with past acts, desires for revenge and perceptions of impunity can be revisited, aired, acknowledged and some of them resolved. Otherwise they are likely to remain embedded in the culture, maintaining the conditions of the societal volatility which makes it prone to outbreaks of violence and capable of regression into war.

Providing access to discourses of the 'other'

In conflicted societies, even the most enterprising citizen who wishes to understand and learn about perspectives of the 'other' must usually overcome many obstacles. First, the *prima facie* risk – real or imagined – of relating directly to those who have been previously regarded as inherently untrustworthy and dangerous must be taken. Then the risk of ostracism by the home community must be faced, since re-negotiating the actual or imagined relationship with the 'other' depends not only on access to and engagement with that 'other' but also on the resilience to take risks in the home community. Yet in deeply divided societies, access to the 'other' and to particular conflict-related discourses and accounts is severely constrained by patterns of spatial and ideological segregation (see Shirlow and Murtagh, 2006).

Risk-takers play a key role in initiating and promoting departures from patterns of exclusionary interaction and dominant versions of truth. Officially promoted truth recovery mechanisms can open up sanctioned spaces for such departures, and play an important role in building complex, multi-dimensional perceptions of the 'other' by improving access to the 'other's' perspectives and experiences. The human consequences of violence for 'the other side' may not be accessible to citizens, preventing even those open-minded enough to engage with such material the opportunity to do so. Ensuring the general accessibility of such discourses across societal divisions is a key function of a valid truth recovery process. Building on Elias' notion of the ability to see oneself from a distance, increasing the ability to project oneself into the shoes of the 'other' and think from their point of view would be a valuable contribution to the process of building political stability. The public process of a truth recovery mechanism which carefully exposes the public to accounts of the experiences of the 'other' offers the potential for the development of empathy across the sectarian divide. In the absence of a stable monopoly of power, perhaps truth commissions have the capacity to promote progress towards pacification, whilst extending emotional identification between previously antagonistic elements.

Creating potential disincentives to violence

Some form of public documentation of the tragedies and losses due to conflict can focus attention on the human costs, and uncover the dimensions of that cost which have been previously ignored or hidden, and the pervasive nature of the damage. Such documentation affords the opportunity for public reflection on the human costs of conflict which may be denied or hidden in a militarised society. During conflict and continued societal division, the suffering of the 'other' is often a cause for celebration, or indifference. Societal reflection on the suffering due to conflict conducted in a comprehensive and inclusive manner and made accessible to the general public can assist with the societal development of compassion across old lines of enmity. Such compassion for enemies can act as a strong counter-indication to and a powerful disincentive from future violence.

Exploring the distribution of damage

Citizens do not suffer equally during periods of conflict. Typically, civilians, the young and those on lower incomes suffer more than other groups. Violence is also concentrated in certain locations and sub-populations, and because of the divided nature of the society, this distribution of damage may be hidden, and erroneous assumptions made about how others have been affected. Some, such as members of the security forces, live secret lives, concealing the realities of their experience from even their closest family members. Elites and more privileged groups may be largely ignorant of life in the epicentre of conflict, yet these same elites may be policy and decision makers. Yet good information about the nature, distribution and effects of the damage is essential to those who would make good the damage and build a peaceful society.

Attempt to synthesise polarised discourses of the past

During conflict, the production of propaganda, and the ongoing hostilities between the various factions lead to the production of a range of diametrically opposed accounts of past events, and interpretations of them. Unless the parties to the conflict can begin to produce a more-inclusive account, the political dynamic and contests over 'truth' in the supposed transition out of violence can resemble a 'war by other means'. The continuation of vigorous contests and the lack of a common framework of meaning in the post-settlement period can impede political progress and tax the patience of intermediaries. This pattern has been apparent in Northern Ireland consistently and increasingly since the Good Friday Agreement, and indeed in the period leading up to that agreement.

Formal truth recovery processes can provide a mechanism where various accounts of the past can be rehearsed and interrogated, and a structure within which irreconcilable accounts can be juxtaposed and compared. Without a formal container for this process, the contest between divergent accounts will occur in a piecemeal and chaotic fashion, with no mechanism for formalising any progress or resolution that might be made, making for a constant reiterating of contested accounts, absorbing political energy and goodwill and maintaining a conflicted dynamic – a 'war by other means'. A formal process with the express purpose of creating an inclusive record according to pre-agreed principles and with a formal imprimatur can channel these energies, focus the contest and remove some of the necessity for these debilitating contests.

The incorporation of new material – towards a common history

In the process of truth recovery, new facts are uncovered and previously unknown or hidden aspects of the past emerge. Of course, this is one of the reasons why former combatants, both those in the paramilitary groups and in the security forces are nervous about truth recovery. There is an appetite amongst some victims for new information about certain events, and about admissions from key actors about their past deeds and misdeeds. In a truth recovery process, aspects of events that have been either concealed or denied emerge for the first time, and change understandings, altering perceptions of culpability and responsibility. This requires a departure from the discourse characteristic of the post-conflict period, which, as was stated earlier is characteristic of a 'war by other means'. Rather, the establishment in the public sphere of an arena where a Habermasian 'ideal speech situation' could be established might facilitate the emergence of new material, and its absorption.

Truth recovery processes can usefully be seen in the light of Habermas' analysis of formal pragmatics, a theory of meaning and understanding, which sets out the conditions under which ideal speech acts can take place. Such acts can lead to a coming to an understanding, with the goal of 'intersubjective mutuality...shared knowledge, mutual trust, and accord with one another'.[4] For Habermas, such understanding was predicated on the social actors sharing the same meanings in language, which in turn matched their social expectations in a 'mutually recognised normative background'.[5]

Habermas set out four factors which influence the understanding of the meaning of an utterance – namely the recognition of its literal meaning; the hearer's assessment of the speaker's intentions; knowledge of the reasons behind the utterance; acceptance of those reasons and the appropriateness of the utterance. His rules of discourse or 'pragmatic presuppositions' are designed to regulate procedures and set out an ethical framework, establishing the conditions under which an ideal speech act can take place. These rules specify: that all subjects who are competent to speak and act are allowed to participate in the discourse; any participant can question any assertion; any participant can introduce any assertion into the discourse; and no speaker may be stopped from exercising these rights either by internal or external coercion.[6] All of this seems instructive when considering the process of truth recovery, and offers a potential framework against which a truth recovery process could be assessed. We can see formal truth recovery processes function by attempting to provide 'ideal speech situations' for participants. Insofar as they produce new and hidden accounts, truth recovery processes offer the potential to 'complicate' over-simplistic accounts of the past and to add the greyscale to the bifurcated picture produced and maintained during the conflict.

Clearly, this is a difficult aspect of truth recovery for many former combatants, and many are reluctant or unwilling to participate for fear of reprisal, prosecution or the stigma that could follow such disclosures. Yet, for many, trust cannot be built on an incomplete picture of the past, where suspicion remains and where responsibility has not been acknowledged. An appreciation of the contradictions of the past, and the incorporation of previously unknown or hidden dimensions not only makes for a more-nuanced understanding, but also affords the opportunity for the parties to build a more solid foundation for future relationships of trust and confidence. Without some form of disclosure about the past, and the incorporation of such a disclosure into official accounts, trust and confidence are undermined. The role of individual confessions of responsibility for deeds in the past in any truth recovery process, and whether such confessions are best obtained in private or in public, remains to be determined. There are, inter alia, legal considerations about such confessions, in terms of self-incrimination. However, such testimonies can potentially perform a significant function in achieving forgiveness, where this is sought and feasible.

The outcome of 'owning up' by perpetrators in the post-conflict period is shaped by the context in which such 'owning up' might occur. Where there is a risk of self-incrimination and ultimately prosecution, prospects are diminished; where there is little or no such risk they are enhanced. Where retributive models of truth recovery are practised, prospects for such disclosure of responsibility remain poor, whereas a restorative focus on mending broken relationships, perhaps with an added incentive of possible forgiveness, may well provide a more-conducive atmosphere to full disclosure by perpetrators.

One of the goals of the work of recovering the past or auditing the damage done by conflict is to produce new official accounts which all parties to the conflict participate in constructing. In Northern Ireland and South Africa there have been attempts made to construct inclusive accounts of the past, in advance of or alongside formal truth recovery mechanism. The process of such construction has involved the forming of close collaborative relationships between those previously alienated from each other. This has involved constructing the 'artificial' groupings that break the norm of segregation and the avoidance of mixing. Much effort has been devoted to establishing working relationships and trust building. Once established, such groups can work to negotiate versions of the past and interventions in the present that take account of the sensitivities and views of their various constituencies. Work produced by diversely composed teams can enjoy wider credibility. It has the potential to be perceived as fair, inclusive and respectful and it can be 'owned' by both sides.

Such history is deployed in socialising subsequent generations and thus serves to compound an ever-deepening division, thus increasing the chances of further conflict. The production of a new, inclusive history that can be more generally accepted is one of the potential fruits of truth recovery processes. Truth recovery processes offer the opportunity for a more synthetic history to emerge, incorporating aspects of previously competing accounts. Older versions of history are often rewritten to suit the position of the victor in situations of conflict, whereas undertaking a public truth recovery offers the potential, at least, of a more-inclusive approach.

Public education

Broadcast initiatives can bring out a diversity of accounts to public attention. Clearly, the print and broadcast media have played a key role in the conflict, and this role should properly be part of the review of any truth recovery process, which can offer a structured context in which disclosures are given a formal public meaning, and contribute to a society-wide process. Giddens (1994, p. 245) has pointed out they can consciously or unconsciously facilitate 'degenerate spirals of communication' between rival communities. Habermas, too, was concerned with 'distorted communication', since 'undistorted communication' is posited as a critical tool for human emancipation. According to Habermas, the ideal speech situation has four validity claims: comprehensibility; truth; appropriateness; sincerity, and those who lay claims to these must have a social context in which they justify such claims. In ideal situations, such claims are rationally debated and consensually agreed. However, in reality the unequal power relations and resource distribution prevent this level of rationality and consensus, and this leads to 'distorted communication'. Alterations in the disposition of the media in the post-conflict period, and their promotion of ideal speech situations is an important aspect of peace-building in the post-conflict period.

Thus, the media, together with other channels of public information can perform a key role during the conflict and their role requires as much critical evaluation as that of any other actor during the conflict. Nonetheless, the media plays a crucial role in disseminating the process and outputs of any truth recovery mechanism in the post-conflict period.

The media can potentially contribute to increased levels of public awareness of the complexities of the past, and place in the public domain a nuanced, complex, diverse and inclusive account of the conflict. (Equally, they can replicate the 'distorted communication' that characterised the period of conflict.) Should they adopt the more positive role, the public education process that results can contribute to shifts in levels of public knowledge, changes in public opinion and public awareness of 'other' perspectives. It could also model for the policy a public discourse capable of containing diverse accounts paying respect to all sides. Public education is an important part of building a new kind of responsible citizenship, which incorporates a thoughtful analysis of the past. There are dangers however in the kind of piecemeal initiatives and journalistic exposés: for example, the death by suicide of Billy Giles following the broadcast of Peter Taylor's *'Loyalists'* in which he was questioned about his involvement in Loyalist paramilitary activity. Equally, as the case of Rwanda illustrates, the media can play powerful roles in fomenting ethnic hatreds. Hence the need for a comprehensive strategy that is designed and coordinated to direct attention to the specific aspects and to support and disseminate this work systematically.

Impunity and the rule of law

Truth recovery is an important part of undermining the sense of impunity that often accompanies the end of armed conflict. The gaps in the justice system, through which many of the events of conflict fall, often leave citizens with a sense of injustice. Victims may be left with a sense that the crimes of the conflict are unaddressed, unpunished, and those responsible for human rights violations or other misdeeds have got away with their transgressions. In the immediate post-conflict period, the criminal justice system can be overwhelmed and incapable of improving this situation, thus compounding the low regard and lack of public confidence in that system. In such circumstances, truth recovery mechanisms can address long-standing unresolved violations and grievances in a way that assists with the reinstatement of a sense of law, order and due process.

Justice is an important aspiration for many who have suffered in political conflict. Yet incentives offered to perpetrators, particularly amnesty, in order to encourage their participation may threaten the prospect of obtaining justice in the eyes of many victims. In South Africa, the Azanian People's Organisation (AZAPO) and the families of the murdered Ntsiki Biko, Mbasa Mxenge and Chris Ribeiro mounted a constitutional challenge to section 20 (7) of the National Unity and Reconciliation Act, the provision permitting the TRC to grant amnesty. The challenge was dismissed in 1996, in spite of the appellants' argument that the granting of amnesty denied them recourse to justice. Amnesty was indeed granted in some cases by the TRC, where perpetrators made application, gave evidence and satisfied the TRC that they had made full disclosure.

Whilst the provision of amnesty may be a valuable incentive to perpetrators to participate in a truth recovery process, the provision of amnesty precludes the achievement of justice for victims. For some victims, the denial of justice prevents the achievement of any kind of closure. Victims in general are seemingly faced with a choice between more information or 'truth' on the one hand and justice on the other.

In reality, justice is often beyond reach in any case – what with the passage of time, perhaps the death or inaccessibility of witnesses and the destruction or disintegration of evidence. In some 2,000 cases in Northern Ireland, the police have instigated a 'cold-case review' procedure, where old unresolved cases from the past will be re-examined by a specially formed team of investigators, some from an outside police force. This kind of investigative work is both labour and resource intensive, yet is often what victims and their families have waited for. It remains to be seen whether the outcome of these investigations will provide victims and their families with any more satisfaction, although they do go some way towards addressing the issue of impunity.

The design of truth recovery mechanisms rarely puts the choice between truth and justice in the hands of the individual victim. Indeed to do so would risk underwriting the impulse in some victims for revenge. Clearly, this would be retrograde for the prospects for peace and stability, and antithetical to the spirit of truth recovery in the transition out of violence. The choice between truth and justice is not therefore placed in the hands of the victim, but is usually is a design feature of the truth recovery mechanism itself. The expressed needs or preferences of victims for either truth or justice, or both, will vary, so some inevitably will be disappointed. The issue of justice is a troubled one. For some, justice is associated with vengeance and retribution, and can therefore be antithetical to peace-building, truth recovery and reconciliation. Yet it is difficult, in a context where the ordinary criminal law provides for retribution and punishment, to persuade victims that they should set aside a right that they see granted to others in the ordinary course of societal processes. However, the practicalities of the large numbers of such unresolved cases, together with the political impossibility of resolving them using an ordinary criminal justice approach calls for extraordinary measures and processes. Truth recovery mechanisms set out to be such extraordinary measures.

The issue of unsolved killings in general and particularly those controversial killings carried out by state forces is something that a publicly sponsored, independent truth recovery process can usefully address. The provision of some forum where those responsible are held accountable in some way, even if prosecution is not available, can not only provide relief to victims' families, but can also lessen the sense that some actors in the conflict have operated with impunity. Bringing all parties to account, with its concomitant universality of accountability, is a function that a truth recovery mechanism could usefully serve. In the case of Northern Ireland, with amendments to legislation on the conduct of public enquiries, and with a queue of controversial cases yet to hear, a comprehensive truth mechanism could potentially serve a useful function in disposing of a large backlog of outstanding cases.

Examine unsolved killings

In the wake of any conflict, a large number of killings remain unsolved, with no perpetrator formally identified or held to account. Even in a low-intensity conflict such as Northern Ireland, where just over 3,700 people were killed over a thirty-five year period, the Police Service of Northern Ireland (PSNI) have almost 2,000 unresolved killings on their books for which convictions were never obtained. The PSNI have instituted an Historic Enquiries Team led by constabularies from outside Northern Ireland. This team's work consists of reviewing each of the cases, including the evidence where it is available, with a view to bringing resolution to at least some of these cases. Such an operation not only provides a model for the kind of investigation that could be conducted under the rubric of a comprehensive truth recovery process, but indeed this operation could be operated under the auspices of such a comprehensive process.

Challenging moral superiority

The moral high ground is often the most overcrowded piece of turf in divided societies. Parties to the conflict tend to focus exclusively on the wrong-doing of the 'other', a focus that obscures the actor's vision of his or her own wrong-doing. Claims to moral superiority and innocence, and denials of responsibility are often the building bricks of conflict. Truth recovery, the placing of new evidence in the public domain, the discovery and revelation of previously hidden or unpublicised accounts of the conflict can create a greater sense of moral equivalence, and illustrate the wrong-doing on all sides. The danger is that truth recovery becomes yet another contest in the conflict. For some it will inevitably be so, since some are unable to stop fighting the war, even though the war is long over. The model of truth recovery adopted is significant here, with a retributive model likely to promote an adversarial approach, and a restorative approach offering more potential for relationship-focus, in which, for example, confessions might be elicited by desires on the part of perpetrators for reintegration and forgiveness. For many, however, the discovery of dark deeds carried out in the name of a cause they supported is a salutary and chastening experience. For others, albeit a minority, confession offers a route to potential forgiveness. The realisation that all parties to the conflict have committed violent acts, broken codes of conduct and inflicted harm can alter the climate of the moral contest in a way that depolarises and is supportive of peace-building.

Learning from the past

The facilitation of learning the lessons of the past can be another function of truth recovery processes, and for those who are open to such learning. For those who are not, exposure to previously unknown accounts of the past can alter perspectives, and in some cases can crack open the resistant shell of denial. If a society is to capture what Appleman describes as the 'wisdom of our losses' then those losses must be known – enumerated, described, documented, examined and acknowledged as a way of signalling their communal significance. The despair and grief associated with the losses suffered, and those inflicted on others may qualify participants in the truth recovery for re-entry into a more humane society. Truth recovery processes demonstrate the value of all human life by offering participants a public and official opportunity to face their own grief and culpability, and respond with emotions appropriate to the ending of human life and the infliction of human suffering. As such, they can be seen as the product of an Eliasian 'civilising process' whereby the importance of emotional life is asserted and emotional identification is potentially stretched to encompass the whole nation.

Containment

Truth recovery processes can also provide a mechanism of containing or drawing a boundary around the pain, conflict, anger and injustices of the past. That truth commissions and enquiries have a beginning, middle – and particularly an end – provides a societal metaphor for managing the past of that society. Many of the grievances addressed in truth recovery are of long standing, and have remained unaddressed for long periods. Some victims have campaigned in the public domain for justice, and have public profiles as victims. Much is made of the need for closure – yet for many involved in political violence, the war does seem to go on forever. A finite truth process, replete with symbolic and ritual significance, can offer a mechanism for transition. This finite process offers the opportunity to examine the past, but places a limit around that examination and the finite quality can offer a sense of closure to victims, airing discourses of grievance, accusation, anger and humiliation. Truth recovery can provide a platform for this discourse to be 'discharged' so that the stage is cleared for discourses associated with the new societal dispensation to emerge. In the case of South Africa, some of these post-TRC discourses shifted in the direction of reconciliation.

Reparations

Truth processes carried out elsewhere have typically made provision for forms of reparations for victims and survivors. Hamber and Wilson (2003) argue that acts of reparation such as reburial, monuments or memorials, or the payment of financial compensation are symbolically important. They are also important in their own right for the value they hold. In Chapter 5, in the discussion on victims and victimhood, the diversity of attitudes amongst victims is explored at greater length. Significantly, victims often judge the reparations made to them in the light of the kind of treatment and reparation made to others, especially those associated with perpetrators, and a formal truth recovery process would provide an opportunity to address any such anomalies.

Acknowledgement and the role of victims

Truth recovery processes are often assumed to be mainly or primarily established to meet the needs of victims. Truth mechanisms play an important part in witnessing and documenting the suffering of individuals and groups and provide acknowledgement for that suffering. This public and formal acknowledgement is in many cases one of the main ambitions of victims, particularly by those who have been responsible for the deeds of the past. However, victims often pay a heavy price for it. The re-opening of old wounds and the frustration of hopes for information, for apology, for forgiveness along with the limited nature of financial reparations, the time constraints, the response of officials, the stress of reliving painful events in order to give testimony are all part of the price that witnesses pay for their participation. This situation of victims is discussed further in Chapter 5.

It is more accurate to describe truth recovery processes as a service that victims (and perpetrators) perform for society, rather than a service provided for their benefit. The work of truth recovery, the giving of testimony, the revelation of secrets, the acceptance of responsibility and the making of statements of regret and apology must occur within a carefully designed, legally constructed context which is equally accessible to all citizens, and in which all human lives are judged to be of equal value. The legal, political, security and psychological consequences must be carefully considered and taken into account in the design of a proper truth process which is tailored to the circumstances of that particular society. Truth recovery is not, and should not be, reality television, although parts of the process may well be televised in order to improve the access to the process itself, and to fulfil the public education function.

The role of institutions and civil society

Truth recovery processes are not necessarily limited to the examination of killings, acts of direct violence or human rights violations. Such processes can usefully examine the role of civil society institutions in the past, how they contributed to or resisted repressive or discriminatory regimes, and the role they played in creating and maintaining the conditions in which citizens resorted to violence. This can include the role of the local state authorities, public bodies providing health, education, housing, social services and so on. Indeed reviews of their past roles can be a valuable part of ensuring that such bodies play a positive role in the transition out of violence. In Antjie Krog's *Country of My Skull*, she recounts that shortly before the deadline for amnesty applications in the South African Truth and Reconciliation process, six young black men went to the Cape Town office of the TRC and applied for amnesty, stating that their crime was apathy, explaining that:

> The act says that an omission can also be a human rights violation. And that's what we did; we neglected to take part in the liberation struggle. So, here we stand as a small group representative of millions of apathetic people who didn't do the right thing.[7]

In any society coming out of a conflict, fostering such reflection amongst the 'silent majority', many of whom have been passively or actively complicit with discrimination, acts of violence or other wrongs in the past, could play a valuable role in a wider societal reconciliation. To narrow the gap between those who took an active part in the violence of the past and those who apparently did not, assists reintegration of former combatants, and reduces polarisation.

Forgiveness

An issue that arises in much of the literature about truth recovery and reconciliation is that of forgiveness. Certainly, great store was set by expressions of forgiveness with the South African Truth and Reconciliation process. Some would argue that this was largely due to the Christian influence of Anglican Archbishop Desmond Tutu and his deputy, Alex Boraine, previously President of the Methodist Church of South Africa. Both these church leaders promoted the Christian value of forgiveness. Boraine, reflecting on his work with the TRC, wrote:

> This concept of forgiveness as a means of assisting individuals and societies to overcome the evil of their past is not a popular concept. Nevertheless, it is an approach without which there can be very little hope in the world.[8]

The danger that victims and survivors may feel under pressure to grant some form of absolution or forgiveness to perpetrators is addressed by Boraine:

> Forgiveness is not something that can be demanded from the victims, but conditions can be created whereby forgiveness becomes at least a possibility. It would be simplistic to argue from the particular to the general, but it nevertheless deserves stating that very few relationships or marriages or partnerships would survive without the quality of forgiveness. We

understandably spend a great deal of time remembering. But this too can be a powerful tool for the continuation of violence. There comes a time when forgiveness needs to take place in order to deal with the past...[9]

Archbishop Tutu participated in a series of three television programmes produced by BBC Northern Ireland in which he and two other panelists, Donna Hicks from Harvard and Mrs Lesley Belinda, whose husband was killed in Rwanda. In these programmes, those bereaved in the Troubles were brought face to face with those responsible for or associated with those responsible for carrying out the acts that bereaved them. In the last programme in the series, Loyalist Michael Stone revealed on camera that he had not, in fact, pulled the trigger that killed the husband of Sylvia Hackett, the woman confronting him.

During these programmes, Tutu repeatedly announced that forgiveness could not be contrived, yet in all cases, the victim shook the hand of the actual or supposed perpetrator. In the third programme, Sylvia Hackett announced early in the programme that she would not forgive Stone, that she had no feelings for him, but after prompting from Tutu, rose and shook Stone's hand, but broke down immediately on doing so. Mrs Hackett said audibly to her brother-in-law during this incident, 'I am lost.' Following the prompts from Tutu, an international figure, and under the glare of television cameras with the question of what millions of viewers would make of a refusal to forgive, the pressure on Mrs Hackett to shake the hand of Michael Stone was almost irresistible. It was almost impossible for her not to shake the hand of the perpetrator.[10]

Whilst the desirability of forgiveness is clear from a societal point of view, it may be too much to expect and unjust to demand. Forgiveness is a highly individual and personal process, and one that not all victims are ready or able to engage in. The 'reality television' aspect of the BBC programmes, where victims were only brought face to face with perpetrators if they agreed to be filmed doing so is hardly respectful of the kind of personal space, support and reflection required by most victims in order to consider issues such as forgiveness. For many, forgiveness is simply too much to expect, and it merely compounds the original victimisation to put pressure on victims to forgive. Some victims require an apology or a sense that there is genuine remorse on the part of the perpetrator. Yet apologies are often hard to come by. Boraine describes how inadequate apology inhibited forgiveness in the South African case .'My experience was that victims and survivors were in the main more than ready to forgive but waited in vain for the *apartheid* leaders to say sorry.'[11]

Hamber and Wilson (2003) are emphatic that victims and survivors should not be expected to forgive simply because of some form of reparation, apology, compensation or acknowledgement of their loss has been provided. Even if forgiveness is seen as some form of prophylactic against revenge and violence, it is by no means experienced by everyone at an individual level. The leadership of the TRC in South Africa, strongly influenced by the Christian ethics of Tutu and Boraine, was keen on encouraging forgiveness. The Judeo-Christian emphasis on forgiveness may not be culturally compatible with all societal contexts.

Arguably, forgiveness does not chime even with the specific brand of Christian fundamentalism prevalent in Northern Ireland, with is closely associated with the 'eye for an eye' retributive approach of the Old Testament, rather than the 'turn the other cheek' conciliatory approach of the New Testament. This issue will be taken up in Chapter 5.

In a society emerging from a period of sustained violence and engaged in an attempt to build a peaceful and cohesive society, the potential role of forgiveness is clear. Arendt describes the function of forgiveness in this context.

> The possible redemption from the predicament of irreversibility – of being unable to undo what one has done though one did not and could not have known what he was doing – is the faculty of forgiving.... Forgiving serves to undo the deeds of the past, whose 'sins' hang like Damocles' sword over every new generation....[12]

However, what has been done cannot be undone. The dead are not resurrected, the broken bodies are not made whole. Forgiveness may relieve the burdens of the perpetrators but the benefits to victims are not so apparent. In the case of Northern Ireland, if, as Kilmurray (NIAC, Q 114) asserts, the aim of reconciliation is setting the bar too high, then to aim for forgiveness is setting it higher still. That is not to say that forgiveness is not desirable, either at an individual or collective level. It is merely to point out that it cannot be legislated for or demanded. Some victims are unable or unwilling to forgive and for some forgiveness might be facilitated by the perpetrator wishing to atone and attempting to make restitution, but many perpetrators are unrepentant and not seeking for forgiveness.

The confusion of individual and collective forgiveness is a further complicating factor. Joyce Mtimkulu lost her son and gave evidence to the TRC and heard her son's killers confess there. She concluded that she could not forgive them. '...they are not asking for forgiveness from us, the people who have lost their loved ones. They are asking forgiveness of the government, they did nothing to the government, what they did, they did to us.'[13]

Mtimkulu's loss was at once the deeply personal loss of her son, yet simultaneously it was a symbolic loss to her community and race. She, like many who have suffered, reserved the right to forgive as a profoundly personal process, predicated in her case, on a sense of remorse on the part of her son's killers. There is an inevitable tension between the personal nature of loss and the political significance of that loss. For Primo Levi, the Holocaust did not cause him to hate the German people, yet he could not forgive it.[14] For some, forgiveness must be personally sought before it can be considered. For others, such requests must be accompanied by apology and remorse, while for others still, none of this seems necessary. Gordon Wilson from Northern Ireland, who lost his daughter in the IRA bomb planted in Enniskillen, announced his forgiveness of his daughter's killers very quickly after her death, and in the absence of any evidence of her killers' remorse. For others, to forgive seems like an act of betrayal. Hamber and Wilson caution against the use of 'narrow Christian and human rights discourses of reconciliation and nation building'. However, the tension between the personal and political dimensions and finding a reconciliation between them is a challenge which is yet to be met, and remains somewhat unresolved.

Private and public roles of victims

Public truth recovery processes offer victims and survivors the opportunity to place their suffering in the context of the broader political upheavals of the nation-state. This, however, may be experienced by victims as depersonalisation and not as such helpful. Yet any resistance by victims to this public positioning may lead to a degree of public censure. A society has expectations of its victims and survivors, discussed in Chapter 5, and if they do not fulfil those expectations or behave in unexpected ways or fail to 'move on' at a recognisable pace, they risk losing public sympathy. This was recognised by William Frazer of FAIR in his testimony to the NIAC: '... everybody sees FAIR as controversial, we are seen as the bad guys within the victims sector and I am sure nobody will say anything different here in front of you' (Q 728).

In the case of Las Madres de Plaza de Mayo in Argentina, the broader political context moved at a different pace than the hearts and minds of individual victims and victim groups. Las Madres refused to see the loss of their children or husbands as a sacrifice for the new society, which they saw as falling far short of their desire for justice, and gradually they became more and more criticised for this stance. They demurred from participating in the arrangements made by government to move the society forward, in relation to past abuses. Thus, victims, whether justifiably or not, can be seen as obstacles to the establishment of a new society, even though they are rarely, if ever, part of negotiating the terms of such a new society. At the point when the victimisation occurs, the vision of a new society is often remote indeed. And even when such transition occurs, very often those who have suffered most during the conflict gain the least under the new dispensation. The continued grievances of victims in the South African process, and the failure to address enormous socio-economic inequalities illustrates this. In Northern Ireland, provision for victims has been more generous in comparison, yet the lack of a public process which addresses the issues faced by groups such as FAIR leaves them both unchallenged and unsupported, and therefore unable to move beyond current entrenched positions.

In summary, a truth recovery process can perform a number of functions. It can: undermine the denial about the past; provide access to discourses of the 'other'; create potential disincentives to violence; explore the distribution of damage caused by the conflict; attempt to synthesise the polarised discourses of the past; contribute towards creating a common, inclusive history; educate the public about the impact of the conflict; address the issue of impunity; examine unsolved killings; challenge stances of moral superiority; address issues of reparation and compensation; acknowledge the suffering of victims and the responsibility of perpetrators; shed light on the role of institutions and civil society in the past and address the issue of forgiveness.

On the other hand, it has been argued that to expose such highly charged issues to a public process is to risk increasing the level of antagonism, and providing a new arena for the continuation of the 'war by other means'. There is a perceived risk that truth recovery will reopen wounds, reactivate old grievances and re-stimulate the desire for revenge. However, it will be argued in subsequent chapters that this fear is partly composed of resistance to exposure and ultimately to entering a situation in which the outcome is not guaranteed; fear that is related to the impact of the conflict on the flexibility and openness of those who lived through it. It will also be argued in Chapter 9 and elsewhere that much depends on the methods and processes by which such explorations of the past are conducted. Careful attention to methods and processes can neutralise some of these risks.

3 Truth and cultures of organised and normalised lying

This chapter examines the nature of truth within the philosophical literature and how religion and law have defined truth, and influenced the way it is popularly conceptualised. The manner in which some populations come to be regarded as more suspect and less truthful is outlined, and the South African Truth and Reconciliation Commission's four definitions of truth are examined; forensic truth, narrative truth, dialogical truth and healing truth. The role of the narrative truth in dismantling cultures of silence is discussed, and the desire of victims for truth is examined. The impact of a bifurcated culture of violence and of repeated exposure to traumatic violence on conceptualisations of truth is described and the manner in which extreme conditions create moral inversions and uncertainties about matters such as truth. The chapter ends with a discussion of the role of truth in politics, political resistance to truth telling, the impact of revelations of truth on political processes and the practice of 'organised lying' as a result of the subterfuges of war and civil conflict. Truth recovery is examined as a possible antidote to the effects of such practices.

Truth

The fraught question of 'what is truth?' – or 'what is the truth?' – is largely avoided entirely in the literature on truth recovery. Hayner (1994, pp. 72–85), for example, devotes a chapter to 'what is the truth?' – a wording that implies a singular truth. However, the chapter does not address the issue of singular or absolute truth as compared to relative or multiple truths, but concentrates largely on the goals, time parameters and remit of truth commissions, and their information management systems.

The nature of truth is not an easy question to address, especially in the context of 'truth' recovery after armed conflict. The philosophical literature engages extensively with the nature of truth, as one of its central subjects, from diverse perspectives: Wittgenstein's *Tractatus Logico-Philosopicus* uses truth tables to place truth functions in a series; Tarski theorised language and sentences as truth bearers; and Kripke asserted that a language can consistently contain its own truth predicate. A wide range of schools of thought can be identified: semantic theorists such as, Davidson, Russell and Whitehead; coherence theorists such as

Spinoza, Leibniz, G. W. F. Hegel, F. H. Bradley, Joachim, Neurath and Hempel; correspondence theorists such as Kant; constructivists such as Giambattista Vico, Hegel, Garns and Marx; situation theorists such as Barwise and Berry; anti-realists such as Putnam; consensus theorists such as Habermas and Rescher; pragmatists such as Peirce, James and Dewey; the performative theory of Strawson; the redundancy theory of Ramsey; prosentential theorists such as Grover, Camp and Belnap, and so on.

Whilst the philosophical literature engages extensively with the issue of truth, it does so in the luxury of abstraction, calling to mind Marx's assertion in his *Thesis on Feuerbach*: 'The philosophers have merely interpreted the world in different ways; now the task is to change it.' Confronted with the myriad challenges of complex, contradictory, emotionally charged competing narratives characteristic of the post-conflict context, the philosophical debate can seem barely relevant to those engaged in the work of truth recovery, and who face the necessity of defining truth in short order. Nonetheless, conceptual clarity is an important underpinning to the work of truth recovery; and central to our concerns is the distinction between relativism and relative truth on the one hand and absolutism and universal truth on the other. The way these concepts are understood and applied by those who engage in truth recovery work, and by the wider society will determine much of the truth recovery process and outputs. There are two key popular influences on thinking about truth; religion and the law.

Religion and truth

Religious use of concepts of absolute truth is a significant influence, particularly in the post-conflict contexts such as Argentina, South Africa and Northern Ireland, where religious ideology has a pervasive influence, particularly where religious fundamentalism is a significant factor. The implicit influence of religion on this and other issues is further discussed in Chapter 5. There is a distinction between absolute truth in philosophy and the way the concept of truth is used in religion. Truth, in most religious traditions may be spiritually revealed or handed down in tradition and comprise the doctrine of that religion. Yet, as Arendt points out, with the exception of Zoroastrianism: 'none of the major religions included lying as such, as distinguished from 'bearing false witness' in their catalogues of the gravest sins' (p. 549).

Truth, it seems, is primarily a doctrinal matter, as opposed to the practice of truth telling. In Christianity, the Bible as a central text provides the source of claims to truth, whilst Catholics additionally hold that the Pope is a source of infallible truth on matters of doctrine. Some fundamentalist Christians believe that the Bible is entirely true – the doctrine of Biblical inerrancy – whilst others see the Bible as true on matters of faith, but requiring contextualised interpretations on other matters. Hence, we see within Christianity, the seeds of a contest between absolutism and relativism, between those who believe in the literal truth of religious texts and those who interpret such texts in the light of historical and cultural differences.

The significance of these divergent approaches, which co-exist within Christianity, albeit often in competition with one another without satisfactory resolution of their differences, for the interpretation of 'truth' or 'the truth' is clear. Barrington Moore (2000) has argued that monotheism, which emphasises virtue in the supernatural without providing any supernatural scapegoats, lies at the root of extreme forms of intolerance and has provided the justification for much persecution throughout the world.

It is only within Buddhism that doctrine attempts to resolve the tension between relative and absolute truth(s) in the Jain doctrine of 'anekantavada' which emphasises the necessity of considering any matter from many points of view. For Troelsch[1] the 'absolutism of Christianity' was a central factor in sectarianism and other writers, such as Moore (2000) have connected absolutism with monotheism and its predominance in Western thought. Indeed, absolute truth is an article of faith within many Christian denominations: the Pope as the source of infallible truth in Catholicism; and the scared text the absolute authority for fundamentalist Protestants.

Truth and law

The second influence on popular thinking about truth is the law and legal approaches. In divided societies in which the law is centrally located within the conflict itself, legal processes and interventions have typically been used to address the conflict. Emergency legislation, suspensions of the normal rule of law and counter-terrorism measures become a pervasive feature of everyday life during the period of conflict. In theory, the concept of truth in law is dependent on the concept of 'fact', where law is based on secular juridical processes and judgements, such as British Common Law. Truth, in such law, is the witness swearing to tell the truth – the witness makes an attempt in good faith to do so, and is tested by the legal process which must determine their credibility and veracity, through testing the facts as they present them.

Otherwise, truth is held to be that which is a fact, or which is verifiable, with an emphasis on the importance of evidence and proof. This Western legal approach implies a process of establishing truth through a process of assemblage of facts, rigorous testing, interrogation of evidence and measured judgment. Where other forms of law, such as traditional law in Africa (or restorative approaches in the West) are applied, priority may be given to other factors, such as the maintenance of peaceable relationships within the community.

Extracting the 'truth'

The lived experience of Western law and legal processes, however, has often fallen short of these abstract standards of truth. This is especially notable in contexts where societal upheavals has meant that emergency laws have altered the rules of evidence or due process, and where credibility and veracity tend to be regarded as inherent qualities in some witnesses, and not in others. In violently divided societies, certain entire populations are regarded as more credible, whilst those from what Hillyard (1993) – writing about the Irish in Britain and the Prevention of Terrorism Act – refers to as 'suspect communities' are regarded with distrust and suspicion.

> The most important feature of the operation of the PTA [Prevention of Terrorism Act] has been the way in which it has constructed a suspect community in Britain. The wide powers of examination, arrest and detention, the executive powers to proscribe selected organisations, the range of specific offences under the Acts, the power to issue exclusion orders and a whole new range of provisions covering seizure and investigation, have all played their part in making the Irish community living in Britain, or Irish people travelling between Ireland and Britain, a suspect community. This community is treated in law and police practices very differently from the rest of the population... the wide powers of examination, arrest and detention have allowed the police to trawl the Irish community for information whether at ports or airports or inland.[2]

Hillyard cites a 1990 article in the British *Mail on Sunday* in which a Deputy Assistant Commissioner in the police is quoted as saying:

> We need the public to tell us about all Irish people who have arrived within the past year or so. They may be living with you, or near you, or working with you. Just tell us, and we'll check it out.[3]

Since the beginning of the Irish peace process, and the IRA cessation in 1996, this pressure on the Irish community has lessened, only to be replaced by a similar situation of pressure on the Muslim community since the beginning of the War on Terror. The Palestinian population in the Middle East, historically black South Africans and a host of other 'suspect communities' report similar experiences.

Thus, the kind of truth that is enshrined in law and upheld by evidence and proof acquires a tarnish amongst those for whom the law is a tool used by a hostile state against them. The power to define truth lies with the powerful, and within such 'suspect communities' another truth, driven underground, often regarded as subversive, dangerous and unpatriotic, provides an alternative discourse. In the post-conflict period, this underground discourse must be heard, understood and integrated into the dominant account, if the perception and practice of law and the understanding of the truth are to move beyond the divisions of the past.

Forensic truth

The South African Truth and Reconciliation Commission, a body whose prominent actors were mainly Christian churchmen and lawyers, identified four types of 'truth' in its final report. The first was objective, factual or forensic truth, also referred to by Albie Sachs as 'microscope truth' which the commission was charged with producing by means of investigation, corroboration and verification. This is the truth familiar to those operating within legal frameworks, and which is manifest by production of evidence, as discussed earlier.

Narrative truth

The second type of truth identified by the TRC was 'narrative truth' or 'personal truth' manifest in the oral traditions of South Africa and the testimonies of victims and perpetrators. The Healing Through Remembering project in Northern Ireland conducted an audit of storytelling, and reported:

> Storytelling was the form of remembering most often suggested to the Healing Through Remember project... it was felt that the process of telling one's story could be a cathartic one. It could equally be inspirational and informative for the listener... Many felt that it would be important to record the stories of individuals' experiences of the conflict as an historical resource, and a way of enabling society to examine the wealth of meanings and learning connected to the conflict. Some... expressed concern that, unless a wide range of accounts are recorded and archived, a singular, exclusive narrative of the conflict will become dominant over time. This appeared particularly important to people who felt their experience of the conflict had been ignored.[4]

In the South African case, both the accounts of victims and perpetrators were considered as truth(s) by Boraine (2001, p. 289) and one of the valuable contributions of this form of truth according to Boraine (2001, p. 290) is to end the silence that often characterises the post-conflict period, permitting the emergence of diverse experiences and perspectives on the past.

Cultures of silence

The silence that is associated with conflict, as a result of taboos that operate in conflicted societies, about open discussion on topics related to the conflict is, in itself a form of anti-truth or non-truth. In situations of war and violent conflict, a culture of silence typically develops around the most dangerous and fearful aspects of the conflict. In Chile, after the retirement of Pinochet, silence about the past prevailed. Censorship, both self-censorship and laws forbidding the newspaper coverage of ongoing trials contributed to this atmosphere of pervasive silence. This culture of silence closes down the possibilities for truth telling, restricting it to a very narrow ground, or relegating it to the indeterminate future.

Even when people do break the silence, the taboo is still felt. As Feldman (1991) writing about Northern Ireland notes, 'The line between *informants* and *informers* was clearly drawn: it marked a division of life and death.' Often, this silence has a wider historical and cultural context, buried in the often-lengthy history of conflict and division. The silence is a taboo about articulation. Such silence is a set of rules, which may relate not simply to political violence, but to loss and catastrophe in general. These rules place a taboo on speaking about the topic, isolate the individual and outlaw or at least severely restrict expressive reactions. Silence and the taboo about speaking becomes pervasive when the reality is distressing and clearly perceived by the individual – the secret is known, but cannot be spoken about, even with those who are closest to you. Deane's (1996) fictional account written from the point of view of a child living through an armed conflict, in a house full of secrets about deaths, guns and betrayal, describes this silence thus:

> So broken was my father's family that it felt to me like a catastrophe you could live with only if you kept it quiet. Let it die of its own accord like a dangerous fire. Eddie gone. Parents both dead within a week. Two sisters, Ena and Bernadette, treated like skivvies and boarded in a hen-house. A long, silent feud. A lost farmhouse, with rafters and books in it, near the field of the disappeared. Silence everywhere. My father knowing something about Eddie, not saying it, not talking but sometimes nearly talking, signalling. I felt we lived in an empty space with a long cry from him ramifying through it. At other times, it appeared to be as cunning and articulate as a labyrinth, closely designed, with someone sobbing at the heart of it.[5]

The taboo on speaking is arguably impossible to break whilst the conflict is ongoing, but as hostilities dwindle, gradually the possibility of 'telling one's story' becomes feasible, and for some, beneficial and desirable. The increasing availability of a diverse and contradictory range of stories acts cumulatively to complicate and often challenge hegemonic accounts of the past.

Dialogical truth

The third kind of truth according to the TRC report is social or 'dialogical' truth – truth or experience arrived at through a social process of interaction, discussion and debate. This kind of truth can manifestly be described as 'socially constructed' in that it results from an interactive collective social process. The model for this process can be found in the work of, for example, Jane Addams' Chicago Hull-House. This was the first settlement house in the United States, where collective inquiry into social problems and issues was promoted and carried out (Addams, 1912). The work of Dewey (1927) also provides an historical base for community inquiry which is seen as a practical and theoretical framework for an open-ended, democratic, participatory collective aimed at collaborative activity that can create knowledge related to the values, history and lived experiences of the community.

This form of truth is promoted by community inquiries into certain events, such as the 2002 New Lodge community inquiry into the deaths of six men in the New Lodge area of Belfast[6] and a more wide-ranging community inquiry and documentation process conducted by the Ardoyne Commemoration Project in North Belfast, culminating in the publication of a book on the subject. Jenkins (2003), reviewing the Ardoyne book, comments:

> This, necessarily, dramatises the complex nature of truth. It is an elusive commodity. The book offers one area's truth, many different people's truths, a truth rooted in republican politics. These do not agree with each other, and are all important and valuable. Between them, and within them there is a reality that has to be attended to and respected if the north of Ireland is to move forward; along with a host of other realities, many utterly different.[7]

This form of truth offers opportunities for popular participation in the process of redefining truth and remaking accounts of the past.

Restorative truth

The fourth kind of truth is 'healing or restorative' truth, aimed at meeting the requirement on the TRC to contribute to repairing the damage of the past and to the prevention of recurrence of future abuses. This typology is related to the concept of restorative justice, promoted by a growing social movement in the United States, Europe and elsewhere. As a practice, restorative justice aims to provide non-violent methods of addressing harm and violations of human rights, through working for a resolution that promotes repair of damaged relationships, reconciliation and reparation for the harm done. Such approaches strive to balance the needs of the victim, the perpetrator or offender and the community, whilst maintaining respect for all parties to the process. In some ways, the South African Truth and Reconciliation Commission was an example of a restorative process, although the discussions of prosecution and amnesty (also part of the TRC process) are not restorative in nature.

The South African TRC typology of truth is aspirational, particularly the last category, 'healing and restorative truth', in that it expresses the desired outcome of the truth recovery process rather than engaging with some of the thornier issues about truth itself. Nor does this typology assist with the central questions about the nature of truth, and the reconciliation of the divergent narratives that are elicited by a call for truth. Is there – or was there – an Afrikaaner truth, a black truth, a coloured truth? In Argentina is there a government truth and a Madres de Plaza Mayo truth? In the case of Northern Ireland, is there a Republican truth, a Loyalist truth, a British government truth and an Irish government truth? And if so, are they all equally credible and valid? And can a truth process be seen, rather, as a process of reaching approximate, contingent, mutable inter-subjective agreements about what is and what was?

Victims' desire for truth

When victims call for truth, they are often asking for 'the' truth, a singular truth. The truth that is desired by victims is often an ideal, absolute truth. This desire is usually informed by and shaped by two main factors. The first of these is a legalistic conceptualisation of the truth, some set of externally valid facts that comprise 'the truth, the whole truth and nothing but the truth'. Yet these facts – where they can be assembled and verified – may confound the desire for that singular truth. Even when it is possible to establish a set of verifiable facts, the statement – the desk is to the right of the chair – is only true if the observer stands in a particular place. Standing in another position, the desk might well be to the left of the chair.

These and other problems with the concept of truth would suggest that the singular, *absolute* truth is not always realisable within the context of truth recovery (or elsewhere), although it is passionately pursued by many in certain political groupings and by certain cohorts of victims such as the Madres in Argentina, Khulamani in South Africa and other victims' organisations elsewhere. For some victims, such as the families of the Madres, or the families of those killed on Bloody Sunday in Northern Ireland, they have already heard or discovered much of what happened, and know a great deal of the 'forensic truth'. In such cases, a public truth recovery process is less about their discovery of what was or what is, and more about public acknowledgement, inserting that knowledge formally into the dominant discourse so that it authoritatively overrides previous problematic accounts of events.

The assertion of the relative nature of truth, or indeed the multiplicity of truths about a particular set of events, and the assertion of their equal value, for example, can be frustrating and enraging for victims. Often they desire the 'silver bullet' of the truth, which will bring with it all manner of magical properties – acknowledgement; closure; healing; reconciliation, reparations and in some cases the restoration of what was lost. In cases such as the 1960 Sharpeville massacre in South Africa or Bloody Sunday, the 'multiple truth' model leaves families to struggle to establish that their sons, husbands or fathers who were killed, were unarmed civilians, since some of the other accounts allege that they were armed and that there were shots fired and so on. As in this case, the dominant account is often resistant to the accommodation of these conflicting accounts, since to accommodate them means to call into question the moral authority of the state and to radically disrupt the dominant discourse about the past. The desires of victims for such acknowledgement, particularly those who are isolated and without political support, are often sadly unrealistic and pathetically unrealisable. That they are entirely oriented to the relatively inaccessible territory of the past rather than the unexplored terrain of the future contributes to a wider societal tendency towards preoccupation with past grievances at the expense of political and other forms of innovation.

The publicly articulated desire of victims is constructed in the public sphere where the dominant paradigm within which victims' experience is a particular context, primarily a legalistic one. In this context, victims often seek or have sought the prosecution of perpetrators, or their holding to account in some formal manner. This legalistic approach to truth, the use of forensic evidence, the method of its testing and verification suggests a hostile world in which lies outnumber and threaten to vanquish truth. It also places the desire of victims in the context of the propaganda, lies and secrecy which is characteristic of the pasts of war-torn and divided societies. It is a medieval battle between good and evil, the process of 'paranoid projection' characteristic of the law court,[8] a form of 'othering'. There, irrespective of the complexity of human responsibility and action, the purpose of legal argument in the adversarial court is to prove the total culpability of the 'other' and the total innocence of the self. Truth is characteristic entirely of one, whilst the other lacks truth entirely. This bifurcated dynamic within an adversarial legal system is antithetical to the reconciliation of divergent accounts of the various actors. Rather, one actor is vindicated, whilst the others are vanquished.

Truth and the dynamic of conflict

The second set of factors which inform and shape the conception of truth is the relative degree of division and conflict or unanimity and consensus in the social and political environment. The dynamic of conflict, the centrifugal force of real, remembered or imagined violence casts most of the society involved into a polarised and bifurcated ideological state. Under the threat of violence, enemies and friends are (apparently) clearly demarcated, with definitive boundaries – indeed clear blue water – between them. There is little room for nuance, grey areas, or ambivalence in a society steeped in political violence. Enemies are enemies, and allies are allies, ambivalence is danger and grey areas are the regions where lethal attacks can most easily be conducted. The ideological force of violence is one which distils and reduces everything into pure black and white.

In this ideological state, absolutism serves to reinforce the boundaries between the self and the 'other', the main mechanism for keeping the self feeling safe. Nor does this ideological – or psychological – state automatically disappear when violence ends. On the contrary, the end of violence may be seen as the latest trick of the enemy, a devious ploy to entrap the victim into even more lethal circumstances. The enemy is incapable of benign action. In this world, the conflict continues, whether in the minds of the victims, or in the external 'real' world matters not. The war may end, but it continues in the Clausewitzian sense, by other means. Thus, the continuing real or imagined conflict continues to shape and construct the discourse and fantasies about truth – truth is singular and desired, and imbued with enormous power to either heal or devastate.

For those who persist in living in the real or imagined conflicted society, factual truth is rare, precious, devastating and rather unbelievable when it emerges. This disbelief is a product of the state of duplicity, the clandestine misrepresented nature of past events and the levels of public and private suspicion and paranoia associated with everyday life in violently divided societies.

Violence and perception

Living in those contested ideological territories is no longer a post-code or zip-code lottery or an accident of birth. It is increasingly, if not entirely, due to an inability or an unwillingness to trust the evidence of declining levels of violence and to see the war as ended. It is not a conscious choice for that significant number of individuals on whom the psychological impact of long-term exposure to political violence has rendered them incapable of psychologically 'leaving the battlefield'. The battlefield is a familiar place where the rules and the enemy are known. For them there is no possibility of re-conceptualising the enemy as less dangerous or more benign. Not only have they have become habituated to what Darby and McGinty (2000, p. 260) called the 'custom of violence', but the imprint of that violence on the psyche may be indelible.

Recent psychological work which examines the effect of repeated and long-term exposure to traumatic events suggests that, unlike discrete exposure to a single traumatic event, recovery from the effects of multiple exposure may not be possible in some cases. Indeed, some such works have suggested that long-term exposure to repeated trauma, which is the experience of those living with armed conflict, may well result in permanent alterations to the personality[9] and long-term damage to mental health. Such alterations and damage may well compromise the flexibility, capacity for change and creativity that is essential to successful adaptations to new societal circumstances, such as the cessation of hostilities. For some who have been so traumatised and for whom no healing has occurred, it seems they may be doomed to continue to live in the fear and anger associated with the past, even in more tranquil times. For them, the truth is overwhelmingly hidden in the past, and the present is not to be trusted.

Truth and politics

Nor is there much consolation for those who seek truth in the political domain. Arendt[10] discusses the age-old conflict between truth and politics, explaining the antipathy between politicians and truth-seekers and truth-tellers. She attributes the conflict between truth and politics to:

> two diametrically opposed ways of life – the life of the philosopher, as interpreted by Parmenides and then by Plato and the way of life of the citizen. To the citizens' ever-changing opinions about human affairs, which themselves were in a state of constant flux, the philosopher opposed truth about those things which in their very nature were everlasting and from which, therefore, principles could be derived to stabilize human affairs. Hence the opposite to truth was mere opinion, which was equated with illusion, and it was degrading of opinion that gave the conflict its political poignancy; for opinion, and not truth, belongs among the indispensable prerequisites of all power.[11]

Truth is posed as durable, universal in the sense that it transcends the vagaries of daily life, and providing a stable reference point, thus acting as a stabilising influence. According to Hobbes only 'such truth, as opposeth no man's profit, nor pleasure, is to all men welcome' – truths relating to specific matters such as mathematics, because they 'cross[es] no man's ambition, profit or lust.'[12]

However, many truths 'oppose some men's profit' after violent conflict, and are therefore not universally welcome.

Yet, it is opinion, according to Arendt, rather than truth, that is the indispensable component of political power. Politicians rely on opinion, and regard truth-tellers with suspicion and hostility. Those who would tell the truth at any cost, whatever is at stake, are considered to be dangerous, undiplomatic, unreliable, even traitors. As Arendt points out: ... 'every claim in the sphere of human affairs to an absolute truth, whose validity needs no support from the side of opinion, strikes at the very roots of all politics and all governments...' (Arendt, 1978, p. 550).

The business of politics, then, is the ongoing resolution and contest between competing and multiple versions of relative truth. It is precisely the impact of truth on opinion that renders it politically sensitive, and a worrying element of public life. Political fortunes, based on public opinion, wax and wane on the emergence of 'the truth' about Watergate, the sexual peccadilloes of prominent politicians, the treatment or condition of prisoners in Abu Graib or Quantanamo, and so on.

The relationship between 'truth' and 'opinion', however, is complex. According to Spinoza, laws prohibiting free thought lead to 'men thinking one thing and saying another', leading to 'the corruption of good faith' and 'the fostering of perfidy.'[13] Kant argued the central importance of the ability to communicate thoughts publicly, since: 'the external power that deprives man of the freedom to communicate his thoughts publicly deprives him at the same time of his freedom to think,' since 'we think, as it were, in community with others to whom we communicate our thoughts as they communicate theirs to us.'[14] This social dimension of thinking, the ability to express and exchange thought is a process of validation, since human reason is fallible, but also socially formed, and requires to be expressed and examined by others. Truth formation, as opinion formation, for Spinoza, is a social, interactive and public process. This implies a certain societal dynamic and civic process through which such ideas are exchanged and tested. For Arendt, too:

> Factual truth... is always related to other people: it concerns events and circumstances in which many are involved; it is established by witnesses and depends on testimony; it exists only to the extent that it is spoken about, even if it occurs in the domain of privacy. It is political by nature. Facts and opinions, though they must be kept apart, are not antagonistic to each other; they belong to the same realm....[15]

These conditions, the separation of fact and opinion, are not usually characteristic of the violently divided society, or the society coming out of conflict, where facts and opinions are not kept apart, but inextricably interwoven in propaganda, and competing accounts of 'reality' mirror the antagonisms of the conflict. Primo Levi[16] reflects this in his note of caution about his own memoir of Auschwitz:

> Please grant me the right to inconsistency: in the camp our state of mind was unstable, it oscillated from hour to hour between hope and despair. The

coherence I think one notes in my books is an artefact, a rationalization *a posteriori*.[17]

Levi draws our attention not only to the vacillating and chimeric nature of thinking in the extreme conditions of the camp, but also to the (re)construction that is necessary in order to produce an account of the past. Such accounts of the past, he cautions, acquire a 'coherence' and perhaps other qualities such as moral authority *post hoc* – what he calls '*a rationalisation a posteriori*'. Yet the past was not coherent, or rational.

Levi[18] goes on to describe the more general moral inversions and reversals that occur in extreme conditions such as those in Auschwitz, where moral judgements and definitions including that of truth are altered by the perverse moral climate:

> We now invite the reader to contemplate the possible meaning in the Lager of the words 'good' and 'evil', 'just' and 'unjust'; let everybody judge on the basis of the picture we have outlined (of the Lager)...how much of our ordinary moral world could survive on this die of the barbed wire.[19]

Societies experiencing deep violent divisions, or involved in armed conflict are also perverse moral climates in which the identification and pursuit of truth is an elusive quest in a hall of distorting mirrors.

Truth recovery and hindsight

Does, then, the business of recovering the truth about the past consist of placing moral templates and frameworks on past circumstances and deeds, templates and frameworks that were not and could not be in place contemporaneously, precisely because of the moral uncertainties, inversions and moral disruptions generated by war and oppression. The general reordering of society and communal life around the moral and discursive demands of war and oppression renders previous moral codes and standards of veracity irrelevant, untenable. This retrospective contest over truth about the past presents a challenge for the political functioning of the society, since the factual truth lies at the core of social, legal and political processes, according to Arendt:

> Freedom of opinion is a farce unless factual information is guaranteed and facts themselves are not in dispute... Factual truth informs political thought, just as rational truth informs philosophical speculation... Even if we admit that every generation has the right to write its own history, we admit no more than that it has the right to rearrange the facts in accordance with its own perspective; we don't admit the right to touch the factual matter itself.[20]

During armed conflict, the process of free inquiry and thought, and therefore of establishing any credible form of truth is impeded by pervasive censorship, and the culture of silence that characterises such societies. In the post-conflict period, therefore, it seems likely that the partial and discredited nature of 'truth' during the conflict will require addressing if there is to be any reinstatement of a more universally credible account. In order to arrive at such a goal, some formal mechanism of 'truth recovery' may well function to establish new patterns of truth-seeking and truth-telling. In the absence of some formal mechanism, 'truth' becomes another contested domain, an opportunity to continue the 'war by other means' unless and until a more authoritative version is established by a definitive and publicly recognised process.

Resistance to truth

According to Arendt, we don't tolerate the questioning of factual matter itself. Yet, this may well be one of the functions of truth recovery: to publish that which has been denied, distorted or repressed, a process which some do indeed find intolerable. Boraine (2001) recounts the words of former South African President PW Botha to Desmond Tutu which amount to his refusal to appear before the Truth and Reconciliation Commission, in spite of his central role in implementing Apartheid:

> You have the truth at your disposal and I am telling you now, I am prepared to speak to you and President Nelson Mandela, but you will not force me to appear before the Truth Commission. I refuse to be humiliated and you people want to humiliate me. And at the same time you also want to humiliate Afrikaners who believe in me just like you have already humiliated others.[21]

Botha, an old, sick man, remained unrelenting and unrepentant till the end. The refusal of truth and resistance to truth recovery is found in all conflicts, where political beliefs and moral status is called into question. For others, discussed earlier in this chapter, whose lives and personalities have been indelibly shaped and reconfigured by conflict, for whom truth is to be found hidden in the past and the present is not to be trusted, truth recovery as a project is fatally paradoxical. Truth lies in the past, which is hidden, yet if it is to emerge, it will emerge in the present, where nothing can be trusted. Thus, truth recovery for some of those worst affected is an impossibility, a kind of reverse alchemy. As long as truth remains untouched in the past it is desirable; brought into the harsh light of the present, it becomes merely another contested uncertainty, another weapon in the war by other means. Some forms of resistance to truth recovery can be seen in this light, whilst other forms are clearly to do with the avoidance of shame, discussed in more depth in Chapter 4. For example, over six decades after the end of World War II, and in spite of the Nuremburg trials, holocaust denial persists. Truth – factual truth – then, is not always embraced, and can conflict with political interests.

Timing

Concerns about truth, and opening up the issue of factual truth can be at one and the same time profoundly compelling and politically disruptive. The timing of the publication of the Report of the Police Ombudsman for Northern Ireland[22] into the activities of police officers in the Special Branch intelligence section in relation to the payment and protection from the prosecution of members of Loyalist militias who committed a series of killings, largely of Nationalist Catholics, is an example. The report was released just as the Sinn Féin leadership sought the support of their membership to endorse the reformed police force, which may or may not have contained some of the police officers implicated in the Ombudsman's report. The endorsement of the police force by Sinn Féin was a prerequisite for Loyalist agreement to sit in government with them. Yet the disclosure of the past 'dirty deeds' of the police jeopardised the chance of party members' support. Such revelations are a regular feature of the political climate in societies in transition, as aspects of the past are uncovered, even without a truth recovery process. With a process, however, the revelations are ordered, contained within a set of parameters and procedures and rendered somewhat more predictable, at least in terms of timing.

The irresistibility of truth and organised lying

Some resistance to truth recovery is based on the notion that truth recovery can be indefinitely postponed or dispensed with altogether. As Arendt points out, the demands of truth can be persistent and hard to resist:

> Unwelcome opinion can be argued with, rejected, or compromised upon, but unwelcome facts possess an infuriating stubbornness that nothing can move except plain lies... The modes of thought and communication that deal with truth, if seen from the political perspective, are necessarily domineering; they don't take into account other people's opinions, and taking these into account is the hallmark of all strictly political thinking.[23]

The demands of truth, then, perhaps must be served before politics can take root with any stability, especially where truth has been repressed or distorted for a protracted period. And such demands can be onerous, disruptive and inconvenient. The extent of the impact of truth seeking and truth telling, according to Arendt, depends on the extent to which truth was suppressed or distorted. Such distortion and suppression are often part of the emergency measures taken in times of war and conflict. Truth becomes a powerful and endangered force:

> Only where a community has embarked upon organised lying on principle... can truthfulness as such, unsupported by the distorting forces of power and interest, become a political factor of the first order. Where everybody lies about everything of importance, the truth-teller, whether he knows it or not, has begun to act; he, too, has engaged himself in political business, for in the unlikely event that he survives, he has made a start toward changing the world.[24]

Yet 'organised lying' is in the nature of war propaganda. In the prelude to the 1994 genocide in Rwanda, Hutu nationalism used the press and Radio Télévision

Libre des Mille Collines (RTLM), then in the ownership of prominent Hutu politicians, to conduct a campaign of hatred directed against Tutsis, instilling fear and enmity against them. Broadcasts and newspaper articles described Tutsi as subhuman and thus incited the violence that was to follow. This form of organised lying contributed to creating the conditions under which genocide could occur. In South Africa, the South African Defence Force (SADF) and various other state agencies that operated under cover during the Apartheid regime continued to deny and cover up their involvement in assassinations, bombings, sabotage and other violations of human rights, sometimes blaming their deeds on others.[25] Similarly, in Northern Ireland, British agents embedded in Loyalist paramilitary groups operated clandestinely and participated in the assassinations of Catholic civilians.

Such 'organised lying', which enters into the dominant discourse, and is part and parcel of the world of espionage, infiltration and intelligence gathering is not, according to Elias' conceptualisation, simply a collective phenomenon. It shapes the individual personality, since developments in social institutions interact with the character and emotions of the individual. Elias argues that there is a 'continuous correspondence between social structure and the structure of the personality' (Elias, 1994, p. 156).[26] Similarly, Weber saw personality as an institutionalisation of the individual, where the personality is shaped by the social forces in its context, reminiscent of Foucault's 'technologies of the self'.[27]

The truth-teller, then, and truth processes themselves, do not merely act at the collective level, but simultaneously hold the potential for individual transformations. By providing an alternative public version to the 'organised lying' which institutionalises the individual, the individual can be altered.

Pham Xuan An, who was the only Time reporter to remain in Saigon after 1975 had spied for the North Vietnamese from the early 1950s. After his true affiliations emerged, fellow reporter, David Halberstam commented:

> An's story strikes me as something right out of Graham Greene... it broaches all the fundamental questions: what is loyalty? what is patriotism? what is the truth? who are you when you are telling these truths? ... There was an ambivalence to An that's almost impossible to imagine.[28]

In situations of protracted armed conflict and violent societal division, there are many examples of those who have lived similar lives, concealing their true roles, creating fictions to cover up their activities, some over many decades, some without the knowledge of their closest family and friends. Bheki Jacobs in South Africa, Brian Nelson and Alfredo Scappaticci in Northern Ireland and 'Omar Nasiri' who infiltrated Al Qaeda are other examples of those who – some for decades – worked as government undercover agents whilst holding membership of an armed non-state grouping.

Clearly, such protracted self-(mis)representation impacts on one's personality, the 'technology of the self' including intimate relationships and identity. A significant number of these people are destined to go to their graves with the secrets of their true affiliations and motivations untold, even to those closest to them. Sanders (2006) raises the question of how and to what extent living entirely within such 'organised lying' and systematically relating to others through falsity ultimately compromises the individual's ability to decipher truth from lies; fact from fiction. However, if one's very survival depends on the repeated telling of lies and maintenance of fictions, then substantial amounts of energy will be devoted to that purpose, perhaps at the expense of self- and personality development.

Those living, working and dealing with such (mis)representations will, if the (mis)representations are successful, believe the fictions told to them. In a society where significant amounts of undercover activity is carried out, then at a collective level, it becomes difficult to tell truth from fiction. In Northern Ireland, the revelations such as that Denis Donaldson, a trusted and prominent Sinn Féin member was a British agent added to previous revelations about Alfredo Scappaticci, codenamed Stakeknife who was a key IRA operative. The role of Brian Nelson as a British agent within the Loyalist Ulster Defence Association had already been revealed, all of which led to an unsettling sense that perhaps very few people were who they said they were, that there were spies in every camp; which of course undoubtedly there were.

At the collective level, all of these individuals contribute to a culture of organised lying which in turn shapes individual perceptions throughout the society. The denigration of truth that is created by these kinds of revelations in the wake of conflict is predictable where undercover operations, disinformation, intelligence gathering and infiltration have been practised. The uncovering of such 'organised lying' can make for a sense of unreality. It is difficult to know who to believe, and as further disclosures are made, the sense of unreality is compounded.

Nor is the 'organised lying' always so dramatic or high profile. In violently divided societies, people routinely manage their identity to avoid the risk of violence or abuse. This may entail providing a false name or address, or inventing an occupation for yourself or your partner. Certain occupations, police officers, soldiers and others associated with the security forces in Northern Ireland routinely concealed their true occupation and identity as a matter of survival. A police officer interviewed for an earlier study,[29] who had been badly disabled in a bomb and grenade attack recounted how he used to explain his callipered legs by saying that he had had poliomyelitis. He was caught out on this fiction a few times, when people asked him about new medication available for the condition. So he developed a new strategy – he subsequently told people that he had been injured in a bad road accident in which no one else was involved and which happened as a result of his own drunken driving, and he didn't want to talk about it.

Nor is 'organised lying' only practised by those in targeted occupations. Children in an earlier study in Northern Ireland described how, in order to use a swimming pool in a Protestant area, they adopted false Protestant-sounding names for the afternoon, so that they would not betray the fact that they were in 'enemy territory' and thus invite attack. In violently divided societies, 'organised lying' becomes less 'organised' and more normalised, made routine for those who feel too vulnerable to reveal their true identity, occupation or affiliations. In a violently divided context, one learns to represent oneself in speech in a manner than minimises danger and threat. The primary concern, then is not the authentic representation of one's opinion, feelings or thoughts, but with the impact of their expression on one's safety. Hence lying becomes normalised, passes into the practices of everyday life. At a societal level, normalised lying is a survival strategy.

Systematic truth recovery provides a context in which such subterfuge can be examined and the truth distinguished from the fiction. Those who would tell the truth, however, on these sensitive matters particularly, often put themselves in great jeopardy. Truth telling is not a safe occupation, yet it seems that in spite of this, the truth will often come out. When it does, there is a need for a collective reassessment of the past, a re-explanation of events in the light of what is now known.

The power of truth and truth recovery

In spite of the danger to the truth-teller, and other challenges, Arendt is convinced of the power of factual truth, attributing to it a kind of political half-life, a resilience and an essential place in social and political life.

> Truth, though powerless and always defeated in a head-on clash with the powers that be, possesses a strength of its own: whatever those in power may contrive, they are unable to discover or invent a viable substitute for it. Persuasion and violence can destroy truth, but cannot replace it...[30]

Truth telling, however, for Arendt is necessarily an extra-political role, which is invalidated should the truth-teller engage in political rhetoric or action.

> To look upon politics from the perspective of truth...means to take one's stand outside the political realm. This standpoint is the standpoint of the truth-teller, who forfeits his position – and with it, the validity of what he has to say – if he tries to interfere directly in human affairs and to speak the language of persuasion and violence.[31]

Arendt, then sees the truth-teller as a lonely outsider, who jeopardises their own wellbeing by naming or revealing the truth in all its volatility and power. We cannot or should not expect politicians to name the truth, but rather it is the role of those who are prepared to risk themselves in the interests of establishing the truth and having it recognised and entered into public discourses about the past. For example, Las Madres de Plaza Mayo in Argentina have lost two of their number, who have 'disappeared' since the beginning of their campaign for truth. Formal truth recovery is a method of institutionalising the role of the truth-teller, as a marker of a society's willingness to change its understanding of itself and its past.

It seems that the truth referred to by advocates of truth recovery is most usefully considered to be factual truth, a statement of what is or was. Such factual truth may contain facts garnered from different standpoints, but there is a core validity to such truth that requires to be established. The establishment of this validity is necessarily a social and interactive process, involving others and their perspectives and knowledge of factual truth. This process is one of definition or re-definition of the truth, which, in the case of a society coming out of conflict, is necessary because of the changed circumstances and context of that society. The new generation of truth-tellers and politicians must be brought into a closer alignment with one another through a revisiting of the factual truth about the past. If a new collective truth is to emerge, it will be produced in an interactive, dialogical process where the history is rewritten to include those aspects of factual truth that have been omitted from existing accounts.

A further area for consideration is the truth of collective responsibility, of our connection, however distant or intimate, with the deeds and campaigns conducted on our behalf by the national, ethnic or political group of which we are members. The establishment of a model of truth recovery that integrates individual and collective responsibility in a way that reflects the Eliasian interconnectedness of the two seems central to the ability of that process to contribute fully to political, social (and personal) reconstruction. This point will be taken further in the discussion on shame.

To embark on a truth recovery process is profoundly politically challenging, yet the maintenance of the status quo by the exclusion of factual truth is no less of a challenge. Factual truth and those who seek and tell it, although outside the realms of politics, are profoundly politically powerful and threatening to a regime build even partly on the exclusion of truth. The choice in post-conflict societies is not between seeking and telling truth and repressing it, but rather between a *laissez-faire* approach where truth emerges piecemeal as new disclosures are made and a pro-active strategy of eliciting and addressing the factual truth about the past in a state-sponsored and orderly process. It is not a choice that factual truth will simply go away and stop bothering us.

4 Shame, honour and cultures of violence and peace

In this chapter, the issue of shame, particularly, following Elias, a personal internalised sense of shame, is asserted as a key factor in self-regulation and ultimately in a societal 'civilising process' which deters violence and killing. This shame, it is argued, is socially constructed, and the role of the observer is crucial to the production of the 'observing self' who anticipates the judgement of others on our actions. The art of politics is often the art of allocating blame and shame to others, whilst avoiding blame oneself, and shame – and the desire to avoid it – plays a major role in the political arena. However, more powerful political actors can avoid shame more successfully than the less powerful.

The chapter describes how shame is altered by the conditions of armed conflict and oppression. Using the work of Primo Levi, it explores the complexities of shame, produced by a sense of generalised shame at the behaviour of other human beings and a sense of common humanity, experienced by victims and observers. Victims also experience shame as a result of the humiliation, lack of agency, weakness and degradation they experience. This complex account by Levi, it is argued, blurs the rigid distinction between innocence and guilt, implicating all in the acts of their fellow humans, and negating totalising analyses of the power of the perpetrator and the helplessness of the victim. The ideology of war is posited as shame resistant, with warrior cultures and notions of honour and duty to fight and use violence providing legitimisation for political and other forms of violence. Just-war theory and cultures of warrior's honour is discussed as the antithesis of Elias' self-regulating and civilising shame, and as gendered cultures permissive of violence.

Following Arendt, it is argued that if societal solidarity that overcomes racial, ethnic and other divisions is to be achieved, then a redefinition of what is shameful and honourable is required in the post-conflict period, and the new shamefulness of violence internalised in a 're-civilising project' whereby society establishes the inhibition against violence through the establishment of new norms and solidarities. In order to achieve this, discourses in the public sphere must alter to provide the conditions for 'undistorted communication'. The chapter considers the lack of trust between former enemies as an obstacle to the recognition of sincerity, and to the emergence of any common definition of truth, the emergence of which could provide the basis for a new societal solidarity. The chapter concludes by considering whether shame can be elicited by purposeful intervention, and whether shame can play a role in post-conflict societal transformation.

Dominant discourses and shame

In the heady days following the fall of Apartheid and the establishment of democratic government in South Africa, the society was abuzz with change. A flourishing of enterprise and optimism was felt, at least amongst those who supported democratic change. Strong emotions of pride and achievement swelled each time the new National Anthem was played, each time Madiba – the father of the nation, State President Nelson Mandela – made a public appearance and each time the new South African flag, symbolic of the new united nation, was flown.

In many white suburbs, however, conversation was almost invariably preoccupied with rising crime rates. These fear-filled conversations provided the backdrop for the exodus of some whites from the country at the time of the political transition. Those who left could see no attractive prospects for themselves in a democratic South Africa. Some feared reprisals and revenge, mindful of the experience of white farmers in neighbouring Zimbabwe. Others predicted economic ruin, skills deficits amongst blacks, mismanagement and corruption. Those conversations after the transition were more careful; there was a need to 'mince' words which previously had not been necessary. Nonetheless, the underlying *swart gevaar*[1] was evident. Now, with the demise of the Apartheid government, the *swart gevaar* merely moved from the public domain of government security policies into private discourses. It crystallised as a fear of crime and attack, fuelled by actual rising crime rates which was partly due to the failure to properly reintegrate former combatants.

This old fear, the *swart gevaar* in its new incarnation, provided business opportunities for the proliferation of private security companies operating in the white suburbs and city centres. Some former combatants have found employment with them. Security fences, watchdogs and 'armed response' security contracts on private houses in these suburbs are *de rigeur*.

As the Truth and Reconciliation Commission had begun its work South Africa was exposed to the brutalities and violations of the past, particularly (although not exclusively) those perpetrated in the name of Apartheid.[2]

An ironic remark encapsulated the changing dominant discourse. 'It is difficult to know how Apartheid lasted so long,' it went, 'since it is impossible nowadays to find one person who supported it'.

Clearly, one could find supporters of Apartheid; former President P.W. Botha and his ilk remained unapologetic about Apartheid or their role in imposing it on the population, but they were no longer in the political mainstream, they were suddenly the counter-culture. So, too, were the armed factions aimed at wrecking the new regime, including the Inkatha Freedom Party (IFP) and more recently the right-wing white-supremacist Boeremag (Boer Force) led by Thomas Vorster.[3]

The remark about the difficulty in finding supporters of Apartheid is worth a closer examination. Apartheid survived on more than the actions of PW Botha and other prominent and elite defenders of that system. It relied on the daily work and compliance of many white, black and coloured South Africans and that of other immigrants living and working in the country. In the old days, support for Apartheid was hegemonic; it was the dominant discourse and defenders of that system were the mainstream. Following the transition, irrespective of privately held views, support for Apartheid was much less commonly publicly expressed. Supporters of the *ancien regime* could no longer express their views publicly with impunity. The dominant discourse had altered radically over the period of the transition. To be associated with the old regime was shameful, not something that one admitted easily or freely. And this shame was a private shame, one that led people to reinvent themselves, and to alter their public pronouncements.

It was also a new shame, a product of the transition itself, and its antithesis was the newly found South African pride in the success in achieving democracy. Racist voices of doubt about the capacity of black South Africans to run their own affairs, if not entirely silenced, were relegated to the private domain. Such views were no longer socially acceptable, there was no place for them in the public domain. This new shame served to regulate the public behaviour of those who embraced the new democratic South Africa with considerable reluctance. Theirs was no longer the upper hand, they could no longer espouse their views without expecting strong challenges and censure. In a few short years, South Africa had made the participation of its own population in Apartheid shameful. This shame served to regulate public behaviour and expressed attitudes so that they complied with the new norms of democracy.

A second example is post-war Germany. As a young academic teaching for a semester in West Berlin in the 1980s, I was struck by a number of cultural differences between German society and my own, chief amongst them was the more *laissez-faire* attitude to students, and what seemed to be a very casual attitude to participation in class. I was cautioned by a colleague about my observations, which would be regarded as 'fascist' by the younger generation of students.

The label 'fascist' applied by a younger generation of Germans, carried enormous power with those Germans old enough to have been alive during the Nazi regime, some of whom were circumspect about their own role or doubtful of the role of their close relatives in the Third Reich. For many of these young students, the past was largely the responsibility of this older generation, and they resented having to live with the smirches on German identity that resulted from Germany's role in the Second World War. Furthermore, the silence of the older generation covered the past with uncertainty. In the university, an undercurrent of shame was discernable in these transactions between the (older) staff and the younger students, with some students vigilant and accusatory at any sign, however slight, of Germany's shameful history of authoritarianism.

It is estimated that only a tenth of the million or so who served in the Waffen – SS ever faced prosecution, in spite of the conclusion at Nuremburg that it was a criminal organisation. For young people, there was no transparent perception of the past roles of members of the older generation that they came into contact with.

Cultures of violence and peace 43

Inevitably, then, some of that generation they dealt with were indeed Fascists, at least in the past. In the eyes of the young people, these were the culprits responsible for the enduring shame attached to German identity. These silences and uncertainties, coupled with the sense of shame, contributed, at that time, to the way intergenerational antagonism played out.

Collective expressions of German shame, necessary in the international arena, at home reinforced this sense of stigma and blame attached to that older generation. The ritual representation of this shame was enacted by German Chancellor Gerhard Schroeder, who in 2004 was the first German chancellor to attend the marking of the sixtieth anniversary of the Warsaw uprising, in which 200,000 Warsaw residents died when the city was destroyed by the Nazis. Schroeder apologised for the 'immeasurable suffering' inflicted by Germans in crushing the uprising.

> Today we bow in shame in the face of the Nazi troops' crimes. At this place of Polish pride and German shame, we hope for reconciliation and peace. Never again must we allow such terrible wrong. This task unites the peoples of Europe.[4]

Buruma (1994) argues that Germans have engaged in a great deal of self-reflection about their past, and the evidence of that past, in the form of Auschwitz and other sites, is left intact as reminders. However, much of this reflection and memorialising, like Schroeder's apology, is carried out by an elite on behalf of the population, without regard for popular involvement in such rituals. Popular perceptions of, and discourses about the past are more diverse, complex and unknown. Some children of Nazi perpetrators and descendants of Holocaust survivors continue to search for healing and peace of mind, and some of them do this jointly (see, for example, Rothschild, 2000)[5]. For others in the next generation of Germans, Buruma argues, the conclusion drawn from German's Nazi past was that pacifism is the only way forward: all war is wrong.

The pacifist conclusion to the assessment of Germany's past has been challenged by a number of factors since the 1980s. First, German reunification was brought in and second East German history, where the East Germans used Buchenwald and other camps to detain Social Democrats and other political opponents right up until 1950. The East German view of the past diverged from that in the West. In the East, the Second World War was seen in class terms, the Fascists fought a war against the people – with Jews, Gypsies and other targeted groups undifferentiated from the mass of the people against whom this war was fought. Revisionists on the right now use this to argue that German actions during the war were not superlatively evil or unique, but rather an aberration in an otherwise honourable-enough history. Post-war German pacifism has been further challenged by the recent argument which justifies violent intervention aimed at dislodging tyrants and this challenge has been compounded by the discovery that German-made armaments have been used in the first and second Gulf wars.

Thus, at a popular level, it is possible to argue that Germany's past remains very much contested and unresolved.

These two examples, South Africa and post-war Germany, of the emergence of shame about the past in the context of political transition, raise important questions which this chapter will now address. What is this shame? What is its role and function? What does it do, and can it be of social benefit? What happens to shame during armed conflict? What is the actual and potential significance of shame in the post-conflict period? And if it is a positive influence, can it be stimulated by some form of intervention? Finally, what are the implications for truth recovery?

What is shame?

Shame, variously defined and understood, has been addressed by a range of authors. Scheff (2004) points out the convergence between Freud, Elias and Goffman in the significance they attribute to shame in social life, seeing it as the 'master emotion'. Freud and Breuer (1895: reprinted in 1966) accorded shame a central role in the causation of psychopathology in the individual, because of its role as the principal agent of repression, although Freud later abandoned shame as a central core to his theory, instead developing drive theory. However, two ideas from this early work influenced the thinking of Norbert Elias: the idea of repression; and the idea that emotions, specifically shame, were agents of repression. In his seminal work, *The Civilizing Process*, originally published in 1939, Elias argues that the acquisition of a personal sense of shame is centrally important as a means of self-regulation of individual behaviour and therefore acts as a mechanism of social control at the societal level.

Elias describes this 'civilizing process' as the acquisition of manners and customs that mediated the acting out of strong emotions and impulses in spontaneous acts, particularly acts of violence and killing. As a result of the civilising process, social control increasingly becomes less reliant on external coercion and more a product of internal discipline, through the acquisition of manners and customs through which impulses were managed internally by personal control. For Elias, shame is the mechanism which activates internalised disgust at transgressions of the manners and customs, and thus prevents such transgression. This internalisation process is so effective, according to Elias that the individual complies with them, even when alone.

> Both rationalization and the advance of shame and repugnance thresholds are expressions of a reduction in the direct physical fear of other beings, and of a consolidation of the automatic inner anxieties, the compulsions which the individual now exerts on himself.[6]

Elias sees a 'continuous correspondence between the social structure and the structure of the personality' (Elias, 1994, p. 156). Inner conflict and self-judgment rather than outside threat and sanction, through this civilising process, produce a sense of shame, which in turn inhibits breaches of norms of behaviour.

Describing the development of the modern urban personality, Elias gives a central role to the development of rationality, and to shifting thresholds of shame, which he argues is an essential feature of modernity. He also examines shame about sexuality and the method of instillation of such shame in children in order to elicit 'modesty'. Here, Elias pointed to adults' shame about being embarrassed to talk about sexual matters, and the denial of such shame leading to complete repression and ultimately to unconscious behaviour.

In terms of accounting for the origins of shame, early work by Cooley (1922) had developed the idea of 'the looking glass self' where both pride and shame arose from perceiving the self as others might see us. Williams (1994), too, later suggested that the emotion of shame requires an 'internalized witness' before whom shame is felt.

> The root of shame lies in exposure in a more general sense, in being at a disadvantage; in what I shall call, in a very general phrase, a loss of power... the loss of power is itself constituted by actually being seen.[7]

For Cooley, there were three dimensions to this business of being seen: what we imagine we look like to the other person; how we imagine the other person will judge our appearance; and an emotion within the self, or what he calls a self-feeling, pride and mortification being the most significant. Cooley emphasises the centrality of:

> the imputed sentiment, the imagined effect on the other's mind... the character and weight of that other, in whose mind we see ourselves, makes all the difference with our feeling. We are ashamed to seem evasive in the presence of a straightforward man, cowardly in the presence of a brave one.... .[8]

This idea of seeing ourselves as others see us as a central influence of social behaviour also arises in Goffman's work. Goffman (1959) developed the idea of 'impression management' to explain the avoidance of embarrassment as a central motivation for human behaviour. Goffman held that the root of embarrassment lay in real, anticipated or imagined slights. He argued that embarrassment was not an aberration from normal social life or a maladjustment, but a part of the system of self-regulation. Shame, for Goffman was to become 'fleetingly for ourselves the worst person we can imagine that others might imagine us to be' (Goffman, 1959, p. 236).

The terms 'shame' and 'embarrassment' appear almost interchangeably in the literature although Elias saw embarrassment as distinct from shame, which he saw as more intense and of longer duration.

Pattison (2000) argues that the world that Elias wrote about in *The Civilizing Process*, in which communitarian norms and values were more prevalent, has changed enormously. However, this may mean that shame is more, rather than less, powerful in the contemporary context. Both Sennett (1993) and Lasch (1984, 1991) argue that in the intervening period, societal change such as the growth of consumerism and new technologies of communication has seen the narcissistic personality emerge as the dominant personality mode. Narcissists are much more shame prone than other personality types. Contemporary narcissists are inveterate consumers of goods, seeking meaning through individual consumption. Lasch notes: 'The consumer lives surrounded not so much by things as by fantasies. He lives in a world that has no objective or independent existence (Lasch, 1984, p. 30).'

Increased mobility and instability in personal life creates a climate of uncertainty and insecurity. In Sennet's (1993) contemporary 'age of shame', individuals see themselves as more and more detached from traditional social structures and relationships. The new levels of individual freedom of self-expression, allied to new technologies of communication and surveillance, create a situation where:

> the modern self is constantly on a stage, under the eyes of a critical audience, trying to improvise the correct performance of a role. All are actors seeking to present themselves credibly on the stage of social expectation. However, they lack clarity as to what social roles and expectations might be in an unstable environment. This creates anxiety, strain and tension.[9]

In an age of narcissism, within a media-driven environment, the avoidance of shame is a significant motivator. Pattison (2000) points out its contemporary significance:

> shame may be differently formulated, construed and exploited now than it was in the past. However it still forms an important part of social life and of social control. In highly individualized capitalist societies, people may be less subject to external humiliation and extrinsic social shame. However, factors such as the reflexive nature of the self, internal referentiality and the nature of narcissism, together with the prevalence of various kinds of surveillance mean that individuals can easily be exposed to a sense of psychological shame and inadequacy.[10]

Consumerism, with its emphasis on possessing certain status-enhancing artefacts, the rise of celebrity culture and increasing access to technologies such as cosmetic surgery all contribute to an environment in which the individual is constantly measuring him or herself against powerful images of the 'ideal'. To fall short of the ideal, to have the wrong kind of sports shoes or mobile phone is shameful, and to be avoided, so conspicuous consumerism is reproduced.

Shame in the public domain

The role of shame in public life has also changed. Whereas in the first half of the twentieth century, politicians were shamed largely for political inadequacies or failures of leadership, personal failings, such as disability (Theodore Roosevelt) excess drinking (Churchill) or sexual impropriety (J.F. Kennedy) remained largely hidden from public view. With shifts in culture but particularly with advances in communication technology, this has changed. Balkin (1999),[11] for example, asserts the central role of the mass media in contemporary Western democracies where political survival increasingly depends on a core political skill – the ability to manipulate the media.

Furthermore, the media increasingly presents legal and political issues within the rubric of entertainment, eschewing in-depth coverage, and operating within what Balkin refers to as 'a self-proliferating culture of scandal', which is shaped by the limited attention of audiences and their appetite for the salacious. Thus coverage of political infighting, political scandal and the private lives of politicians take precedence over coverage of more substantive policy questions. According to Balkin this, in turn, shapes political life, which increasingly resembles the way in which politics is represented in the media, and thus both public discourse and political life are transformed.

Political scandal is not new, or a recent influence on political careers. Two factors characterise political life in the early twenty-first century: first, the power of the mass media to make or break political careers, and the centrality of media management skills; and second, the changing nature of the scandals themselves. The late Robin Cook in a speech to the House of Commons on 26 February 1996, following the publication of the Scott Report into the 'Arms-to-Iraq' affair, introduced the issue of shame, implying that it was the proper (but absent) response to findings of government wrongdoing:

> no one is going to accept responsibility – no one is going to go. As the Secretary of State said a week ago, there are to be no regrets, no resignations. This is not just a Government who do not know how to accept blame: they are a Government who know no shame.[12]

A similar speech could have been elicited over Tony Blair's decision to go to war in Iraq based on erroneous reports of weapons of mass destruction, but there, too, no shame was apparent.

In the earlier case, Cook was invoking shame, which, if felt, he implied would lead to government taking responsibility, to resignations tantamount to admissions of responsibility and guilt. Yet political life is the struggle to avoid shame, to be seen to operate within the rules of probity and legality, if not actually to do so. The battle to allocate blame and shame, and to avoid it increasingly comprises the rough and tumble of political life. Avoidance of shame in political life, it seems, is achieved through robust responses, access to power, control and manipulation of the media, rather than any adherence to standards of behaviour.

Shaming at the international level was examined by Lebovic and Voeten (2006) who studied the operation of 'naming and shaming' in the United Nations Commission on Human Rights. There, violators of international standards are named and one of several courses of action taken against them, the most severe of which is to have a resolution passed that publicly condemns a state violator. From their examination of voting records over a thirty-year period, encompassing both the cold-war and post-cold-war periods, they concluded, *inter alia*, that since the end of the cold war, it is the human rights records, rather than the power-base or political alliances of a member country that determine whether or not it will be targeted and punished by public shaming by the Commission. Significantly, they found that although powerful states were targeted by the Commission, they were better able to avoid public shaming. Nonetheless they concluded that public shaming was an effective way of putting pressure on states who fail to deliver on their treaty commitments.

The avoidance of shame, then, can be achieved by the powerful, and is often more a matter of failures or successes in media management rather than any particular adherence to standards of good behaviour. An increasingly common strategy in public life is to simply challenge and deny allegations of misdeeds, whether or not they are justified. Thus the commission of shameful acts and processes of shaming have, to some extent independent existences. Where processes of shaming follow shameful acts, then this raises the expectation that the shameful acts will be acknowledged, and steps taken to ensure they will not be repeated. This may involve a range of measures – apologies, resignations, even prosecutions or new legislation, depending on the scale of the revelations.

Shame, then, and the avoidance of shame is a powerful dynamic in politics. The power of the truth-teller discussed in Chapter 3 is precisely their shame-wielding power, exercised by telling the truth. Certainly, shame is a powerful, if complex, force in politics, and has made and broken political careers, as well as that of regimes and administrations. Those in positions of political power have much to lose by being shamed, so they are ever conscious of the dangerousness of truth-tellers. Watergate brought down Nixon, revelations of corruption dogged the Thatcher government; and within civil society, shame in post-war Germany and in post-Apartheid South Africa was discussed at the beginning of this chapter.

What happens to shame during war and armed conflict?

Post-Apartheid South Africa and the generational dynamic within West Germany offer illustrations of a kind of collective guilt, albeit individually felt,[13] yet shaped by the experience of a generation whose past behaviour has fallen into disrepute. This collective kind of shame, marked by silences, the emergence of new myths, and the subversion of authentic opinion and memory is one manifestation of how shame is produced as a result of conflict and war in these cases during the post-conflict period.

Shame in a variety of forms also appears during war and conflict, and is not only experienced by those labelled as perpetrators but also by victims. A highly differentiated and nuanced account of shame as experienced by those in victim roles is provided by Levi, who documents several types of shame experienced by prisoners in the death camps of the Second World War.

Shame at non-participation

Writing about his time in Auschwitz, Levi gives an account of seeing a fellow inmate hanged publicly[14] by the Germans for conspiring with inmates in Birkenau to blow up the gas ovens there. After the execution, Levi recounts his mood:

> Alberto and I went back to the hut and we could not look at each other in the face. That man must have been tough, he must have been made of another metal than us if this condition of course, which has broken us, could not bend him. Because we are also broken, conquered; even if we know how to adapt ourselves, even if we have finally learnt how to find our food and to resist fatigue and cold, even if we return home. We lifted the menaschka on to the bunk and divided it, we satisfied the daily ragings of hunger, and now we are oppressed by shame.[15]

This account describes a shame, born of a sense of the paucity of Levi's attempts at resistance, in the face of the evidence of the more robust resistance of the condemned man. Levi is shamed by the seeming inadequacy of his own efforts in comparison to the superior efforts made by the executed man. Elsewhere, Levi returns to this theme, this time examining a more generalised shame, including a rationalisation of his (and others') seemingly inadequate efforts at resistance, but failing nonetheless to vanquish that shame.

> What guilt? When all was over, the awareness emerged that we had not done anything or not enough, against the system into which we had been absorbed.... Anyone who made the attempt knows that there existed situations, collective or personal, in which active resistance was possible; and others, much more frequent, in which it was not.... Therefore on a rational plane, there should not have been much to be ashamed of, but shame persisted nevertheless, especially for the few, bright examples of those who had the strength and possibility to resist.[16]

Here, Levi is engaged in a tussle with his own 'internal witness' who judges him harshly, demands more – perhaps the impossible – and leaves Levi feeling the shame of his inadequate efforts at resistance.

Shame at failure to help others

Shame was also produced by not helping others in the camps. Levi recounts how he found some precious water, a commodity in very short supply, but did not share it with another prisoner, Daniele, whose need was possibly greater than his own. In retrospect, he muses on his sense of shame at this decision:

> Is this belated shame justified or not? I was not able to decide then and I am not able to decide even now, but the shame was there and is there, concrete, heavy

perennial. Daniele is dead now, but in our meetings as survivors, fraternal, affectionate, the veil of that act of omission, that unshared glass of water, stood between us, transparent, not expressed, but perceptible and 'costly'.[17]

In this case, Daniele knew that Levi had found water, and did not share with him, thus performing the role of the external witness, and Levi's shame is the imagined reflection of his own behaviour in the eyes of that witness, who is also the one wronged by the refusal to share the water.

Thus, in conditions of severe depredation such as armed conflict, the location of shame operates a warped normative system that shames weakness, degradation and humiliation rather than shaming those who degrade, humiliate and oppress. The configuration of shame during armed conflict will be explored in greater depth later in this chapter. In 'The Drowned and the Saved', Levi[18] graphically sets out the degradation of social and moral life, and the destruction of *geschellschaft* promoted by the savage struggle for survival in conditions of extreme hardship in the Lager. This state is recognised by Levi as a shameful corruption of values and bonds of humanity and respect for the other. It is achieved through a process of degradation, in which the individual is reduced to some primal state in which individual survival takes precedence over all else.

This process whereby weakness amongst the beleaguered is regarded by them as despicable, not a trigger to solidarity or the provision of assistance, can also be observed in other extreme contexts. The collective cannot afford a weak member who may jeopardise them all. Many societies practise forms of excising the weak from their ranks as a way of avoiding the vulnerability that the presence of the weak entails. In South Africa, those suspected of collaboration with the enemy, or of threatening the interests of the township were 'necklaced' – killed by having a tyre filled with lighted petrol placed around the neck; or in the 1970s in Northern Ireland, young girls who associated with the enemy had their heads shaved and were then tarred and feathered, and latterly those suspected of being informers or agents were shot, typically after being hooded, with a bullet to the back of the head. Even within the war-torn or besieged community, there is no haven of safety. Bonds of solidarity disintegrate, anyone may be – or be mistaken for – a traitor.

Suspicion of even those closest to you compounds the isolation of the individual, which in turn shapes the appalling individualism described by Levi as the stuff of which the survival instinct is made. Levi records the shame of this state of affairs, a shame which was never more apparent for Levi than at the end of his incarceration in Auschwitz. Then, through the imagined eyes of those discovering them in the camp, and gradually as they emerged from incarceration, the extent of his degradation became apparent to him:

> Coming out of darkness, one suffered because of the reacquired consciousness of having been diminished. Not by our will, cowardice, or fault, yet nevertheless we had lived for months and years at an animal level: our days were encumbered from dawn to nightfall by hunger, fatigue, cold, fear and

a space for reflection, reasoning, experiencing emotions was wiped out. We endured filth, promiscuity, and destitution, suffering much less than we would have suffered from such things in normal life, because our moral yardstick was changed. Furthermore, all of us had stolen: in the kitchen, the factory, the camp, in short, 'from the others'. From the opposing side, but it was theft nevertheless, some (few) had fallen so low as to steal bread from their own companions. We had not only forgotten our country and our culture, but also our family, our past, the future we had imagined for ourselves, because, like animals, we were confined to the present moment. Only at rare intervals did we come out of this condition of levelling, during the very few Sundays of rest, the fleeting minutes before falling asleep, or the fury of the air raids, but these were painful moments precisely because they gave us the opportunity to measure our diminishment from the outside.[19]

Although Levi's description is specific to the camps, in all situations where individual survival takes precedence, degradation to a greater or lesser degree takes place. To be compelled to submit to body searches, to the removal of one's clothes and shoes, to have one's house invaded in the dead of night, one's children terrified by the presence of armed men, to have one's home destroyed and to be made homeless, to find oneself enraged and full of hate as a result of these experiences, all reduce the dignity and control of the individual. This subjugation to strong adverse influences, as Levi's account documents, leads people into a state and to behaviour that – at least in hindsight – is degrading and shameful to them. An independent, wealthy individual rendered homeless and penniless by an act of war, experiences such degradation, and the shame of having nothing after being proud of their achievements and possessions in the past. It is of no consequence that such losses are occasioned through no fault of the loser, the loser may still experience shame at their reduced circumstances, because they are 'out of character', demonstrating a vulnerability that should be kept out of the public sphere. The social persona prior to the humiliation of loss is compared with this new reduced state in the mind's eye of the humiliated, who anticipates what they must look like to others, and thus, they experience shame.

Shame at the deeds of others

Shame takes many forms, and yet another form of shame, experienced by the prisoners in the camps and documented by Levi was the prisoners' shame at the deeds of others:

It was not possible for us, nor did we want, to become islands; the just among us, neither more nor less numerous than in any other human group, felt remorse, shame and pain for the misdeeds that others and not they had committed, and in which they felt involved, because they sensed that what had happened around them in their presence, and in them, was irrevocable. It would never again be cleansed; it would prove that man, the human species – we, in short – were potentially able to construct an infinite enormity of pain; and that pain is the only force that is created from nothing, without cost and without effort. It is enough not to see, not to listen, not to act.[20]

The prisoners are linked by their common humanity to the perpetrators of foul deeds, even though they themselves had no responsibility for such deeds. Nothing they could do, or fail to do, could change the relentless manufacture of pain. Levi describes this shame on the faces of the first Russian soldiers who came into Auschwitz and were confronted with corpses, the dying and the barely alive. He described how the Russian soldiers treated the prisoners:

> did not greet us, nor smile; they seemed oppressed not only by our pity but also by a confused restraint that sealed their mouths, and kept their eyes fastened on the funereal scene. It was the same shame which we knew of well, which submerged us after the selections, and every time we had to witness or undergo an outrage: the shame that the Germans never knew, the shame which the just man experiences when confronted by a crime committed by another, and he feels remorse because of its existence, because of its having been irrevocably introduced into the world of existing things, and because his will has proven nonexistent or feeble and was incapable of putting up a good defence.[21]

These varieties of shame described and experienced by Levi describes and blurs the strict demarcation between innocence and guilt, implicating all humans in the acts of others. They encompass not only deeds of depravity, but the failure to act to prevent such deeds. It questions the nature of power and agency. Are we truly powerless in the face of oppression? Could we have done or could we do more? Levi presents a nuanced account of where power lies, refusing totalising analyses of power that allocate all to the perpetrator and none to the victim. Enloe (2004) criticises the omission of 'the myriad strands of power' in contemporary accounts of power which: 'too often end up looking like a Superman comic strip, whereas it probably should resemble a Jackson Pollock painting' (Enloe, 2004, p. 23).

Levi's account of shame is a Jackson Pollock painting. All of these questions and self-interrogations point to varieties of little shames that living with war, violence and societal upheaval produces even in the lives of the victim, apparently innocent. Levi's account places this in the context of a nuanced scale of responsibility and shame. Having examined his and his fellow prisoners' responsibilities to resist, to attempt the apparently impossible, to find new and cleverer ways to undermine the regime in the camps, he does not lose perspective on the responsibilities of others who were not suffering the depredations of the camps. Nor does he ignore the responsibilities of those who designed and inflicted this regime of pain on their fellow citizens.

Instead, he provides an account of shame that refutes totalising analysis, that identifies potential sites of resistance in his own camp, interrogating himself and his comrades about their responsibilities, and finding himself, however harshly or unrealistically, also lacking, also culpable in some degree. Levi has reminded us that these accounts are produced *post hoc*, and Levi has cautioned us that the analysis is perhaps 'a rationalisation *a posteriori*' (Levi, 1996, p. 181), produced in the luxury of hindsight, after the liberation. Such self-interrogation is perhaps only possible after the war is over, however, when the demands of survival are not so urgent, and when there is time for reflection.

The shame of the perpetrator and the shame of the world

Levi finally addresses the shame of the Germans, which one might expect would be the main or only shame he need address, alongside the shame of the world:

> And there is another, vaster shame, the shame of the world. It was memorably pronounced by John Donne, and quoted innumerable times, pertinently or not, that 'no man is an island', and that every bell tolls for everyone. And yet there are those who faced by the crime of others or their own, turn their backs so as not to see it and not feel touched by it: this is what the majority of Germans did during the twelve Hitlerian years, deluding themselves that not seeing was a way of not knowing, and that not knowing relieved them of their share of complicity or connivance.[22]

Levi's is an appeal to the humanity that he holds in common with his German torturers, and which they denied. Using Donne, he points to their common human condition, and to the interdependence of humanity, a commonality that the Germans denied those in the camps, and an interdependence that they refused in their attempts to obliterate Jews, Communists, homosexuals, Catholics and other 'sub-humans' – in their terms. The assertion of this common humanity is, in itself, a subversion of Nazism; it is a commonality between the humanity that Nazism was at pains to deny, instead demonising Jews and others in an assertion of the superiority of the Arian race. Scheff (2003) has defined shame as a signal of a threat to a bond. Whereas Levi asserts a common human bond, and can thus feel shame, the Nazis' denial of such a bond (which cannot therefore be threatened) renders them shame-free.

For Levi, this denial of common humanity is shameful in itself: for avowed Nazis, it is self-evidently common sense, and therefore not shameful at all. Levi goes on to discuss German denial, how they turned their backs on the events of the twelve years of the Third Reich, fooling themselves that they knew nothing and that this exonerated them. It is unlikely to have been entirely due to psychological processes of denial, but rather to strategic decisions about what was advisable and inadvisable to say if one wished to survive and prosper in post-war Germany – and survive and prosper they did. In Chapter 3, the phenomenon of normalised or organised lying is put forward. In post-war Germany, the presentation of the past, where it was presented at all, was shaped by such practices.

In the absence of a society-wide truth recovery process aimed at eliciting accounts of the roles of the generation implicated in the Third Reich, which might challenge these practices, some determined members of the later generations became the recoverers of truth. It was they who were the German excavators of the past, uncovering for themselves the shame of their parents, burdened and shaped as they were by the deeds of that previous generation.

The ideological structures which support the persecution of wars and violent campaigns are 'shame resistant' in two ways. First, such violence or the prosecution of war is presented as the defence of one's country, one's culture or one's community, and is therefore of itself honourable – which is the antithesis of shame; and second, to fail to respond robustly to such threats is in itself shameful, therefore violence and attack is necessary in order to avoid shame.

Shame and honour

According to just-war doctrine, to declare and wage war under certain conditions is a moral and just response. Judgements about the justice of waging war are focused on two aspects; *jus ad bellum* the justice of the decision to wage war and *jus in bello*, justice in the methods by which war is waged. As Walzer (2000) points out, these two judgements are independent of one another: it is possible to fight unjustly within a just war, and conversely it is possible to fight justly, according to the rules of engagement within an unjust or immoral war. Some, such as Clausewitz, argue that war, as an act of force, can have no limits, and the idea of restraint on the military methods is absurd. Nonetheless, the rules of engagement as an ideology persist, and contests over the justification for the second Gulf war, particularly the moral challenge to Prime Minister Tony Blair's judgement to go to war, illustrate that the idea of *jus ad bellum* has not fallen out of modern use. Similarly, public disquiet about the methods of interrogation and conditions under which prisoners were held in Abu Graib and to a lesser extent in Quantanamo Bay are examples of the application of the principles of *jus in bello*, that is, if we accept that President George Bush's 'War on Terror' is indeed a war.

All of these rules, whether or not they are adhered to, contextualise certain acts of violence in a moral framework in which certain acts are not only moral, but virtuous. To wage war to defend one's country, and to do so within the rules of fair play, is to be a hero, to earn a debt of gratitude from your fellow citizens. It is an honourable calling. The dead are listed in rolls of honour, memorialised as 'fallen heroes' and commemorated annually.

The roles of honour are no more apparent when we consider those who are excluded from such memorialising, and shamed by such exclusion. In November 1998 the BBC reported[23] that the families of soldiers executed during the First World War for cowardice or desertion had been permitted for the first time to lay wreaths for their loved ones at the Cenotaph at Whitehall. That year, members of the War Pardons Campaign publicly honoured for the first time over three-hundred men who had been executed during the first world war. These men had, for the most part, been shot at dawn for 'dishonourable conduct' of one kind or another, most often associated with what was called at the time 'shell-shock' and more recently post-traumatic stress disorder.[24] On 7 November 2006, the

British government agreed to grant all those executed, a posthumous conditional pardon. The Shot-at-Dawn Campaign responded to the pardon: 'The State now acknowledges that the executed were undeserving of their fate and their *honour* and dignity is restored'[25] (my emphasis).

Other forms of dishonourable conduct also disqualify combatants from their place in the roll of honour. Those who 'turn', who spy for the enemy, who desert or betray their comrades or community are similarly cast out. Honour then, is an integral part of the soldier's status. It provides legitimacy for acts of violence, delineates the parameters of the warrior's acceptable behaviour and binds the soldier to fellow soldiers in bonds of loyalty and selflessness. Rewards and decorations for bravery are part of the honour system, marking out certain behaviours – risking one's life for others or other displays of bravery – are designated as patriotism and are particularly laudable.

These honour codes are to be found not only amongst state armies, but are also prominent in the ideology of non-state militias. A black granite memorial behind an ornamental iron gate in Walnut Street in Belfast, Northern Ireland, commemorates the local members of the Ulster Volunteer Force killed in the Northern Ireland conflict with the words:

> In proud memory of our fallen comrades from the officers and members of South Belfast 2nd Battalion Glorious on the graves of heroes kindly upon all those who have suffered for the cause, thus will shine the dawn. They gave their tomorrow for our today. Lest we forget.[26]

In a similar vein, the words of Velupillai Pirabakaran, Commander of the Liberation Tigers of Tamil Eelam (LTTE) in Sri Lanka claims an almost superhuman and eternal place for 'liberation warriors':

> A liberation warrior's death is not a normal death occurrence. This death is a historical incident. It is a miracle of high ideal becoming a reality. In fact a liberation fighter does not die. The fine ideal which was his life never burns out. That fine of ideal becomes a historical force and captures the heart of others. It wakes up the national spirit of a race.[27]

Of course, gender plays a key role in the ideology of warrior honour, and often the sense of honour is competitive with the enemy, who is seen as weak, corrupt or, in this quote from Osama bin Laden, unmanly: Our brothers who fought in Somalia saw wonders about the weakness, feebleness and cowardliness of the U.S. soldier. . . We believe that we are men, Muslim men who have the honour of defending [Mecca] (Judt, p. 4, cited in Braudy, 2003).

Understanding of this honour code is not limited to state soldiers and non-state combatants. The wider society plays a key role in creating and maintaining the ideology of honour, of supporting 'our boys', of defending their actions, celebrating their victories and of honouring them when they die in battle or when they return from the battlefield. The ideology of war pervades the whole society during wartime. This ideology, a feature of both combatants and non-combatant consciousness, renders moral and admirable acts of violence and war that otherwise would be regarded as abhorrent. It accords status and honour to those who commit such acts, and shames those who undermine the 'war effort' whether that effort is a state-sponsored war or an insurgency. It is shameful not to fight or to fail to support those who do.

This ideology, which relies on the notion of honour and redefines acts of violence as moral acts is not exclusive to societies at war. It can also be found outside of war-torn or divided societies. For example, Cohen *et al.* (1998) conducted studies in the American South on honour-related violence and cultures of honour, which they define as: 'a culture in which male strength and power are highly valued and in which men are prepared to kill to defend their status as honourable men' (Cohen *et al.*, 1998, p. 262).

Here, a particular form of masculinity is implicated in the ideology, a tough, strong masculinity that strikes when angered, that brooks no slight or opposition, that relies on Old Testament values of 'an eye for an eye and a tooth for a tooth', operating within an ideology of retributive justice, where wrongdoing is punished, revenge is exacted and anything less is weakness. Cohen *et al.* cite Fischer who describes this system of retributive justice thus:

> The prevailing principle was *lex talionis*, the rule of retaliation. It held that a good man must seek to do right in the world, but when wrong was done to him, he must punish the wrongdoer himself by an act of retribution that restored order and justice in the world.[28]

Cohen *et al.* argue that such violence is a defence of honour and a method of avoiding the shame that would follow if honour was not defended. They point out that such honour codes develop in civil society in circumstances where adequate law enforcement is not available. Informal codes and norms develop, whereby males must defend their families, specifically their womenfolk. They argue that the prevalence of such codes in the American South, which are tied into cultures of masculinity and are collectively held, explains the higher level of interpersonal violence that occurs there. These codes define 'shared expectations, rules and scripts for a given situation' (Cohen *et al.*, 1998, p. 267).

Thus, cultures of honour and the concept of the shamefulness of weakness can be located in parochial groups and cultures or appropriated by them as support for specific cultures of masculinity and violence. However, these parochial occurrences of shame cannot, by their very parochial nature, be linked with wider societal solidarities, except in times of war.

In the post-conflict society, cultures of warrior's honour[29] that support continued hostilities and celebrate successful attacks on the 'enemy' generally present challenges to the prospects of peace-building. A society that remains saturated with the ideology of war cannot see its own violence as a problem, only that of the 'enemy', and therefore the ideology itself poses a threat to peace and stability. Furthermore, warrior cultures pose a threat to prospects for truth recovery and reconciliation, since the violence of the past, however horrific its effects, will continue to be regarded as justified, even heroic when carried out by one's own side. Only the violence of the enemy can be regarded as transgressions of human rights standards. In the heat of battle, the enemy has no human rights, according to this mentality.

Yet, this ideology does not automatically disappear with the announcement of cessations of violence. Whilst media representations of the arrival at peace or settlement may alter the discourse in the public domain, the ideology of war remains in the minds of many former combatants and in many civilians alike. The remnants of this ideology provide an impetus for the continuation of 'war by other means' – the war of words and politics, and on occasion it can provide justification and comfort for those who would break ceasefires. At the political level, it prevents the self-interrogation or critical reflection on one's own past behaviour that Elias places at the core of the 'civilising process'. That observing self or superego is disarmed and tamed, by immersion in the ideology of war. Shame is an attribute of the enemy's behaviour – honour a mark of our own. The question in the post-conflict period, is how to support the 're-civilising process' of constructing new meanings and associations, for example, violence with shame rather than honour can be activated and supported. In order to understand how such 're-civilising' might take place, it is necessary to examine in more detail the process of 'de-civilising' that takes place during armed conflict.

What happens to shame during armed conflict?

Under conditions of political violence and war, individuals must live with the experience of a sense of personal danger and threat to life. Although experienced individually and managed privately, these threats are not personal to the individual. Rather, they are directed at a group; Shia or Sunni in Iraq, Catholic Nationalists or Protestant Unionists in Northern Ireland, Serbs or Croats in Bosnia, Tutsi or moderate Hutus in Rwanda. Under conditions of political violence and war, social and spatial polarisation and segregation occurs, embodying the antipathy between the parties and facilitating the differentiation between enemies and friends. Identification with the group, bearing the appropriate ethnic markers, can be – and has been in too many cases – a matter of life and death.

This privileging of ethnic identity over other forms of identity in ethnic conflicts serves to reinforce that very ethnic identity, at the expense of individualisation and perceptions of diversity or differences within the group. Ethnic labels are used to describe hostilities, and the population is fractured and bifurcated into 'us' and 'them', 'ourselves' and 'others'. Deep societal divisions are constantly reinforced and reified by ongoing political violence, which drives people more and more into even more tight-knit, exclusive communities. In protracted conflicts, the cohesion, solidarity and exclusivity of these communities forms part of their survival strategy. Outsiders are regarded with suspicion, particularly if they have any association with the 'other'. New norms and values emerge, displacing those associated with peacetime.

These threats and fears are also represented in the public sphere in particular ways, which either validate and reinforce the fears and terrorise the population, whilst denying and minimising threats to 'suspect communities'. In Northern Ireland during the 1970s and 1980s, for example, random sectarian assassinations of Catholics in Northern Ireland were described in the mainstream media as 'motiveless killings' and for a time, the media were reluctant to identify those killed as Catholics.

In societies in conflict, public discourses about the conflict are severely constricted, with dominant discourses prevailing in the public sphere. These discourses tend to be characterised by expressions of anger, condemnation, blame and grievance. To depart from those themes, to question, for example, the state's adherence to human rights standards is to give comfort to the enemies of the state, and this is unacceptable and will attract sanction.

Alternative discourses are produced in minority and insurgent communities, also characterised by similar expressions of anger, condemnation grievance and blame, but with the anger, blame and grievance being directed at rather different targets. There are powerful pressures within both the dominant and minority communities to conform to the underpinning 'truths' and assumptions within that discourse, and to adhere to the constricted themes. It is not acceptable, for example, to express sympathy for the 'other', or to question or criticise the activities of the armed defenders of one's community, or to feel ashamed by what one does to the 'other'. For example in the atmosphere within the United States particularly during the early stages of the second Gulf war in Iraq, to express doubts about the war itself or about US troop behaviour in Iraq was to invite severe censure and the label of 'unpatriotic' and 'unAmerican'.

The missing dimensions of such discourses are those expressions of the other strong emotional responses to violence, such as fear, grief, loss and despair. A kind of stoicism develops, where those who suffer must speak briefly, if at all, of their suffering, unless such suffering can be deployed as propaganda or to illustrate the barbarism of the 'other'. Individual expressions of grief, fear or despair are relegated to private domain, to be rehearsed in the privacy of the home, within the confines of the family and intimate friends. This creates and maintains a false impression of the damage done by violence, the silence masks the human consequences.

Allied to this, individuals and communities habituate to violence, violence becomes normalised, part of everyday life. In situations of ongoing violence, people acquire knowledge about the *modus operandi* of the protagonists, about patterns of violence both spatial and temporal. For example, violence in Northern Ireland tended to intensify during the summer marching season, and in Sri Lanka and Colombia intense violence tends to occur in certain locations, the north of Sri Lanka, and Chocó, Putumayo and east of the Andes in Colombia. This knowledge appears to make the violent context more predictable, creating the impression of the possibility of exercising more control over exposure to violence. For example, avoidance of certain times or taking extra precautions at times when violence is typically intense, or avoidance of the regions where violence is concentrated will be safer. This increased sense of control makes living with protracted violence more tolerable. Other psychological adaptations also render life more tolerable. Habituation to seeking troops with guns or armed insurgents on the streets, to the point where it is unremarkable, part of daily life, reduces the stress experienced. One simply gets used to witnessing violence, hearing shots and explosions, and listening to news of more deaths and injuries.

All of this combines to effect a kind of transformation of personal life in violently divided societies. A kind of stoicism, dark humour, avoidance of certain issues and topics marks daily discourses.

Hopelessness, a sense of powerlessness and the unpredictability of the future, coupled with the avoidance of thinking about certain things, are features of the adjustments made by populations who must learn to live with ongoing danger and violence. The ability to see the future as distinct and different from the past and the present, or indeed the ability to contemplate the future at all, is essential to the transition between war and post-conflict peace and stability. If ethnic, national or racial fault-lines of enmity are to be displaced or transformed, and violence diminished, and its meaning changed, then dominant discourses which regard violence as honourable, and non-participation shameful must be displaced with new discourses that invert these norms. Violence itself must become shameful, and non-violent management of difference must become an honourable *modus operandi*.

Using Elias, Wacquant (2004) has powerfully described the process of 'de-civilising' undergone by America's black ghetto, a process accompanied by the demonisation of the black urban proletarian. He describes three further inherent processes: the depacification of everyday life; social dedifferentiation; leading to organisational desertification and informalisation of the economy as characteristic of the transformation of the ghetto into what he refers to as 'these veritable domestic Bantustans such that are the ghettoes of the old industrial centres' (p. 96).[30] Wacqaunt points out that this process is not unique to the United States alone, but is also observable in working-class estates in France's large cities, and indeed elsewhere. He describes in detail what is entailed in this 'de-civilising process', which is a reversal of Elias' civilising process, and attributes this trend to the: 'multifaceted retrenchment, on all levels (federal, state and municipal) of the American state and the correlative crumbling of public sector institutions that make up the organisational structure of any advanced urban society' (p. 98).

This state retrenchment, he argues, leads to three trends that enact the de-civilisation process: the depacification of society and the erosion of public space; the organisational desertification and the concerted abandonment of public services in Black areas; and changes in social differentiation and growing informalisation of the economy.

Wacqaunt's description is impassioned and striking, because he describes conditions that are to be found in urban-war zones in Northern Ireland, in Apartheid South Africa or in the Occupied Territories. There, everyday life is depacified, killing, robbery, gunfire, high rates of imprisonment and casual violence are commonplace, usually targeting the local population. There too, businesses withdraw. Churches and religious organisations, if they operate at all, perceive their operations as missionary rather than pastoral work, and leisure and neighbourhood associations struggle and falter. Health and educational facilities are basic, and are so preoccupied with the basic human needs of local residents, so that they can barely deliver the range of functions they were established to perform. Wacqaunt particularly points to the: 'pauperisation of the public sector that has debased the schools to the level of mere custodial institutions, incapable of fulfilling their pedagogical function' (p. 102).

Finally, he points to the trend of 'social dedifferentiation and economic informalisation'. Social dedifferentiation is, according to Wacquant, a movement towards occupational uniformity of residents of the ghetto. In Northern Ireland, similarly, Murtagh (1994) and others have pointed to the exodus from frontline communities of any resident with the economic resources to get out, leaving behind an increasingly homogenously impoverished population. Alongside this, economic informalisation entails the collapse of the job market due to disinvestment and relocation to sites where cheaper labour is available, a rise in small local businesses where pay is low, and a growth in the 'grey economy' such as racketeering and drug dealing and selling.

Wacquant's description of the black American ghetto would be familiar to the resident of the segregated community in a number of war-torn societies. Even the levels of violence are directly comparable. The processes of state retrenchment are similar, and indeed the process of demonisation of the black ghetto is also to be found in insurgent communities in war zones.

War-torn communities are de-civilised, and this de-civilisation is enacted in the social, personal, economic and political life of its citizens, as Wacquant as described. The presence of violence, the disengagement of benign attentions and services of the state and the militarisation of communities all serve to consolidate this process of de-civilisation. And the state of de-civilisation is both cause and effect of war and socio-political chaos.

The question is this: is the reversal of that process possible, and if so how can it be achieved? Some of the reversals merely require the removal of the conditions of war, and the reduction or end of violence. Levi describes a shift during the last ten days of Auschwitz. Before the 'liberation'[31] when the Germans had abandoned the camp, and inmates struggled to survive until the arrival of the allies. Levi records a critical moment in that transition, a shift in the norms in the relationship between inmates, following the efforts of some inmates (including Levi) to find and prepare food for the others:

> Towarowski (a Franco-Pole of twenty three, suffering from typhus) proposed that each of them offer a slice of bread to us three who had been working. And so it was agreed.
> Only a day before a similar event would have been inconceivable. The law of the Lager said: 'eat your own bread, and if you can, that of your

neighbour,' and left no room for gratitude. It really meant that the Lager is dead.

It was the first human gesture that occurred among us. I believe that that moment can be dated as the beginnings of the change by which we who had not died slowly changed from being Häftlinge to men again...[32]

The changed circumstances and understanding of the inmates led them to alter their behaviour towards Levi and the others who were working on behalf of the weaker and more vulnerable prisoners. A new solidarity was consolidated with the new prospect of liberation.

Yet the world of Auschwitz is only a microcosm of the shifts required in a whole society moving from what Roy calls 'the terror of war' to 'the horror of peace' (Roy, 1998, p. 20). Peace is horrific, because the familiar order (war) disappears and new uncertainties and insecurities accompany the ending of hostilities. In the public sphere, which Habermas[33] defines as 'a network for communicating information and points of view' which eventually forms public opinion, some new discourses appear, although the old discourses of war, which do not entirely disappear, compete with them. Spoilers, those who would wreck the peace initiative, adhere to the old way; and public opinion is typically sceptical about the possibility of settlement, at least initially, given the disappointments and ferocity of the enmity of the past. Yet, as Habermas points out, only 'undistorted communication' can emancipate, in this case from the violence of the past. So discourses in the public sphere must be substantially transformed if they are to serve the purpose of an Eliasian 're-civilising' process.

Elias (1994) argues that in the course of the civilising process, the emotions are gradually deployed in the service of social control. Shame is central to this transformation. Pattison (2000) summarises Elias' ideas on the role of shame in this transformation process:

> Elias convincingly shows that the objects of shame, the experience of shame, and the uses to which shame is put, evolve over time as personalities are shaped by social arrangements. One vital continuity remains. Shame, whether internally or externally experienced is one of the supreme means of ensuring social order, social control and individual conformity.[34]

Sennett (1993), like Elias, sees that a decline in physical violence as a means of social control does not represent a diminution of coercion, but rather the replacement of physical violence with other methods of control such as shame. These replacement methods, he argues are equally effective in effecting social control. He argues that socially engendered shame is deployed in emotionally managing and controlling individuals and groups through increasingly sophisticated psychological forms of manipulation.

Pattison (2000) following Scheff (1997) argues that shame 'helps define social boundaries, norms and behaviours, and signals the state of social bonds.... Thus shame is an indispensable and necessary part of the socio-emotional architecture of any social order.'

Pattison also argues for the 'overt use of shame as a tool of social control' and sets out to show how shame has moved from being understood as a social condition extrinsic to the personality...to being a psychological condition located in the discourse about the self...' (p. 132).

Other writers locate shame in the social domain. Scheff (2003), as stated earlier, defines shame as a signal of a threat to a bond, and argues that shame is central to the understanding of human systems. Thus, in a divided society, since bonds do not exist with the 'other' side, there can be no shame in attacking the 'others'. A sense of shame, according to Scheff, leads to the belief that such is the mortification and degradation involved, that human bonds and relationships will be damaged or will end, and social isolation will result, because of the reduced state that shame produces. Who would wish to be associated with a shamed person? Indeed, there is good evidence that shame does alter the pattern of relationships and alliances and there is a tendency to dissociate from traitors, or those who bring the family or community into disrepute, however that is judged.

Shame and the post-conflict period

For violence to be relinquished, mechanisms of social control must develop to regulate the behaviour and attitudes of the society and the individuals within it who have acquired the 'custom of violence'. Norms and values must change; violence must become shameful even – and especially – violence directed against opponents.

One of the significant challenges of the post-conflict period is the problem of how to move people out of what Darby and McGinty (2000) call 'the custom of violence' into the mode of 'the resolution of differences through negotiation' (p. 260). They see peace processes in general as the playing out of the tension between these two factors:

> The relative strength of each...determines the pace of a peace process and ultimately its success or failure. Its central task is to alter human behaviour from a helpless acceptance of fell deeds to the civilized conduct of human relationships.[35]

Darby and McGinty further define what they mean by 'the custom of violence':

> Many people...do not live in the war zone, but all are also affected by the custom of violence. This does not mean that large numbers of people become engaged in violent actions. It does not even mean that they acquiesce in those actions. It means that violence and its effects have worked their way into the very fabric of society and become part of normal life so that they become accustomed to the routine use of violence to determine political and social outcomes.[36]

Cultures of violence and peace 63

How and with what can this 'custom of violence' be replaced when the de-legitimisation of political violence occurs? (One might ask how can this shift occur even before this de-legitimisation occurs, but that is a question about conflict management rather than one about post-conflict reconstruction.) After conflict, what social and political processes will support the shifting of community norms, rules and attitudes in the direction of establishing a 'custom of non-violence?'

Elias' 'civilising processes' are proposed as methods of regulating behaviour and diminishing tendencies towards destructive or anti-social behaviour. It is an internalised sense of shame that prevents individuals from transgressing the social norms of *civilité* and as such provides a much more elegant and effective process of social control than policing of behaviour by others, according to Braithwaite (1989).

Establishing a new discourse based on solidarity in the post-conflict period would require what Habermas calls 'undistorted communication', which, according to Habermas has four characteristics: comprehensibility, truth, appropriateness and sincerity, all to be judged in the context in which the communication occurs. Already, in the post-conflict context, difficulties arise with at least two of these: sincerity and truth. The chronic lack of trust in divided societies impedes the recognition of truth and sincerity, even on the occasions when they do occur. Take, for example, Northern Ireland Unionist reluctance to accept the word of the Independent International Commission on Decommissioning headed by General John de Chastelain that they had verified the decommissioning of the total arsenal of IRA weapons in Northern Ireland. Unionists' fears and distrust were such that the decommissioning was seen as merely the latest IRA trick, and that they continued to suspect that the IRA could not possibly have fully decommissioned their weapons. All of this speaks to a significant problem with issues of trust.

However, the difficulties with truth are even more profound. Where there has been a strongly hegemonic dominant discourse, to stay with the example of Northern Ireland, which, for example disallows any validity to claims of wrongdoing by the state, then strong contests over truth are inevitable. On the release of Police Ombudsman Nuala O'Loan's report which found collusion between the security forces in Northern Ireland and illegal Loyalist paramilitaries, Prime Minister Tony Blair's spokesperson said: 'This is a deeply disturbing report about events which were totally wrong and should never have happened. The fact that they did is a matter of profound regret and the Prime Minister shares that regret.' http://news.bbc.co.uk/1/hi/northern_ireland/6286657.stm

Chief Constable of the Police Service in Northern Ireland, Sir Hugh Orde responded by saying that the report made: 'shocking, disturbing and uncomfortable reading. It does not reflect well on the individuals involved, particularly those responsible for their management and oversight...I offer a whole-hearted apology for anything done or left undone.' http://news.bbc.co.uk/1/hi/northern_ireland/6286657.stm

Yet, in spite of the acknowledgement of the validity of the report by the state and the police, Jimmy Spratt, a politician from Ian Paisley's Democratic Unionist Party challenged the veracity of the report.

If this report had had one shred of credible evidence then we could have expected charges against former Police Officers. There are no charges, so the public should draw their own conclusion, the report is clearly based on little fact. This report is another clear example why both serving and former Police Officers have no confidence in the Police Ombudsman or her office, the government should immediately appoint an independent body to investigate complaints made against her and her office. http://news.bbc.co.uk/1/hi/northern_ireland/6286657.stm

Jimmy Spratt's response to the accusation of wrong doing by police officers, which is to disallow any validity to them, can be seen as successful shame-avoidance. Were the claims to be admitted, they would bring shame, not only on the officers responsible, but also on their staunch Unionist defenders, who regularly assert the bravery, loyalty, unimpeachable conduct and dedication of the police. Spratt's response is contrasted to that of the Prime Minister and the Chief Constable, and illustrates the lack of consensus about the nature of truth, and severe disjunctures between these actors, who are all working on behalf of the state, on how to recognise the truth. This lack of consensus about the validity of an accusation against the police, even in the face of an acknowledgement of that veracity by those representing the state, Habermas called 'distorted communication'. In the absence of any resolution of the contest about truth, it is difficult to see how communication can be anything but distorted.

Thus, some resolution to the issue of truth could possibly elicit a new 'economy' of shame, a more inclusive dominant discourse, which countenances a more equal distribution of culpability across all the parties to conflict. The refusal of any culpability is thus rendered more and more difficult as the truth about the past is excavated, publicised and corroborated. The redistribution of shame about the past demands an adjustment to political attitudes in the present and increased self-interrogation in the future. All of these developments are positive contributions to the consolidation of peaceful relations based on undistorted communication.

Can shame be stimulated by intervention?

Can shame, and hence certain collective behaviours be engineered by some form of intervention? Contemporary experience in crime prevention and public health would suggest that such engineering is not only possible, but ongoing. Attitudes to drinking and driving in Britain have changed substantially over the last twenty-year period. Shifting public attitudes to drink driving were arguably engineered by public campaigns aimed at shaming those who engaged in it. A similar campaign on smoking in the United Kingdom and in Ireland, coupled with legislation restricting the locations where smoking can take place is altering public attitudes to tobacco consumption. Increased attention to, and public discussion of obesity, alongside debates about children's diets and school meals, and supermarkets' coding systems for healthy food is another area where attempts are being made to alter attitudes to food, eating habits and exercise. It does seem that concerted efforts in the public domain holds potential for shifts in the dominant discourse, which in turn has consequences, at least in the medium term, for behaviour patterns at a societal level.

At an institutional level, shame has also been used in school league tables with the naming and shaming of underperforming schools. However, Pattison (2000) argues that the use of this strategy by government in an attempt to improve school performance was ineffective, in that it led to the stigmatisation of certain schools and their damaged morale. Thus, whilst shame may well be of use in establishing systems of social control aimed at ending violence and 're-civilising' societies coming out of conflict, there may also be contraindications to its use.

Alterations and distortions take place in the nature and thresholds of shame during conflict. Although shame exists during conflict, behaviours that are considered shameful, such as non-participation or betrayal are often dealt with in terms of further acts of violence. This kind of shame carried over into the post-conflict period undermines efforts to end and de-legitimise violence. In the post-conflict period, if collective redefinitions of what is construed to be shameful can be achieved, then shaming those who carry out continuing hostilities holds potential value in terms of underpinning new norms of non-violence in the process of peace-building.

Implications for truth recovery

It has been argued that shame can play a significant role in social control in general, and when incorporated into dominant discourses and integrated into conscience can be a very effective form of social control and alter norms of behaviour. In the society coming out of conflict however, the redefinition of what is shameful and what is honourable is crucial to the transition out of violence. The 'warrior honour' associated with the past can jeopardise the prospects for peace unless honour is redefined.

If one examines accounts of those implicated in violence and destruction – whilst in retrospect some may regret their past actions and recalibrate their moral assessment of their past involvements – many do not. Shame, which in the past was associated with non-participation in hostilities, or betrayal of those who were, must now be redefined, if peace is to be consolidated. Shame must become shame at non-compliance with new non-violent norms and a new reflexivity about past behaviour must undermine some of the past rigidities and moral certainties associated with the conflict.

Truth recovery can assist the societal move towards such reflexivity. Cooley (1922) identified three dimensions to the 'looking glass self': what we imagine we look like to the other person; how we imagine the other person will judge us; and what he calls a self-feeling, and he singles out two, pride and mortification as the most significant. Truth recovery can be used as a process of reflecting back to a society the deeds of the past in all their horror and complexity. Examining the past can make for a 'looking-glass society' where, finally, the evaluation of others of one's past behaviour is distilled, how one is viewed by others is apparent, and sometimes attitudes are altered. Truth recovery can enter into the dominant discourse emanating from the past new accounts which problematise and complicate the simple, polarised histories on which conflict has fed.

This is an ideal role for truth recovery, in the best possible scenario. Clearly, there will always be resistance to the exploration of the past, usually from those with the most to lose by such exposure. Their fear is one of humiliation, of being shamed, since they have usually been able to avoid such shame until then. Yet the allocation of responsibility, the sharing out of shame, which as Levi has powerfully illustrated leaves no one untouched or untainted, is a crucial step in the path towards a less-polarised future. It is a levelling process, it bulldozes the moral high ground into more even terrain. Whilst truth recovery, at worst, can be merely a contest for control of the contents of the dominant discourse, at best it can enter into the public domain of new discourses and perspectives, unheard stories, which have been hidden and unheard. In the process it can sometimes move hearts and alter minds.

5 Victims, healing, forgiveness and truth

Victims are seen as of central importance in matters of truth recovery, which is often presumed to be for their benefit. In this chapter, some of the assumptions made about victims and their role in the post-conflict period are examined, the nature and prevalence of political victimhood and the experience and needs of political victims are reconsidered. The chapter critiques the manner in which victims are often stereotyped and cast in the role of 'moral beacons'. Qualifications such as innocence which are often required in order to attain victim status are examined, and victims' roles as iconic representations of the suffering of their community and the political appropriation of that suffering for use in propaganda, is explored in the context of post-conflict contests over truth. The manner in which cultures of victimhood can be used to legitimise violence is set out alongside Bouris' (2007) argument for a re-conceptualisation of victimhood as complex and inclusive. The assumption that truth recovery necessarily assists victims' healing is questioned and the role of victims as sources of forgiveness is critically examined in the light of victims' iconic role in representing suffering of their communities. Seen in this light, forgiveness, it is argued, might be seen as betrayal. The effectiveness of reparation as a way to recognise and address victims' suffering is examined, and finally the often-marginal position of victims within peace processes and the effect on and benefits of truth recovery for victims is explored.

Victim identity and status

In situations of political conflict, political violence visits harm on all sections of the population – civilians, combatants, state forces, even journalists and foreign visitors. However, the effects of such violence are not evenly spread amongst the population. Typically, civilians suffer more than combatants, men are more likely to be killed or injured, and women are likely to become carers of the survivors.

In Northern Ireland, where reliable data on the distribution of the fatal effects of conflict are available, 53% of those killed have been civilians, British forces account for a further 16%, local security forces for almost 15%, Republican paramilitaries for 10% and Loyalist paramilitaries for just over 3%.[1] Those killed were overwhelmingly male (91.1%) and disproportionately Catholic (43%), with

Protestants accounting for 30% of those killed and those from outside Northern Ireland, mostly British soldiers, accounting for 18%.[2] In terms of injuries, the official figure of 40,000 injuries[3] is likely to be an under-representation, since not all injuries will have been reported.

The Northern Ireland conflict is increasingly typical of contemporary armed conflicts, which are overwhelmingly intra-state. The civilian casualty rates indicate that it has been more 'targeted' than some other such conflicts, with a comparatively low percentage of civilian casualties, compared to civilian casualty rates as high as 85% elsewhere.[4]

The effects of political violence are also spatially concentrated in certain geographical locations and within certain communities. Again in Northern Ireland, the conflict-related death rate overall is 2.2 per 1,000, whereas in Ardoyne in North Belfast, it is five times that figure,[5] whilst similar patterns of concentration are discernable in the Israeli–Palestinian conflict, with areas such as Gaza experiencing high concentrations of violence. Multiple bereavement, where two or more people from the same family have been killed, is a common phenomenon in such areas. Residents also experience attacks on their homes, high levels of displacement, much greater exposure to violence and higher levels of witnessing violence, all of which can have deleterious effects on physical and mental health. Residents in such areas are often fearful about being outside their own area and are acutely wary of outsiders. These are often heavily militarised communities, with high levels of security force and militia activity, and high levels of male imprisonment. It is very often within these communities, blighted by violence, that the highest levels of socio-economic deprivation can also be found.[6]

Those who have been bereaved or injured in political violence often reported isolation, even within their own families, where often there was an unspoken rule of silence surrounding the violent event. Some live with strong feelings of injustice and resultant anger at the failure to apprehend the perpetrator, and in cases where the perpetrator is apprehended, at the leniency of the punishment. For some affected by state violence, they do not trust the authorities to treat them like other victims, and some feel stigmatised. Lack of trust in authority is often widespread.

Emotions are usually characterised as individual phenomena, yet they are also powerful forces in inter-group transactions and arguably are experienced collectively. The collectivisation of emotions arising out of victimisation that is experienced as targeting a group or nationality is particularly powerful and binding of the individual to the group. The role of collective emotion in social movements is explored theoretically by, for example Emirbayer and Goldberg (2005)[7] and Gabriel (1992)[8] has examined pubicly displayed and politicised collective emotions of grief and rage in the context of the vigils of Women in black in the West Bank and Gaza, and opposition to such vigils. Patočka (1996) has referred to the 'solidarity of the shaken'[9] as the collective experience of catastrophic events such as war.

Anger, both collective and individual, at past and current neglect of victims and their rights can be seen amongst some of victims' organisations, who give voice to certain cohorts of victims' frustrations and conduct campaigns of various kinds. For example *Khulamani*[10] (tr. Speak Out) in South Africa which campaigns on impunity and has legally pursued banks and other business that operated during Apartheid, Las Madres de la Plaza de Mayo[11] campaign on the return of their 'disappeared' relatives, and Families Acting for Innocent Relatives (FAIR)[12] in Northern Ireland, challenge Republicans, particularly those in public office, on their past involvement in Republican violence. Unresolved issues of justice; the wish to have a dead relative's body returned, or a lack of acknowledgement that prevents some victims from coming to terms with past loss, and this draws some victims into an involvement campaigning, which in turn focussed past losses and injustices and can further fuel their anger and frustration.

Early research (Smyth, Hayes and Hayes, 1994)[13] and subsequent research by Hayes and Campbell (2005)[14] has found that the emotional effects of violent bereavement do not necessarily resolve over time, and many psychological symptoms may appear for the first time, many years after the trauma. Edkins (2003) has usefully pointed to the profoundly disorganising and disorienting experience that the term 'trauma' has come to represent.

> What we call trauma takes place when the very powers that we are convinced will protect us and give us security become our tormentors; when the community of which we consider ourselves members turns against us or when our family is no longer a source of refuge but a site of danger.[15]

Trauma, then, is a kind of betrayal of our expectations of security and protection. Psychological injuries sustained during conflict include phobias, anxiety-related conditions, agoraphobia and the bereaved or injured often reported depression, and sleep disturbance. Alcohol and drug misuse, including misuse of prescribed medication are often attempts to cope with psychological sequelae. Those injured by gunshot wounds, the management of chronic pain and acquiring appropriate prostheses are challenges. Physical disablement by conflict or the loss of the bread-winner can lead to financial problems associated with the loss of job or career or the ability to work. Where governments, such as in South Africa or Northern Ireland, operate schemes for providing compensation or reparations, complaints about manifest inequities and delays in such schemes proliferate. Those owning or working for businesses that have been damaged or destroyed similarly report difficulties in obtaining compensation, where it is available at all. These difficulties arise in an atmosphere that often precludes these issues being openly addressed or acknowledged until violence subsides.

Humanitarian assistance

The needs of victims can be seen in three categories: provisions for humanitarian needs including physical and psychological health, shelter and financial support; provisions for issues of justice and human rights and provisions for public acknowledgement.

Most immediate are the medical needs of those injured, and from the outset, the medical profession have adapted their methods and documented their response to political violence.[16] There has been a growing interest in the psychological and emotional needs of those affected by political violence. This can be accounted for by several broader social trends, such as the psychologising of everyday life;[17] the decreased tolerance for psychic pain involving increased general expectations of happiness;[18] the proliferation in the West/North of the use of psychotropic drugs for the management of unhappiness, and an increasingly individualised and narcissistic culture in which large numbers of people can acceptably claim to have been traumatised by events that seem trivial in comparison to the trauma of war.

Arguably, the scale and diversity of the psychological needs can only be assessed and attended to in a situation of decreased violence. There has been an increased tendency to apply psychiatric formulations to those with emotional or psychological distress as a result of political violence. One particular psychiatric diagnosis, Post Traumatic Stress Disorder (PTSD) has been commonly applied, without regard to the lack of field testing of the diagnostic framework (Diagnostic and Statistical Manual of Mental Disorders of the American Psychiatric Association – the DSM) in situations of war.

War-related trauma entered the diagnostic system through a series of debates surrounding the American experience of returning Vietnam War veterans, on whom the PTSD diagnosis as it appeared in the DSM is based. The standard tour of duty in Vietnam was a year to thirteen months, with a majority of the veterans serving only one tour of duty, although some served two or three. Most returned to the United States between 1964 and 1975, and the PTSD diagnosis appeared in 1980 for the first time. Its appearance provoked anxiety on the part of the authorities about the fiscal implications of providing treatment for service-related disorders of which the new, formalised PTSD now was one. Unlike the average length of tour of duty in Vietnam, exposure to conflict has been ongoing in conflicts such as those in South Africa, Israel/Palestine and Northern Ireland for almost three decades, which may well merit an examination of the applicability of PTSD as a framework in long-standing civil conflicts. Furthermore, and perhaps more significantly, populations experiencing such conflict – particularly those in the security forces, combatants and those who live in militarised areas – have not left the war zone. There is no '*post*' trauma experience.

Young (1995) contextualises current thinking about trauma and traumatic memory in the emergence of new concepts of human nature and consciousness and in the emergence of psychiatry as a medical specialty.[19] PTSD does not exist as an independent fact: it has been invented it as a way of summarising and bringing together things that were understood differently,[20] variously dealt with, or perceived as unremarkable, in the past.

War-induced fear produces a range of effects, which have been variously described over the last century, largely in soldiers of the First World War: cowardice; shell shock; hysteria; malingering; commotional shock; soldier's heart; disordered action of the heart (DAH) and latterly PTSD. During the First World War, such conditions were dealt with by a range of methods ranging from court martial and summary execution to psychiatry. The psychiatric approach was rather inconsistent and sometimes very brutal. Sufferers could be treated by electric faradisation at the hands of Yealland, or by the talking cure advocated by W.H.R. Rivers (Showalter, 1987). Hunter (1946) has pointed out that it was the army who was the patient even though the individual soldier was being treated. The ultimate goal of treatment was to get the soldier back on duty so that the war could be won.[21] A fictionalised account of the moral and clinical dilemmas of this situation is provided in Pat Barker's novel, *Regeneration*.[22]

A further difficulty with the diagnostic category of PTSD lies with its origin in military psychiatry. It has emerged from the history of PTSD briefly outlined above, that combatants' and soldiers' experience has played a defining role in the definition of a set of diagnostic criteria and concepts that are then applied broadly to civilians and combatants alike. It is noteworthy and not surprising that in this field, as in many others, it is those with the power of weaponry and relationships with political leaders whose experience is seen as the defining factor. However, it seems likely that significant departures between civilian and combatant experience exist, and that frameworks derived from civilian experience of armed conflict would look rather different, but the relative lack of control and power in civilian experience results in the military paradigm exerting a dominating influence on dominant discourses on the effects of war.

However, under the Criminal Injuries Compensation Scheme in Northern Ireland, eligibility for financial compensation as a result of conflict-related emotional distress depended entirely on acquiring a diagnosis from a psychiatrist of PTSD. Psychiatrists were employed as expert witnesses by both plaintiff and the state. Preliminary studies of regional differences in diagnostic practice indicate that psychiatrists in Northern Ireland avail of the PTSD diagnosis much less than their counterparts elsewhere in the United Kingdom. Should a lower level of PTSD diagnosis be found, it would lead to the conclusion that such practice may well have assisted the state in limiting its expenditure, and thus would have had ramifications for the distribution of compensation.

Straker (1987), writing in Apartheid South Africa, finds existing psychiatric frameworks inadequate to situations of armed conflict. She argues that the diagnostic category of post traumatic stress disorder is inapplicable in situations of ongoing violence and proposes instead the term *continuous traumatic stress syndrome*[23] to encompass the continuing nature of the violence and stress.

Straker's (1987) proposition of the term *continuous traumatic stress syndrome* demarcates two polarised views of trauma. The first view sees the sufferer's context as the society in which political violence is ongoing, and the other sees the sufferer's context as the psychiatrist's consulting room. The second view, sees the solution for the sufferer as lying in the consulting room whilst the first would tend to look for social and community resolutions.

Even in the mainstream of psychiatry and psychology, that tends to accept without question the edicts of the DSM, mental health professionals have been divided in their approach to PTSD and its antecedents from the outset. The 'talking cure' of WHR Rivers, compared with the shock treatment of Yealland is still reflected in debates today, albeit in a less-extreme form. On the one hand, the psycho-dynamically inclined tend to the view that exploration of the experience through telling and re-telling the story of the trauma will 'wear it out' and achieve therapeutic results. Those with a more behavioural bent challenge this, favouring instead a 'reprogramming' approach in which the goal is the extinction of unwanted or dysfunctional responses or behaviours. Other treatments, (Eye Movement Desensitisation & Reprocessing – EMDR, for example) offer seemingly technical solutions which focus on seemingly unrelated issues such as eye movement.

Denial, as a coping mechanism, is widespread amongst populations living with armed conflict. People living in ongoing violent conflicts will typically say, for example, that things are not as bad as they appear, that everyone is learning to live with the situation. Significantly, in both South Africa and Northern Ireland after cease-fires and peace accords were put in place, a sharp increase in numbers of people seeking help for difficulties as a result of the conflict was noted. Whilst the conflict is ongoing, people cannot afford to 'feel' how difficult things are, so they employ denial and stoicism as coping mechanisms. Human service practitioners, as citizens themselves, can be part of this trend, and in their professional practice can overlook or minimise the impact of the conflict on their service users or patients. The normalisation of unduly high levels of anxiety makes this almost inevitable.

A further area of concern is the role of psychotropic drugs in 'treating' the distress associated with trauma. Many were shocked by a scene broadcast from Russia, where a woman bereaved by the loss of a nuclear submarine was apparently injected with a tranquilliser in full public view after she expressed her anger at a senior politician (BBC World News Saturday, 26 August 2000 http://news.bbc.co.uk/1/hi/world/europe/897467.stm). Yet more subtle and hidden forms of such medication have been ongoing in conflict zones for the last three decades. Evidence from South Africa suggests that drug companies regard the medication of, for example, adolescents diagnosed with PTSD as worthy of investing in research on the application of an exclusively chemical intervention. Yet these adolescents have been traumatised by political violence and live in continuously violent environments. The prospect of regarding the medication of people living in such settings as a solution clearly presents a new emerging market to pharmaceutical companies. However, it presents a social and moral conundrum for the rest of us.

In many situations of political conflict, it is neither financially feasible nor socially desirable to offer clinical psychological treatment to all those who suffer psychologically from exposure to violence. Certainly, from available evidence,[24] a relatively small number will require intensive and highly specialised psychological help, but for others who may well have symptoms of trauma, and who can be sustained within community and family networks, perhaps other group and community interventions can prove less stigmatising and more empowering. Yet even where the more specialist kind of intervention is appropriate, accessibility to such services (for civilians) is often difficult. It is a paradox of modern warfare that whilst provision is often made by armed parties to the conflict for the care and psychological rehabilitation of their members, it is overwhelmingly civilians who suffer, and for whom provision is often scant.

It might therefore be assumed that flying in plane loads of psychologists, psychiatrists and social workers to a war zone will help with the emotional or psychological distress experienced by victims. However, the Cost of the Troubles Study survey in Northern Ireland found, overwhelmingly, that those who had direct experience of the conflict there sought help within their own families – from spouses, parents and children (Fay *et al.*, 1999). Given that violence disproportionately affects certain specific geographical areas, then those communities not only contain the highest level of need, but also have to provide the greatest amount of support for their bereaved or injured neighbours and kin. Smyth, Hayes and Hayes (1994) found that although people living with the long-term effects of political violence are often isolated, many are unwilling to use psychiatric services because of the stigma of being seen as mentally ill, given that they may be reacting normally to abnormal circumstances.

The other two categories of victims' needs, the expressed need for 'justice' and the need for acknowledgement are connected. If we take the examples of the Sharpeville massacre in South Africa, or Bloody Sunday in Northern Ireland, in both these cases, local communities knew what had happened, large numbers of people had witnessed the events. In the case of both the South African Truth and Reconciliation Commission and the Bloody Sunday Inquiry, the families of those killed were not hearing much, if any, new information about the events of those days. In both these cases, the public rehearsal of evidence in an official investigation into the events, created for the relatives of the bereaved a sense that their grievances had been acknowledged and taken seriously, and were now being dealt with. The establishment of a public process may or may not yield much by way of singular truths, as discussed in Chapter 3, but they have value in terms of public acknowledgement.

The outcomes of such inquiries are also of central importance in the delivery of another kind of acknowledgement, that of the responsible party acknowledging their role in the event. In the case of the Sharpeville massacre, the regime had changed, and responsibility was laid at the door of the old regime. In the case of Bloody Sunday, the outcome is yet to be declared. However, the situation is much more complex. The British government remains responsible for the actions of its troops, there has been no regime change and the government is sensitive about creating a liability for themselves to compensate the bereaved families, not merely in this case, but in the substantial numbers of other cases where harm has resulted from the actions of its troops.

For some victims, financial compensation for wrongs committed is of central importance, particularly in cases such as those in South Africa, where many communities live in conditions of near destitution, or where disability has changed the financial circumstances and prospects of a family. For others, compensation is seen as 'blood money' and in some cases, such as that of one faction of Las Madres de la Plaza de Mayo – Mothers of the Plaza de Mayo Association – victims have refused to accept or use compensation money.

Similarly, some victims wish to see perpetrators punished, before they can feel that justice has been done. They wish to see some legal process and verdict and the perpetrator sentenced for the wrong they have done to them. For others, an acknowledgement, for some in public, for others in private, of responsibility by the perpetrator would suffice to resolve the past wrong. For many victims of past abuses who seek resolution, whether it be justice or acknowledgement or both, the path to achieving these is strewn with obstacles. Even where there is a willingness to reinvestigate the past, and a process within which this can take place – the passage of time, the location of evidence, the death of important witnesses and perpetrators' fears of incriminating themselves, all make satisfactory outcomes very difficult to achieve. Where a conflict has been protracted or on a large scale, the likelihood of being able to re-examine all cases deserving of attention is a further challenge. In the case of the South African TRC, some victims missed the deadlines, or did not hear about the process until it was over. In Northern Ireland, where certain incidents in the past have been investigated by public inquiry on a case-by-case basis, it is unlikely that the demands for further inquiries into a long list of incidents will all be met. Indeed, the British government has altered the legislation pertaining to public inquiries to limit their remit and powers as a result.

The victim as stereotype

These discourses of victimhood largely depend on stereotypical conceptualisations of the victim. Elsewhere (Smyth 2000; 2001; 2003), I have argued that victims are represented stereotypically as innocent, passive, suffering, bereft, powerless, helpless, dependent, absolved from responsibility, needy and morally entitled to help. Stereotypical victims are expected to suffer, to be inconsolable and to remain in that state. Social pressures may be exerted on bereaved victims by some victim groups to conform to certain norms, and 'never to forget'. Behaviour that shows signs of a less-than-total engagement with the past can attract censure. For example, FAIR in Northern Ireland has equated remarrying after the violent loss of a partner as tantamount to wishing 'to forget everything' including the lost partner. http://www.victims.org.uk/29.11.06.htm

Victimhood can be seen as a kind of childhood, where the stereotypical victim is regarded as lacking agency, their foibles and excesses are tolerated because allowances are made for them, and they are regarded as having a diminished facility for taking responsibility for their actions and words. The amount of toleration of victims' challenges is likely to be directly related to the extent to which they direct their efforts against the existing or emerging *status quo*, with scant toleration for those victims who threaten to derail the momentum of any political settlement, or who challenge the dominant – or emerging – discourses about the past.

Victims also acquire a status as 'moral beacons' (Thomas, 1999).[25] Consideration of Holocaust survivors, for example, stimulates a sense of awe at their apparent resilience and strength of purpose, just as Levi himself was overawed by the resilience and metal of the executed fellow prisoner who plotted to blow up Birchenau (Levi, 1995). When Levi compared his efforts at resistance to those of the condemned man, they seemed paltry. We try to imagine ourselves undergoing what Levi and his fellow-prisoners have undergone, and we find ourselves wanting. In the mind's eye, we fall short of the Herculean strength that we calculate is necessary to survive the ordeals that they have survived. This attributed Herculean strength assigns to the victim a superiority over our (presumed) weakness. We cannot imagine ourselves enduring what they have endured.

Victims are thus held up to the rest of society in order to provide role models, to illustrate some higher state that others should aspire to, some feat of self-control and self-mastery that should be aimed for. Their stories lead us to marvel at the resilience of the human spirit, and perhaps see something of the better part of ourselves in them. Victims such as Mandela, or Gordon Wilson in Northern Ireland, whose daughter, Marie, was killed in an IRA bomb and who forgive without hesitation, bear no animosity and are conciliatory in their political attitudes are implicitly models of moral superiority and self-control.

During the early stages of the conflict in Northern Ireland, the media adopted a practice in interviews with the newly bereaved, of asking immediate family members, sometimes hours after a shooting or a bombing, if they forgave the perpetrator. Many called for no retaliation, and some demonstrated great magnanimity and some, such as Gordon Wilson forgave the perpetrators very quickly. The response of the bereaved person becomes a moral benchmark by which the public can gauge their own entitlement to anger, desire for revenge or retaliation. Through the victim, a signal is broadcast in the public domain about how to measure one's response against that of those who are most entitled to blame and seek revenge – those closest to the loss. It is this function, this power of victims that politicians have striven to appropriate. By association with victims, they bring unassailable moral authority to their cause. The entry of the 'qualified' victim onto the political stage is, perhaps, always only a matter of time.

Victims' authority and status derives from what Thomas (1999) calls the 'Principle of Job', the (questionable) idea that 'great suffering carries in its wake deep moral knowledge.'[26] There is no reason to suppose that suffering necessarily morally improves the sufferer or victim. The evidence is equivocal. For each example of a victim being improved by suffering, there is another of moral degeneracy, retaliation and hatred resulting from victimisation. Yet in spite of these contradictions, there is a continued tendency to appoint victims as 'moral beacons' for the wider society. Although there are examples of victimisation motivating victims to become peace activists, there is little systematic evidence about the political opinions or roles of victims, which one is tempted to assume to fall along as broad a spectrum as those in the general population.

Thomas (1999) also raises the issue of the eligibility for such appointment. He argues that, whilst Jews in the United States have been elevated to such positions, African-American blacks, although qualified by the suffering of slavery to fill the role, are not regarded as moral beacons. Suffering *per se* is not a sufficient qualification, nor is sustaining loss in armed conflict. The widow of the alleged informer, the victim of a necklace killing in South Africa, or the wife of a political prisoner are unlikely to qualify as moral beacons, in spite of their endurance of suffering, unless – as in the case of South Africa – there is an overturning of the dominant values, and yesterday's terrorist becomes today's statesman and hero. The moral beacon must be congruent with the dominant political values, which may change, as in the South African case.

The suffering must be recognised as 'undeserved' according to dominant values, and the victim must belong to a group that is not stigmatised. Therefore, as Thomas points out, certain identities or races are precluded by racism and prejudice from being regarded as 'moral beacons'. In deeply divided societies, attitudes to suffering are similarly divided; the suffering of one side is not easily recognised or acknowledged by the other. The experience of this in Northern Ireland will be explored further below. The production of a 'moral beacon' about which there is consensus is therefore problematic in such circumstances of division, since one side's suffering can be a source of the other side's triumph. The inversion of this triumph over the suffering of the 'other', and its transformation into what De Swaan (1995) refers to as 'widening circles of identification'[27] so that the suffering of the 'other' is recognised as suffering, allows empathy and compassion to be experienced.

'Real' and 'innocent' victims

The increasingly political role of victims groups, some of which argue that certain bereaved or injured people should not be entitled to victim status is a feature of post-settlement Northern Ireland. These groups, largely based in the Protestant Unionist community argue that only 'innocent' victims should be considered as true victims. Elsewhere,[28] I rather idealistically proposed that in order to qualify as a legitimate victim, it was sufficient to be a human being and to have suffered as a result of violent conflict. Whilst this definition may assist with questions of entitlement to support services, it does not reflect the way in which victim status is accorded to or withheld from sufferers in the *realpolitik* of the society coming out of conflict.

In Northern Ireland, this inclusive approach met with strong opposition from those in the Unionist community who had to countenance the inclusion in the same 'victim' category as themselves, those from the community that had harmed them. The attempts to draw distinctions between categories of victims became particularly marked as radical Unionist opposition to the settlement consolidated.

A growing number of new voluntary groups, FAIR (Families Acting for Innocent Relatives) and HURT (Homes United by Republican Terror, later changed to 'Homes United by Recurring Terror') for example, began to be formed from mid-1998 onwards. Many of these groups sprang up in the border regions, where the deaths of members of the predominantly Protestant local security forces had been concentrated. Many of these groups adopted 'exclusive' approaches, saying that they represented 'victims of terrorism', 'innocent victims' or 'victims of Nationalist terror'. The use of the terms 'innocent' or 'real' as qualifications for victimhood were adopted by some groups as a means of excluding others. De Swaan usefully describes this as the process of disidentification[29] which he applies to the case of Rwanda. Their activities were mainly meeting politicians and voicing opposition to prisoner releases. By November 1998, FAIR had been invited to join the Touchstone Group, a group established at Bloomfield's recommendation to advise the government on victim issues. In the end, they did not take up their seats. From another quarter, the government's Victims Liaison Unit had been under a different kind of pressure, this time to include prisoners in their remit. With the increasing pressure from these new victim groups, the inclusion of prisoners became increasingly less likely.

Legitimate victimhood is a contested category, and the contest centres on how certain associations – with insurgency, for example – disqualify those who have been harmed by conflict from the acquisition of legitimate victim status. This means that the true diversity of those suffering harm is not admitted into the category of 'victim' – at least not without a struggle. Victimhood, according to this model, is one-dimensional: one cannot have a complex relationship to conflict, and one cannot be both a perpetrator and a victim. Association with, for example, insurgency, disqualify those who have been harmed from the acquisition of victim status (Smyth, 2003).

The victim may become an icon of grievance for their entire community. The harm done to them may come to symbolise the historic, multiple wrongs perpetrated against their community. The construction of the narrative about the victim's experience plays a central role in both individual and collective identity formation. The victim's identity can become bound up with the communal grievance, particularly if media attention is intense. Some victims become well-known as spokesperson for their family, or are expected to perform the role of moral beacon described earlier in this chapter. This can place an unsolicited burden of responsibility on certain victims, and their feelings and decisions are shaped by the expectations of their own community. The son of a man killed on Bloody Sunday described his experience of identity following his father's death, by explaining that, on Bloody Sunday his own name changed. Prior to Bloody Sunday his name was 'A.N. Other', and after Bloody Sunday, his name became, 'A.N. Other whose father was killed on Bloody Sunday'.

Arguably, victim identity should ideally only be a temporary position, and with support, successful coping skills and the passage of time, the victim is transformed into a survivor. However, in some cases, such as those who are put into iconic roles or those for whom disablement has resulted from the violence, the alteration brought about by the violence is not merely in living circumstances and health, but identity itself is significantly and permanently altered; nor is the welfare of the victim or their identity unfolding in a vacuum. The interplay between the success or failure in the quest for justice and acknowledgement has significant effects on victims' well-being and identity. However, it is a tragic feature of victimisation itself that some victims' quests are doomed to failure. Los Madres de la Plaza de Mayo (founding line), who campaign to be reunited with their loved ones, who are clearly dead, or others' demands for the re-imprisonment of political prisoners released as part of a settlement are examples of such campaigns. Indeed, the then Secretary of State for Northern Ireland, Mo Mowlam met with prisoners during the Irish peace negotiations in January 1998 in order to encourage their support for the peace process and apologised to those bereaved and injured for doing so, justifying her actions by referring to support for the peace process.

There is a clear relationship between victim welfare and the achievability of their goals, yet lawyers or other advisors may shy away from spelling out the harsh realities to the already-vulnerable victim. Those victims, such as Khulamani's litigation, or the Bloody Sunday families' successful campaign for a public inquiry, who undertook the Herculean task of campaigning for justice and acknowledgement often paid a heavy price emotionally and sometimes financially and in health terms. They must remain in close touch with perhaps the most painful event of their lives, where other victims may succeed in achieving some emotional resolution as time passes, since the events are not so close to them in time. For some victims, building a new life is possible with the achievement of resolution, but for those denied justice and who campaign for such justice, these achievements are more difficult.

Discourses of victimhood play a central role in the propaganda war in the determination of which side in a conflict is deserving of sympathy; which is most profligate in inflicting harm; which has violated the rules of war; which is guilty of human rights violations. The propaganda war – the war for hearts and minds – is of central importance in reinforcing the political and moral strength of each party to the conflict. Discourses of victimhood often figure centrally in the propaganda war because they potentially perform a number of functions: they gain sympathy for suffering and hardship endured; they demonstrate the degeneracy of the 'other' side in inflicting such suffering; they highlight the injustice of the victimisation and the need to protect against further victimisation and avenge that which has already taken place. Harm inflicted on children by the 'other' side features prominently in both Israeli and Palestinian propaganda, for example. Such representations of victimisation helps to consolidate the political and moral strength of a party to the conflict.

Thus, the propaganda war, and representations of victims in both dominant and subaltern discourses largely depends on a one-dimensional representation of the victim, as a simple suffering creature, without agency, politics or associations with the conflict itself. This obscures any representation of the diverse characters, histories and affiliations of those who are harmed by political conflict. According to Bouris (2007) it has several other effects in the political sphere. First, it prevents the international community and peace-building scholarship from recognising those in more complex situations as victims. Second, and consequentially, this may prevent a response to the needs of such victims who are not recognised as such, and third, the creation of a stable peace may be prevented by overly simplistic or stereotypical representations of victims. Bouris (2007) argues that victim discourses play a key role in the formation of post-conflict institutions and practices.

This is illustrated by the work of Borer (2003) who proposed a taxonomy of victims and perpetrators based on the South African Truth and Reconciliation Process. Borer (2003) challenges the assumption of the homogeneity of the categories 'victim' and 'perpetrator', arguing that they are heterogeneous categories. She identifies a range of categories which illustrate this, for example perpetrators who became heroes, heroes who became perpetrators, perpetrators who were victims, victims who were heroes and so on. She goes on to point to the three main errors in the conceptualisation of victims and perpetrators in human rights scholarship. These are:

1   Most often they [victims and perpetrators] are referred to as two distinct groups: in situations of Gross Violations of Human Rights you have victims and you have perpetrators.
2   Implicit in this approach is the assumption that both groups are homogenous: victims and perpetrators are referred to as if they are all the same. The victims. The perpetrators.
3   In the worst case, the two are set up as diametrically opposed – for example, victims vs. perpetrators.[30]

Nor are these matters of semantics or fine sociological distinctions, as Bouris has pointed out. These categorisations determine access to compensation, for example in Northern Ireland, where those involved in 'terrorist' activity – and their relatives – are debarred from compensation. Borer describes how the South African TRC process depended on individuals identifying themselves as *either* victims *or* perpetrators in order to fit into the categorisations of the TRC and its processes. Applicants could not be both victim and perpetrator, nor could they refuse these categories, therefore those who could not identify themselves under one or other of these labels could or would not participate in the TRC process. In order to qualify for reparation, for example, applicants had to be certified as victims by the TRC, and in order to apply for amnesty, applicants had to identify themselves as perpetrators. Borer points out that: 'Many would-be applicants for amnesty never applied because they could not identify with the process – they were not perpetrators, they were defenders of the nation' (Borer, 2003, p. 1115, quoted in Bouris, 2007).

Nor was it only perpetrators who were resistant to the process of labelling. Others, ascribed the role of victim, such as Andre Du Toit in South Africa, refused to be presented as 'victims in need of healing' (Minow, 1998, p. 28), preferring to be seen as freedom fighters. Some victims wish to avoid being seen as vulnerable, whilst others in the South African case wished to avoid the pressure on victims to forgive which is promoted within the South African process.

Cultures of victimhood

Within conflicted societies, the experience of victimhood is often self-defined and individually experienced. A useful sample survey of Northern Ireland[31] some

80 *Victims, healing, forgiveness and truth*

seven years into the peace process found that 12% of the sample saw themselves as victims of the conflict, that those who considered themselves victims were older, less likely to be in professional/managerial occupations and less likely to live in areas of low violence. Furthermore, seeing oneself as a victim was always associated with lower levels of psychological well-being.

As distinct from the experience and actions of actual victims, cultures of victimhood develop within violently divided societies. Victimhood is experienced and claimed by 'both sides', with combatants referring to acts which victimised them or their constituency as the stimulus for their taking up arms. Thus, combatants, too, commonly lay claim to victimhood. (This is one of the issues which enrages some victims' organisations – even a significant number of those who take up arms do so because of a previous experience of victimisation or humiliation.)

In this way, victimhood is deployed as a legitimisation of further violence, which is cast as retaliation for the original victimisation, and ultimately blamed on the original perpetrator. Thus responsibility for acts of violence is separated from those who commission them, rendering them shame-free (Smyth and Morrissey, 2002). It is not shameful to retaliate when one's family or community is attacked. Thus, a strong collective identity whereby individuals identify with wrongs done to their identity group, coupled with ongoing violence, creates the conditions for a pervasive culture of victimhood, where 'everyone is a victim.' Such universal definitions of victimhood are powerful agents in the erosion of shame in a society, since a victim's retaliation is understandable, not shameful. In Chapter 4, the role of warrior's honour was also discussed in relation to the neutralisation of shame. Prospects for a self-regulated society with inhibitions about violence depend on the presence of shame, which was shown to be a central factor in effective social control in the form of self-regulation.

In Northern Ireland, for example, both contemporary Loyalism and Republicanism[32] are cultures of victimhood in that paramilitaries on both sides refer to their status as victims in order to justify their recourse to armed conflict. Loyalists describe their victimisation at the hands of the IRA, whereas Republicans describe their victimisation by British Imperialism and Loyalist sectarianism. In a society with a strong culture of victimhood, acts of violence are cast as retaliation and perpetrators of violence deploy their victim status to explain their acts of violence. Such a society is violence-prone, since violence is understandable – if not honourable – rather than shameful. The implications for political culture where victimhood becomes a socially institutionalised way of escaping guilt, shame or responsibility are far-reaching. A political culture, based on competing claims to victimhood will support and legitimise violence, and fail to foster political responsibility and maturity.

Deconstructing the victim stereotype

The earlier description of the victim stereotype as innocent, passive, powerless and so on is problematic in a number of ways. First, since victimhood in certain post-conflict situations has come to be an all-encompassing and one-dimensional identity, victims cannot be anything other than victims, particularly not simultaneously. Even the idea that a soldier shoots dead an innocent child, and subsequently is, himself, severely injured in a bomb attack usually gives rise to the pro-state faction seeing him as a victim, whilst those in the dead child's community may see him as an enemy rather than a victim. When that dead child's brother, who was traumatised by witnessing the shooting, joins an armed group to fight against the soldier's army, the state will see this traumatised brother of the dead child as a terrorist, but not as a victim. This unipolar view of combatants (and victims) denies the complexity and diversity of experience which can be of both perpetration and victimhood.

Popular perception, public policy and many truth recovery mechanisms, such as the South African TRC, do not permit recognition of such concurrent identities, or take into account the complexities and diversities of experience of armed conflict that can be built up, particularly over protracted armed conflicts. Yet the victims and perpetrators of any armed conflict can provide a plethora of examples of such complexities. Furthermore, the tendency to see victims (and perpetrators) as one-dimensional and homogenous identities further compounds the polarisation of conflict itself.

A major source of resistance to a closer examination of victim identity and this deconstruction of the stereotype of victimhood is the fear of such a process spilling over or contributing to victim-blaming. Bouris describes the common aversion to embarking on such an enterprise:

> Precisely because of a deep and real concern with victim blaming, much scholarship on political victimization does not simply overlook or oversimplify issues of, for instance, victim responsibility, but rather such issues are purposefully suppressed. Victim blaming has made the lives of victims and their advocates tremendously difficult. ... Insofar as unlinking victim innocence, purity, moral superiority and lack of responsibility is seen as a gateway to blaming victims, it is certainly justifiable to refrain from tampering with the constellation of the victim that protects her from such assaults.[33]

Clearly, victim-blaming is a risk against which vigilance is required. Equally, Bouris (2007) argues that to interpret a critique of the stereotypical attributes of the victim as an attack on actual victims is equally problematic. Victims' suffering is not denied or minimised by a perception of those who suffer as complex human beings, some with diverse and complicated histories, in whom – like the rest of us – virtue and fault can coexist. Rather victims are restored as three-dimensional, complex personas, each of whom has diverse connections with the conflict, and unique ways of understanding these connections.

Within dominant discourses and in popular attitude, there is a tendency for victimhood to subsume all other aspects of identity, which are read and re-interpreted in the light of the victim stereotype. Victim identity can thus become all-consuming, masking other aspects of the sufferer, some of which – like creativity – can be crucial to the sufferer regaining a sense of control over his or her life (Smyth, 1999). Elsewhere I have argued, (Smyth, 2003, p. 140) that stereotypical perceptions of victims lead to the silencing and isolation of those victims that do not conform to the stereotype, de-legitimising the real feelings and desires of actual victims. For example, victims are supposed to recover within a set time period, and those who cannot, feel weak or inadequate.

A more sensitive perception of the complexity of victim identity would be greatly facilitated by a more careful assignation of victimhood to certain parts of individual identity, leaving other parts to coexist. Thus, the individual is a victim during the period he or she experiences victimisation, and at other times may define his or her identity without reference to victimhood; the individual is a victim by virtue of the specific status acquired by the process of victimisation – the status of widow or of disabled person, and other statuses – football supporter, pigeon fancier, jazz singer, hill walker – held by the sufferer are not subsumed or smothered under the mantle of victimhood. This looser and more focused manner of defining victimhood also affords much greater flexibility to victims in terms of expressing the diversity of their experiences and needs, but also 'unfixes' victim identity, providing for the possibility of change, and movement beyond victim identity. This would entail, however, shifts in forms of social power that operate to perpetuate insider–outsider dualisms to allow the development of an enlarged collective which is capable of including the outsider.

Bouris (2007) argues that victimisation discourses shape the institutions and practices of the post-conflict society (Bouris, 2007, p. 6). She sets out to critique discourses of victimhood, a process which, she argues, will: 'disturb those practices that are settled, untie what appears to be sewn up, and render as produced that which claims to be naturally emergent' (p. 6).

She sets out to deconstruct the black and white accounts of victimhood, demonstrating the overlaps and complexities of accounts of victimisation, and using Arendt, she argues for the emergence of what she calls the 'gray victim' – a more complex, nuanced and three-dimensional character than the stereotypical victim; a character not only with the potential for being victimised, but also with the potential for victimising and for participating in wider social and political processes which support victimisation.

Constructing the complex victim

Arendt's work represents a challenge to simplistic and static accounts of evil persecuting the innocent. Arendt, arguing for a more nuanced analysis, explains the 'foul deeds' of men not by reference to some absolute form of superlative evil, but rather to the 'banality of evil' which, referring to Eichmann, she explains as:

> The phenomenon of evil deeds, committed on a gigantic scale, which could not be traced to any particularity of wickedness, pathology, or ideological conviction in the doer, whose only personal distinction was perhaps an

extraordinary shallowness. However monstrous the deeds were, the doer was neither monstrous nor demonic, and the only specific characteristics one could detect in his past as well as in his behaviour during the trial and preceding police examination was something entirely negative; it was not stupidity but a curious, quite authentic inability to think.[34]

Arendt, like Levi, eschews the simple bifurcated and fixed accounts of the roles of both victims and perpetrators, but rather lays bare the complexities of roles and responsibilities of both perpetrators and victims of the Holocaust. For many Jews, Arendt's approach was a betrayal, a travesty, which undermined the healing of the wounds of the Holocaust and compromised the rebuilding of a Jewish people. Objections to Arendt's work included criticism of her analysis of the alleged collaboration of the *Judenrat* with the Nazi regime, and her reading of other historical events. However, in Levi's analysis of shame, and his identification of various subtle varieties of shame amongst those who were clearly the victims of the Holocaust yet perhaps did not resist enough, one can see a parallel with Arendt's analysis of responsibility. Levi's first-hand account of life in the Auschwitz Camp provides a self-reflexive interrogation of his own role as a victim of the Nazis, in which he raises questions about his own responsibility, creating a portrait of himself as a victim, but still possessing some limited agency, and still experiencing shame and guilt.

Both Levi and Arendt refute the 'Superman comic strip' representation of power and responsibility where powerful and powerless are clearly differentiated in favour of the Jackson Pollock painting analogy, where power is layered and dispersed.[35]

Arendt, like Levi, asserts the concept of a common responsibility created by an imagined common humanity, an identification with other members of the species, whereby one experiences shame, for example at the 'foul deeds' of others. This identification has the effect of blurring the demarcations between victim and perpetrator and also provides an alternative to the discourse of race.

> [P]eoples have learned to know one another better and learned more and more about the evil potentialities in men. The result has been that they have recoiled more and more from the idea of humanity and become more susceptible to the doctrine of race which denies the very possibility of a common humanity. They instinctively felt that the idea of humanity, whether it appears in a religious or humanistic form, implies the obligation of a general responsibility which they do not wish to assume. For the idea of humanity, when purged of all sentimentality, has the very serious consequence that in one form or another men must assume responsibility for all crimes committed by men and that all nations share the onus of evil committed by all others.... Those who today are ready to follow this road in modern version do not content themselves with the hypocritical confession, "God be thanks, I am not like that," in horror at the undreamed of potentialities

of the German national character. Rather, in fear and trembling, have they finally realized of what man is capable – and this is indeed the precondition of any modern political thinking... This, however, is certain: upon them and only them, who are filled with a genuine fear of the inescapable guilt of the human race, can there be any reliance when it comes to fighting fearlessly, uncompromisingly, everywhere against the incalculable evil that men are capable of bringing about.[36]

The realisation of the evil that all humanity is capable of, and fearful vigilance over this capability is, for Arendt, the basis for building the future. To build a community on a unilateral claim to the moral high ground, based on rigid distinctions between the innocent and the guilty, rather than on a concept of a broader identification with other human beings and comprehensive vigilance, for Arendt endangered the project of rebuilding a Jewish community. Only by engaging with the complex nature of victimisation and of evil, according to Arendt, could such a community be built on solid foundations.

Healing, identity and victims' needs

One of the concerns that properly emerges in the post-conflict period is attention to victims' needs, and the discourse about victims frequently refers to the facilitation of victims' healing. Hamber (2001) argues that the South African process did not deliver healing to all those who participated in it. It could be reasonably argued that expectations of the South African process were unrealistically high, but this is to obfuscate the real shortcomings and political compromises in any truth recovery process that compromise matters such as prospects for healing, which Hamber, Kulle and Wilson (2001) argue, are inevitable:

> In questions of post-war justice, there is only the political. That is not to say simply that expediency is supreme. Moral decisions are certainly made within the context of political struggle and negotiation... in the case of South Africa, such decisions have stemmed less from universal principles of rights and duties and more from within a vision of a free, self-governing community of citizens seeking to build a different kind of *res publica*.[37]

The obligation to address victims' needs is often expressed in moral terms, as a collective obligation to those who have suffered most, or who have paid the highest price for the emerging new dispensation. For some, questions of truth recovery in general are dominated by moral concerns, establishing justice, culpability and absolute truth. However, Arendt has cautioned us about the disconnect between opinion and truth, which suggests that politics and morality occupy two separate and sometimes conflicting spheres. For others, the business of truth recovery is properly concerned with rehabilitating a sense of order and accountability and undermining impunity with processes such as lustration. In this, the allocation of responsibility, acknowledgement, apology, forgiveness and reconciliation are central. From those approaching truth recovery from a moral perspective, the adulteration of 'pure' truth recovery with the considerations of political expediency seems sacrilegious. Elements of this tension are observable in the processes in South Africa and Argentina, and to some extent account for the dissatisfaction of many, especially victims, with those processes.

In terms of the prospects for Northern Ireland, there is still a substantial amount of moral absolutism in the way in which some in Northern Ireland pursue – or refuse to pursue – questions of truth recovery. There has been an undue focus on validating historical political positions and exposing one's enemies to the exclusion of a focus on reconciliation or the shared experience of loss and damage that spans the societal divide. These tendencies have been crystallised by the political appropriation of suffering, which has been an increasing feature of political contests in Northern Ireland and elsewhere. As Wilson, Kulle and Hamber have cautioned, the uses to which suffering has been put in Northern Ireland have often served an agenda more preoccupied with political advantage than with healing or reconciliation.

Perhaps the bifurcation of society that occurs during an armed conflict is so profound that the creation of new collectivities and solidarities should be framed as an intergenerational project, which the process of formal truth recovery can merely initiate. The erosion of layers of enmity and the establishment of new forms of identification and relationship across the fractures in society is a bigger task that any time-limited formal truth recovery process can deliver. But it can provide the conceptual framework, the language and the opportunity to begin such a project.

Healing

There has been an upsurge in interest since the cease-fires in attending to the damage done by the violence of the past. One tendency has been to pathologise this damage and see it exclusively in mental health terms, with counselling as the solution. This privatises and depoliticises the past in a manner resisted by many victims, who see their suffering in a communal context and the solution similarly lying in a collective approach. Ettin's (1988) seminal article, 'By the Crowd they have been broken, by the crowd they shall be healed' explores further this collective dimension of healing, which addresses the damage to relationship sustained by the process of victimisation.

The issue of agency in relation to healing is a central one. The demands on families and communities that have been worst affected by an armed conflict in terms of care and support for victims have been heavy indeed. These communities bear a disproportionate burden of grief and loss over several decades and also the day-to-day support for victims' physical and emotional needs. The issue of healing, therefore, is not an individual or indeed a family issue. It is not simply the victim's problem. It is a community issue, with an individual and family aspect to it.

Professional support services are often not equipped to deal with the emotional and psychological sequelae of armed conflict in other than in a pathologising manner. The stigma associated with using such services, together with their slowness to engage with the community dimension of victims' experience has meant that the relevance and take-up of professional services has been low, especially during the period of active conflict. That victims should seek to avoid what Goffman (1963) referred to as the 'spoiled identity' associated with the use of support services is a further illustration of the configuration of shame, even in the post-conflict period. As discussed in Chapter 4, the danger is that it is vulnerability, not violence and aggression that is shameful, The culture of silence and denial, once a 'coping mechanism' that prevented victims' needs being identified or met, continues to operate on a smaller scale in the post-conflict period. Whilst there are dangers in assuming that demolishing denial and ending silence is necessarily a universally beneficial intervention, continued silence can compound the isolation of victims and victim communities, and prove a block to individual and collective healing.

A further block to healing can be the fixed nature of victim identity, particularly if the victim has taken on an iconic significance for their community. To heal or recover a quality of life, even to a limited extent, can compromise their value as an icon of suffering. There is a permanence to the status of certain victims such as certain Holocaust survivors or Las Madres de la Plaza de Mayo; victimhood and activism on issues arising out of it, almost becomes a full-time occupation. Individuals and groups who campaign for justice can find themselves in this position, where a continuing focus on the victimisation inhibits or prevents healing or a new start after the shock and a period of grieving.

Who needs forgiveness?

In Northern Ireland, where there has been extensive research and documentation into victims' needs, those needs are usually expressed in terms of the desire for justice – truth, healing and closure. Victims have rarely expressed a need to forgive, although doubtless some have done so. Rather, it is usually outside or professional observers who raise issues of reconciliation and forgiveness. The issue of reconciliation will be taken up later. Here, forgiveness will be examined and related to the situation of the victim.

Some advocate forgiveness because of its alleged role in the victim's healing process and a growing literature in psychology (Freedman and Enright, 1996; Harris *et al.*, 2006) argues the therapeutic benefit of 'forgiveness therapy' whereby the victim is encouraged to forgive the perpetrator. Others (Smyth and Graham, 2003) argue the Christian duty of forgiveness and some (Tutu, 1999) argue that there is 'No Future without Forgiveness', pointing to an imperative to forgive in order to underpin peace in a society and to achieve reconciliation.

Victims in the South African process were ascribed the role of 'forgivers' and in the religious ethos of the TRC process, much emphasis was placed on the value of Christian forgiveness and its role in reconciliation. The role of victims as role models of forgiveness in Northern Ireland was discussed earlier. All of this cast victims in the role of dispensing forgiveness – in the South African case often at the prompting of Archbishop Tutu. Some victims refused to be categorised as victims, so strong was their objection to the ethos of forgiveness in the TRC process, preferring a political analysis which emphasised their role of political opposition against an abhorrent regime.

Earlier in this chapter, the role of victims as 'moral beacons' for the wider society and their real or assumed moral superiority was outlined, and the manner in which victims expressions of forgiveness or aversion to revenge sets a tone for the rest of society. Gobodo-Madikizela (2004) argues that the expression of forgiveness by the victim is evidence of that moral superiority, but that during the South African TRC process, some victims found themselves able to forgive, whilst others could not. Gobodo-Madikizela argues that the choice by the victim to forgive or not to forgive was determined by which course of action would preserve the moral superiority of their identity.

> the decision to forgive can paradoxically elevate a victim to a position of strength as the one who holds the key to the perpetrator's wish. For just at the moment when the perpetrator begins to show remorse, to seek some way to ask forgiveness, the victim becomes the gatekeeper to what the outcast desires – readmission into the human community. And the victim retains that privileged status as long as he or she stays the moral course, refusing to sink to the level of evil that was done to her or him... forgiveness does not overlook the deed: it rises above it "This is not what it means to be human," it says. "I cannot and will not return the evil you inflicted on me." And that is the victim's triumph.[38]

Primo Levi takes a different view, pointing out that the mere achievement of understanding of the perpetrator does not necessarily lead to forgiveness, and he himself finds forgiveness difficult, because of the impossibility of true reparation or restitution. He says 'I am not inclined to forgive... because I know no human act that can erase a crime' (Levi, 1989, p. 110).

Victims, then, are not merely individuals with individual affective processes and engagements with their victimisation. They are also iconic figures with a moral status, and as such are an integral part of the communities for which they may symbolise historic grievances. In this context, forgiveness may be a betrayal of the community. For other victims, forgiveness is predicated on apology or being asked for forgiveness, and where no such request has been made, forgiveness is not possible. The withholding of forgiveness may be one way in which the victim feels that they can exercise power over the perpetrator, and the victim may be reluctant to relinquish this power. Perhaps the withholding of forgiveness as a way of maintaining guilt and perhaps an associated shame is paradoxically one of the dynamics that might force a society to face its past squarely. Forgiveness that easily comes by, arguably permits a pre-emptory reckoning with the 'foul deeds' committed by all sides, facilitating at least partial denial and avoidance.

Yet religious approaches emphasise that the duty to forgive lies with the victim, whether or not they have received an apology, or a request for forgiveness. Bouris (2007) points out that Christian advocacy of forgiveness relies on 'the evil perpetrator/ideal victim dyad' (Bouris, p. 168) so this form of forgiveness leaves intact the polarised black and white understanding of the dynamic of the conflict itself. It requires no rethinking of the stereotypical victim and therefore does not promote a concept of the complexity of victim identity. Even a more secular, restorative justice reading of forgiveness relies on the ability and willingness of the victimiser to take full responsibility. If responsibility is spread, then so is blame, and so then, too, must be forgiveness.

Reparations

The provision of some form of financial compensation or pension to victims is often a part of truth recovery. In some contexts such as South Africa, reparations provide desperately needed financial resources, and in others, victims' compensation is awarded alongside or as an alternative to state financial provision. The Northern Ireland provision, however, was established during the period of conflict. Even when the violence was at its peak, there was a Criminal Injuries Compensation Scheme (which was reviewed after the ceasefires)[39] and a Criminal Damages scheme for the compensation for damage to property.

Whilst reparations and financial assistance to victims can provide the much-needed assistance, it also raises a number of thorny issues. The refusal of some victims to accept reparations, seeing any financial compensation as 'blood money' has already been referred to. The acceptance of financial reparations from the state is also resisted by some, since it may imply the acceptance of a 'full and final settlement' of the wrong done.

The South African case that the qualification for reparations is also an admission to formal victim status was certified by the Truth and Reconciliation Commission. Such admission is a form of acknowledgement of victims' suffering and may be welcomed as such. Yet other victims are disqualified, refused such acknowledgement, sometimes because of their involvement in 'terrorism' as in the case of the Northern Ireland scheme, or because the circumstances of their victimisation does not meet the criteria or time frame of the scheme, such as in the South African case. The actual amounts of money dispensed is also a source of distress and conflict. Differences in the amounts of compensation for the death of a family member, for example, arguably values some lives more than others, and this has caused great resentment. In Northern Ireland, lump-sum amounts were paid to bereaved families, but some received substantially more than others. Those bereaved later in the conflict did better than those who lost a family member in the early days of conflict, and police widows received more than civilian widows. A recent proposal in Northern Ireland to compensate the widows of those killed whilst serving in the Ulster Defense Regiment,[40] has drawn protests from those who suffered at the hands of rogue elements of that regiment.

For most victims, the losses sustained in an armed conflict are irretrievable, and reparations can never truly compensate for those losses. Nonetheless, reparations can have a practical value to some victims in need of financial support, and for others, the symbolic acknowledgement is the most important aspect of reparation. Nonetheless in the pecuniary aspects of reparations lie many pitfalls, with much potential for renewing grievance as well as for soothing it.

The role of victims

All of this pre-supposes a focus on the victim, and a concern with the role of the victim in any settlement and in post-conflict developments. However, not all transitions out of violence have been managed so that a victim focus can be maintained. In Northern Ireland, for example, the Good Friday Agreement contains no provision for victims' rights or for truth recovery, and victims are mentioned in only two paragraphs in the context of the benefits of the overall settlement to them, and an exhortation to provide for children and young people affected by the conflict, is largely unaddressed. It was only after the Agreement, when victims organised themselves to lobby for their needs that the government began to put in place a range of measures. This was organised with support from a strong NGO sector and involved some cross-community lobbying, with victims' groups from the opposite sides of the divide working together on matters of common interest.

This relative inattention to victims in the process of negotiations is not uncommon. Williams and Scharf (2002, p. 27)[41] have pointed out that a narrow focus on peace, particularly if this focus contributes to measures of appeasement in order to achieve peace, not only risks failure to fully address issues of justice and victimisation, but will create a discourse of moral equivalence and moral duplicity between victim and perpetrator. This, in turn, can lead to an erosion of the distinction between victim and perpetrator, spreading culpability between them. Whilst this erosion may speed the movement towards the end of violence settlement, in the long-term it may undermine the stability of peace. Some have recognised this danger, and Holbrooke (1999) acknowledges that, although he was a committed advocate of 'getting to peace' in Bosnia, that unless war criminals were identified and subjected to a process of justice as part of the peace process, the prospects for the stability of the settlement were likely to be undermined (Holbrooke, 1999, p. 261).[42]

Using Holbrooke's approach to the Bosnian negotiations, which demonstrated a strong commitment to victims, whilst not engaging explicitly in discourses of victim and aggressor, Bouris sees three images of the victim emerging from this method of peace-building:

> A victim eroded as a result of a platform of moral equivalence; a discourse that recognizes some degree of victim complexity though purposefully does not develop this in the context of peace-building; and lastly a strong, moral commitment to the victim that can motivate movement towards peace even if it does not feature prominently in the peace negotiation dialogue.[43]

The possibility of placing these three images of victims within a process of truth recovery, where the victim in all his or her complexity can contribute from a moral ground that permits questioning and exploration of moral complexity and yet where the victim's suffering, needs and desires are central and respected might well contribute to the dismantling of old bifurcated camps of enmity and the consolidation of a new societal solidarity in which old patterns of division are eroded, and thereby the risk of future victimisation is minimised.

The enemy of this possibility, of course, is the culture of blame, where all responsibility for the wrongs of the past is denied and allocated to the 'other'. Alongside this, the competition between the protagonists to lay claim to the largest amount of victimisation also impedes the emergence of more-inclusive practices of dealing with the hurts of the past. Hence, dialogic engagement in the public sphere, within a structure that facilitates ideal speech acts, and aimed at interrogating the past may be one key contribution to the 're-civilising process' after conflict.

6 Framing the grievances of the past

Northern Ireland since the Belfast Agreement

Introduction: the case study on Northern Ireland

In this section of the book a detailed case study will be undertaken, examining the feasibility of establishing truth recovery and addressing the issues of timing and 'readiness'. It focuses on the conditions which predispose or prevent embarkation on a truth recovery process and the rationale for that process, arguing that there is no magic moment of 'readiness' for truth recovery, but that the conditions are constructed rather than spontaneously occurring. The role of the state and the concept of political 'willingness' are placed at the centre of the analysis.

The subject of the case study is Northern Ireland, where a formal political settlement was reached on Good Friday 1998, and continuing difficulties with establishing a viable parliament have been produced by the deadlocked dynamic between the various political protagonists. Haunted by the violence of the past, there is resistance to the embarkation on a formal truth recovery process. As the society struggles to move forward, the next three chapters consider if the entrenched positions of some in Northern Ireland, and the failure of the key parties to understand and recognise the positions of others can be shifted by a society-wide revisiting and re-evaluation of the past. This chapter provides a background to the Northern Ireland peace process, Chapter 7 provides a detailed analysis of the Northern Ireland Affairs Committee's Inquiry into dealing with Northern Ireland's past, and Chapter 8 considers the issue of readiness, how is it defined, diagnosed and constructed.

The grievances of the past: Northern Ireland since the Belfast Agreement

In Northern Ireland – in spite of complaints about the lack of progress on the peace process, the suspicions of Unionists and Loyalists, and their mistrust of the stability of the situation – levels of political violence have declined steadily and substantially since the mid-1990s and the initiation of the formal peace process which led to the signing of the Good Friday Agreement in 1998. Success in establishing a stable devolved government for Northern Ireland has eluded participants in the process. The establishment of a local Assembly has been stymied by a range of factors.

From a Unionist point of view these are: issues of decommissioning, especially of Republican weapons; various outbreaks of violence, notably the murder of Robert McCartney allegedly by members of the IRA in January 2005; allegations that Republicans were engaged in spying within the Assembly and latterly the exposure of the senior Republican involved as a British agent; the involvement of former – and perhaps current – members of the IRA in senior positions in Sinn Féin and the resultant appointment of 'terrorists' to ministerial positions in the Assembly; a massive bank robbery carried out allegedly with either IRA involvement or complicity; the alleged continued involvement of the IRA in criminal activity, extortion and money laundering; the continued existence of the IRA, and a lack of faith in their intention and capacity to forswear all violence; failure of Sinn Féin to participate in the new policing structures; and opposition to certain aspects of the Good Friday Agreement, and in some cases comprehensive opposition to that Agreement.

From a Republican and Nationalist point of view, the obstacles to establishing a devolved Assembly are: Loyalist, especially the DUP's long-standing opposition to power-sharing with the Nationalists of any hue; shifting goalposts in demands for measures such as decommissioning; the Loyalist desire to humiliate the IRA; a desire on the part of the British government to maintain the alleged impunity in relation to a number of deaths in which the security forces have been implicated, evidenced by their lack of enthusiasm for further public inquiries or a truth commission and the alleged lack of cooperation from the British government with the Bloody Sunday Inquiry; a lack of attention to the decommissioning of Loyalist weapons and continued killings by Loyalists, thus operating double standards; incomplete reform of the criminal justice system, especially the failure to deal with the issue of lustration with regard to policing; lack of resolve on the part of the British government to challenge Loyalism, and pressure them into a deal. In summary, a seemingly ever more polarised political culture, characterised by blame, accusation and an inability to understand or accommodate the 'other's' stance, renders political progress painfully slow, if not impossible, and maintains a political stalemate.

That stalemate which has more or less persisted since the fall of the Assembly in 2001 has not been assisted by a steady stream of revelations of, for example, British agents who have operated within Sinn Féin, the emergence of various pieces of evidence about the role and behaviour of the British Army and of Martin McGuinness' role within the IRA during the Bloody Sunday Inquiry. Alongside this, the efforts of various relatives of those killed by various parties including the security forces to obtain justice, if necessary through civil proceedings, have continued. This last issue, coupled with the regular emergence of sporadic revelations about clandestine deeds and relationships during the conflict has set up a pattern of a continuing drop-feed of disclosures of spying, collusion, double tricks that has created a sense of distrust and doubt about the past, and a questioning of any or all of the political and military actors involved.

This pattern has established a dynamic of low-grade tension about a range of issues and cases that seems to be sustainable over the medium and the long term.

Coupled with this, the opposing parties are involved in an adversarial dynamic and the political atmosphere is not one that facilitates parties to take any responsibility for their errors or misdeeds, since to do so would provide ammunition for the opposition, and to be seen as 'letting down' their community, which would have negative electoral consequences. Political discourse is bifurcated, and political positions polarised, as political generosity, introspection or self-critical reflection are largely absent from the discourses of all the main parties. All of this is contextualised in a wider pattern of intensified sectarian violence, including the purging of some areas of the 'other' and increased racism against black, ethnic minority and migrant populations in the wider society.

Political violence may have been substantially reduced, the IRA may have ceased military operations, British troop numbers may be drastically reduced, but the conflict continues, largely by other means. The prospects of success for the British government's attempts to open negotiations between the parties, and to move towards the re-establishment of a devolved administration seem slight, in spite of the relatively feeble reassurances of the British minister.

Nonetheless, in certain strands of civil society and in various institutions, there is an appetite for movement beyond the conflicted dynamics of the past, an appetite that is, more often than not, thwarted by the efforts of politicians, leading to a general political cynicism and a reluctance to engage with politics or politicians. Such cynicism notwithstanding, various civil society initiatives have aimed at de-polarising the political discourse, uncovering the legacy of past violence and reconciling victims and perpetrators. Some of the proliferation of victims groups, community relations initiatives, storytelling and community inquiries have revisited past events, eliciting new discourses and shifting marginalised discourses towards the centre ground. The Saville Inquiry into the events of Bloody Sunday in 1972 has concluded hearing, and the Omagh families and others are intent on pursuing civil cases against those they hold responsible for planting the Omagh bomb.

Yet, all of these disparate initiatives have failed to achieve a comprehensive paradigm shift in the wider society, but rather have been configured into the conflict itself, which persists, at least in the minds and rhetoric of the main protagonists and their followers. All feel wronged, distrustful, aggrieved and all are inclined to blame the historic enemy for the woes facing them and the body politic. The situation tends to be portrayed by the various protagonists as simple, straightforward and the villain as easily identifiable. There is precious little by way of reflexivity, remorse for past deeds, reconciliation with former enemies or acceptance of responsibility for past acts. Some would argue that this stalemate is the inevitable outcome of an Agreement where nobody won, and where no one has the upper hand. In the perception of all the parties they are relatively powerless to achieve progress since the 'other' holds all the cards. This is profoundly paradoxical, resulting, as it has, from an Agreement which set out to avoid making winners or losers of any of the parties, yet the current perception would indicate that this aim has failed.

The concept of the 'societal security dilemma' (Posen, 1993; but also Mearsheimer, 1990; 1992; Snyder, 1993) offers a perspective on the dynamic between the two main blocs in Northern Ireland. The concept of the 'societal security dilemma' borrows from the original concept of the 'security dilemma' (Butterfield, 1951; Herz, 1951) which describes a dynamic within inter-state relations. Herz described a security dilemma as:

> a social constellation in which units of power... find themselves whenever they exist side by side without higher authority that might impose standards of behaviour upon them and thus protect them from attacking each other. In such a condition, a feeling of insecurity, deriving from mutual suspicion and mutual fear, compels these units to compete for ever more power in order to find more security, an effort that proves self-defeating because complete security remains ultimately unobtainable.[1]

According to the theory, whilst none of the state parties wish relations to deteriorate, or escalate, yet as each state acts to increase its own security, the other states interpret its actions as threatening, thus establishing an ironic dynamic of unintended provocation. This dynamic results in the escalation of the conflict, and may lead to war. Herbert Butterfield's description of such a dynamic sets out the danger posed to the international community by it:

> the greatest menace to our civilization today is the conflict between giant organized systems of self-righteousness – each system only too delighted to find that the other is wicked – each only too glad that the sins give it the pretext for still deeper hatred and animosity.[2]

Others, (Posen, 1993; Roe, 2004) took Buzan's (1991) concept of societal security, later developed by Waever as threats to a society's identity, defining society as civil society, as distinct from the state. Waever holds that security action is always taken on behalf of a collectivity, and Buzan (1993) points out that '[W]hat is perceived as a threat and what can be objectively assessed as threatening, may be quite different. Real threats may not be accurately seen. Perceived threats may not be real, and yet still have real effects'[3] (Buzan, 1993, p. 43).

According to the Copenhagen School, the major contemporary threats to European security lie in 'the societal security dilemma' – the threats to ethnic, religious and national identities – rather than in the conventional military, state-centric security dilemma. These ideas were developed in the light of the wars in former Yugoslavia, but offer potential insights into the Northern Ireland conflict.

A societal security dilemma exists when the efforts of one society (or ethnopolitical group) to improve its own sense of security and strengthen its identity triggers a reaction in another ethno-political group which ultimately has a detrimental effect on the security of the first group, because of the adverse reaction of the second (rival) group. The attempt to improve the group's sense of security can be through armaments or through cultural Nationalism, aimed at uniting the group and regenerating it as a political community. However, as

Waever points out this affirmation of identity forms part of the societal security dilemma, in that affirming one identity may weaken that of the 'other'.

> [The] logic of identity means that some other often enters as part of the self-identification...[As] one's identity depends on this other, the other ends up in the dual role of being necessary for my identity and the one who fully prevents me from being fully myself.[4]

The problem with this dynamic is that the space for the realisation of identity is potentially limitless, and both sides can achieve identity security, but this is not apparent to them. In Northern Ireland, the perennial disputes over parades, the proliferation of flags and political wall murals, and competitions over language and resources can be interpreted as expressions or reflections of, and contributions to a 'societal security dilemma'. That the respective sense of insecurity of Nationalists and Unionists appears asymmetrical, and that the Nationalists seem to be more effective in their pursuit of identity security are partly a construction of the dynamic between the two blocs, and serve to perpetuate the competition by equalising the power bases between a skilled, effective, up-and-coming but minority Nationalist community and an aggrieved, depleted, suspicious and recalcitrant Unionism.

The predominating discourses in Northern Ireland are firstly those of the aggrieved Unionist victim,[5] outraged at the inclusion of Sinn Féin in public life, and determined to 'out' those they consider to be terrorists in public positions. Their outrage is fuelled by a number of factors.

First, the dismantling of the *ancien regime*, particularly that of police reform and the disbandment of local security forces are seen as victorier for the historic enemy the IRA. Negotiated by their surrogates Sinn Féin, such disbandment appears to cast doubt on the heroism and honour of the past performance and ignores the threat and suffering that they endured at the hands of the IRA.

Second, the broader programme of the institutional change ushered in by the Good Friday Agreement has, according to some, little to offer Unionists, and largely consists of measures designed to placate Republicans, leading to a sense of the post-Good Friday Agreement Northern Ireland being 'a cold place for Protestants'.[6]

Third, the large number of killings outstanding in police files for which no perpetrator has ever been found contributes to a sense that there is impunity for terrorist deeds committed by the Republicans in the past, and this has been exacerbated by concessions to prisoners such as early release, and the proposed but defeated legislation on the return of the so-called on-the-runs.

Fourth, there is a vocal and active cohort who style themselves the 'innocent victims' and who act as the conscience of Loyalism to some extent, snapping at the heels of any Unionist or Loyalist politician who might be tempted to even consider power-sharing with Sinn Féin. Such politicians can be in no doubt that should they go down the power-sharing route, they will inevitably incur the wrath of this faction, who enjoy the moral authority that their victim status affords them. Their portrayal of the conflict in Northern Ireland is one of a terrorist campaign waged by the IRA against innocent Protestant civilians and the forces of law and order, and there is substantial representation in their ranks of former members of the security forces. Loyalist violence is disowned, and any allegations of collusion between the Loyalists and the security forces disregarded. Few other dimensions of the conflict are included in this discourse, which is increasingly dominant amongst key proportions of the Unionist electorate.

This latter perspective is underpinned in some cases by the fundamentalist Christian belief which casts the conflict in Northern Ireland as part of the grand battle between good and evil, with the Catholic church and armed republicanism cast as the twin evils with whom there can be no compromise, for to do so would be to do a deal with the devil. This grand battle is increasingly conducted in a context of profound political loss, where the old (desirable) order has been dismantled and its proponents humiliated and without true friends or allies.

The second increasingly dominant discourse amongst the Nationalist electorate, accounting for the growing success of Sinn Féin, is that of substantial proportions of the Nationalist electorate who regard the stalemate with increasingly jaundiced eyes. In this discourse, the Unionist veto and the lack of political will to challenge it, is the explanation for the stalemate. The Unionist refusal to date to resurrect the Assembly is a consistent refusal on the part of Unionists to share power with Catholics.

According to this perspective, the escalating demands of Unionists for the decommissioning of IRA weapons, then photographs of such decommissioning, and then bringing to an end the racketeering and other criminal activities by the IRA and so on are seen as goalposts constantly being shifted by Unionists. Their conclusion is that the Unionists cannot be satisfied, since their goal is to avoid sharing power, which entails remaining dissatisfied. There is a firm belief that there have been killings and other dirty tricks carried out by the security forces with the collusion of the government and the Loyalist paramilitaries. Consequently, the Republicans have a difficulty in trusting the not-entirely-reformed Police Service of Northern Ireland, especially the Special Branch, because of what they see as the incomplete implementation of the Patten reforms and the incomplete process of lustration. They also mistrust the intentions of the British.

The failure of the British to fully cooperate with the Bloody Sunday Inquiry, to pursue the issue of Loyalist decommissioning of weapons are not so much issues in themselves, but provide further illustrations of a British disposition to minimise the Loyalist violence whilst seeking to humiliate the Republican paramilitaries, and to cover up their own human rights transgressions and culpabilities. IRA decommissioning and other measures undertaken by Republicans are seen as genuine efforts on the part of Republicans which are met with the ever-escalating demands by the insatiable and therefore disingenuous Unionists.

Although some Republicans have attempted to understand Unionist grievances, there is scant sympathy and much scepticism about the alienation claimed by Unionists, which is often reinterpreted as sour grapes. Ultimately, many

Republicans suspect the ability of Unionists either to live comfortably with the idea of Catholics as equal partners in the state, or to adjust to the loss of the dominant position they enjoyed in the *ancien regime*.

Aspects of the stalemate

Evans and Duffy (1997) have pointed to the structural factors underlying the increased polarisation and inability to reach compromise. Political parties in Northern Ireland compete within Unionist and Nationalist blocs rather than with each other, since the ethno-political makeup of the population determines the size of their respective 'fields' and there are negligible amounts of cross-communal voting. Evans and Duffy point out that it is therefore the working through of divisions within each of these blocs that 'constrain parties' electoral strategies and thus facilitate or inhibit cross-communal compromise' (p. 47). Their analysis of Northern Ireland Social Attitudes Data concludes that the competition between parties within Nationalism was characterised by polarisation along constitutional lines, with most Nationalists taking a moderate line on the constitutional issue. Amongst Protestants, 'left right ideology has a far stronger impact than constitutional position on patterns of partisanship.... Most Protestants, whatever their partisanship, also express strongly Unionist constitutional preferences.' They argue that, as a consequence of this differentiated pattern:

> within the unionist bloc the pattern of intra-communal party competition militates against constitutional compromise as a solution to 'the troubles', whereas among nationalists the unidimensional structure of competition for electoral support and the distribution of attitudes towards the constitutional issue are likely to have influenced the adoption of compromise strategies by Sinn Féin.[7]

Subsequent to the Good Friday Agreement, the Unionist electorate's priority of the constitutional 'safety' of Northern Ireland combined with a Unionist leadership who feared that others in their ranks would oust them for 'selling out' contributed to that leadership's failure to 'sell' the Agreement to their constituents. This Unionist disposition and leadership combined to produce a climate of palpable and growing Unionist fears about the impact of the Good Friday Agreement on that very constitutional safety, in a context of the rising electoral and demographic fortunes of their constitutional enemies.

Back in 2002, Richard Haass, then Bush 'Pointsperson' for Northern Ireland, briefed the United States Foreign Affairs Committee on the Northern Ireland situation. Much of what was said then can still be seen to apply up until 2007:

> I would go so far as to say that the glass is probably more than half full. But if this is the case... why is public support for the Good Friday Agreement

slipping?...Why do so many people in Northern Ireland look at the same environment I just described and see a glass half empty – or worse?

Every time I ask myself these questions, I come back to one answer. There has been a failure at all levels in Northern Ireland – but particularly at the level of political leadership – to acknowledge that the fates of the two communities are tied to one another. Unless both communities share the benefits of peace, neither will know lasting security or prosperity. The leaders of Northern Ireland must resist appealing only to the dissatisfied. The challenge now is to create a common vision that serves all the citizens of Northern Ireland, not just individual constituencies....

The pattern of politics-as-usual keeps many of us from seeing Northern Ireland for what it has become. It has also kept us from recognising the passage of an old paradigm and the emergence of a new one....

...In this new paradigm, all communities share a common future. A majority in both communities must be satisfied and have a firm stake in society and its future for both to be comfortable. What comes to mind is nothing so much as the old adage that we can either hang together or hang separately. [8]

Haass and others (e.g. Gormley-Heenan, 2005) have focused on the effectiveness – or more frequently the ineffectiveness – of political leadership to explain the *impasse*. Yet it is clear from the practice of politics, evident in the shifting fortunes of the parties in electoral competitions since the Good Friday Agreement and the work of Evans and Duffy *inter alia*, that political leadership is, in many ways, *led* by the opinion of their polity rather than the converse. Political leaders ignore such shifts in constituents' views at their peril. And opinions are moving further to the extremes, with the prospects for the emergence of the new paradigm referred to by Haass and others (Meyer, 2003) seemingly growing more and more remote.

Nothing – not written guarantees contained in the Agreement, not reassurance from any quarter, not Republican gestures such as decommissioning otherwise credible to outside observers,[9] nor recognition and acknowledgement of their fears and grievances – seems to alleviate Unionist fears or allow movement in the Unionist stance. They baulk at the new dispensation, at the new roles of former enemies, and suspect that the apparent new tricks performed by the old dogs are all designed to hoodwink them into a false sense of security. Thus hoodwinked, they fear, the Union will be systematically dismantled and they will suffer as the new minority in a united Ireland, annihilated, humiliated, stripped of their proud identity, legacy of power and sacred political purpose.

This Unionist analysis is supported by a number of ideological factors: a sense of being an integral part of a wider 'imagined community'[10] of the 'British'; a heroic sense of mission and righteousness involving the defense of Protestantism and the Union; nostalgia for their version of the *ancien regime* in Northern Ireland; recent vivid and traumatic memories of violence, threat, death and destruction including that of the largely Protestant Northern Ireland security forces at the hands of the IRA; a palpable fear of being overwhelmed by Republicans, the enemies of Ulster; and a framing of the past that portrays Unionists exclusively as victims and Nationalists exclusively as subversive and dangerous. Certainly the last two of these elements are not overtly challenged by dominant discourses, which have either reinforced these two perceptions, or as Crooke (2001) points out, avoided 'controversial' issues altogether. This 'silence' about the conflict has enabled protagonists to fill the gap with widely divergent accounts, leaving the dominant discourse relatively unaffected whilst the competitive rewriting of histories continues.

Towards a comprehensive picture of past grievances

The grievances of the past play a key role in the perceptions of the protagonists. Arguably, the balance of power that creates and maintains the stalemate is supported by the failure to comprehensively engage with and dispose of such grievances, and reveals how all parties are variously implicated in wrongs, abuses and misdeeds. We have argued that hard evidence is necessary to illustrate this point, and elsewhere (Fay, Morrissey and Smyth, 1999) have established that deaths in the Northern Ireland conflict can act as a competent surrogate for other effects of that conflict. Consequently, for the purposes of this discussion, deaths in the conflict have been disaggregated by the perpetrators, showing the status of the victims, whether they were civilians, security forces or paramilitaries (Table 1) and showing the politico-religious label associated with the victim in Table 2. The overall pattern of violence has altered in the period 1994–1998, with security-related deaths falling, and non-fatal security-related incidents increasing. This indicates a changing pattern of violence, away from high levels of fatal violence, with increased levels of parades-related and interface street disorder sectarian and internecine violence, the latter almost exclusively on the part of the Loyalists. Patterns of violence have moved from one of organised and strategic violence associated with the active phases of the conflict, to a more opportunistic and disorganised form.

The majority of deaths, injuries, disasters grievances and hurts that compose the 'past' that Northern Ireland must now manage, fall within the period 1969–1999. As we have argued elsewhere,[11] an examination of the pattern of deaths can shed light on other effects of the conflict, and significantly, on the distribution of those effects and the apportionment of responsibility for them. Perhaps one way of approaching the design of any comprehensive truth recovery process in Northern Ireland is to ensure that it reflects that distribution and apportioning. Perhaps a transparent approach such as this would offer a way forward.

Patterns of suffering

In relation to the overall pattern of violence from 1969–1999, it is apparent from Table 1 that civilians make up the largest category of victims, accounting for

Table 1 Deaths in the Northern Ireland conflict 1969–1999 by perpetrator and status of victim

Organisation responsible	Political status										
	British forces	Civilians	IRA	Other republican paramilitary	RUC	UDR/RIR	UVF	UDA	Other Loyalist paramilitary	Other	Unknown	Total
British Army	(4.4%) 14	(53.0%) 169	(32.3%) 103	(4.4%) 14	(0.6%) 2	(1.0%) 3	(1.3%) 4	(1.9%) 6			(1.3%) 4	(100%) 319
RUC	(3.6%) 2	(60.0%) 33	(21.8%) 12	(7.3%) 4	(1.8%) 1		(3.6%) 2	(1.8%) 1				(100%) 55
UDR		(81.8%) 9	(18.2%) 2									(100%) 11
All security forces	(4.2%) 16 (3.1% of all British Forces deaths)	(54.8%) 211 (10.7% of all civilian deaths)	(30.4%) 117 (39.8% of all IRA deaths)	(4.7%) 18 (25.7% of Republican Paramilitary deaths)	(0.8%) 3 (0.9% of all RUC deaths)	(0.8%) 3 (1.2% of all UDR/RIR deaths)	(1.6%) 6 (13.6% of all UVF deaths)	(1.8%) 7 (9.5% of all UDA deaths)			(1.0%) 4 (68.8% of all unknown killings)	(100%) 385
IRA	(27.2) 465 (89% of all British Forces deaths)	(31.4%) 536	(7.4%) 126	(0.3%) 5	18.3%) 313 (89% of all RUC deaths)	(13.1%) 223	(0.4%) 7	(0.9%) 16		(0.4%) 6	(0.7%) 12	(100%) 1709
Other Republican paramilitary	(8.4%) 28	(64.6%) 215	(1.55) 5	(8.7%) 29	(6.3%) 21	(3.9%) 13	(0.6%) 2	(1.5%) 5	(0.6%) 2 (40% of all other Loyalist deaths)	(0.6%) 2	(3.3%) 11	(100%) 333

	British Forces	Civilian	IRA	Republican Paramilitary	RUC	UDR/RIR	UVF	UDA	Other Loyalist paramilitary	Other	Unknown	Total
All republican paramilitaries	(24.1%) 493 (94.3% of all British Forces deaths)	(36.8%) 751 (38.2% of all civilian deaths)	(6.4%) 131 (44.6% of all IRA deaths)	(1.7%) 34 (48.6% of Republican Paramilitary deaths)	(16.4%) 334 (94.9% of all RUC deaths)	(11.6%) 236 (96% of all UDR/RIR deaths)	(0.4%) 9 (20.5% of all UVF deaths)	(1.0%) 21 (28.4% of all UDA deaths)	(0.1%) 2	(0.4%) 8 (88.9% of all other deaths)	(1.1%) 23 (35.9% of all unknown killings)	(100%) 2042
UDA		(87.7%) 171	(1.5%) 3	(0.5%) 1	(0.5%) 1			(7.7%) 15			(2.1%) 4	(100%) 195
UVF		(81.0%) 222	(2.9%) 8	(1.5%) 4	(0.7%) 2		(8.4%) 23	(4.0%) 11			(1.5%) 4	(100%) 274
Other Loyalist paramilitary	(0.4%) 2	(90.3%) 484	(1.7%) 9	(0.7%) 4	(1.1%) 6	(0.7%) 4	(0.7%) 4	(2.6%) 14	(0.6%) 3		(1.1%) 6	(100%) 536
All Loyalist paramilitaries	(0.2%) 2 (0.4% of all British Forces deaths)	(87.3%) 877 (44.6% of all civilian deaths)	(2.0%) 20 (6.8% IRA deaths)	(0.9%) 9 (12.9% of Republican Paramilitary deaths)	(0.9%) 9 (2.6% of all RUC deaths)	(0.4%) 4 (1.6% of all UDR/RIR deaths)	(2.7%) 27 (61.4% of all UVF deaths)	(4.0%) 40 (54.1% of all UDA deaths)	(0.3%) 3 (60% of all other Loyalist deaths)		(1.4%) 14 (21.9% of all unknown killings)	(100%) 1005
Other	(3.7%) 3	(55.6%) 45	(21.0%) 17	(8.6%) 7	(1.2%) 1	(1.2%) 1	(1.2%) 1	(6.2%) 5			(1.2%) 1	(100%) 81
Unknown	(6.6%) 9	(61.0%) 83	(6.6%) 9	(1.5%) 2	(3.7%) 5	(2.2%) 3	(0.7%) 1	(0.7%) 1		(0.7%) 1	(16.2%) 22	(100%) 136
Total	(14.3%) 523 (100%)	(53.9%) 1967 (100%)	(8.1%) 294 (100%)	(1.9%) 70 (100%)	(9.6%) 352 (100%)	(6.8%) 247 (100%)	(1.2%) 44 (100%)	(2.0%) 74 (100%)	(0.1%) 5 (100%)	(0.2%) 9 (100%)	(1.8%) 64 (100%)	(100%) 3649 (100%)

Table 2 Deaths in the Northern Ireland conflict 1969–1999 by perpetrator and religion of victim

Organisation responsible	Religious status				Total
	Unknown	Non Northern Ireland	Protestant	Catholic	
British forces	(1.3%) 4	(5.0%) 16	(10.3%) 33	(83.4%) 266	(100%) 319
RUC	(1.8%) 1	(3.6%) 2	(12.7%) 7	(81.8%) 45	(100%) 55
UDR			(36.4%) 4	(63.6%) 7	(100%) 11
Subtotal All security forces	(1.3%) 5	(4.7%) 18	(11.4%) 44	(82.6%) 318	(100%) 385
IRA	(15.5%) 264	(32.7%) 556	(33.7%) 573	(18.1%) 307	(100%) 1700
Other Republican Paramilitary	(4.0%) 13	(13.8%) 46	(54.7%) 182	(27.6%) 92	(100%) 333
DAAD*				(100%) 9	(100%) 9

Subtotal	All Republican	(13.6%) 277	(29.5%) 602	(37.0%) 755	(20.0%) 408	(100%) 2042
	UDA	(3.6%) 7	(0.5%) 1	(17.4%) 34	(78.5%) 153	(100%) 195
	UVF	(2.2%) 6	(1.5%) 4	(27.4%) 75	(69%) 189	(100%) 274
	LOY	(2.4%) 13	(2.1%) 11	(19.6%) 105	(75.9%) 407	(100%) 536
Subtotal	All Loyalist	(2.6%) 26	(1.6%) 16	(21.3%) 214	(74.5%) 749	(100%) 1005
	Other	(4.9%) 4	(6.2%) 5	(30.9%) 25	(58.0%) 47	(100%) 81
	Unknown	(15.4%) 21	(13.2%) 18	(31.6%) 43	(39.7%) 54	(100%) 136
Overall total	Total	(9.1%) 333	(18.1%) 659	(29.6%) 1081	(43.2%) 1576	(100%) 3649

Note
* DAAD = Direct Action against Drugs, a Republican grouping.

almost 54%. Loyalists killed the largest share (almost 45%) of civilians, followed by Republicans (38%) and the security forces killed almost 11% of the civilian total.

The data points to the fact that, during the period of the Troubles, civilians rather than any of the armed groupings or security forces saw the largest impact. If a truth process were to reflect this, primacy would be given only to ordinary people who do not align with the various factions – the very people who have often been pushed into the margins and who are not represented by any of the lobby groups, and who do not wish to be located in the political silos that compose Northern Ireland politics.

The second largest cohort of victims was the security forces, who make up almost a third (31%) of victims, with British soldiers alone making up over 14% of the total. Police and police reservists account for just over 9.6% of all victims, whilst the local regiments of the British army account for almost 7%. Republicans have been responsible for over 95% of security forces deaths, and the IRA alone have been responsible for almost 90%. The loss of life sustained by the British Army, and indeed the experience of British soldiers serving in Northern Ireland is, similarly, a marginalised account. Within Northern Ireland, it is rather the experience of the locally resident police and local regiments of the British Army that are heard. The inclusion of the substantial experience of the British Army would diversify the security forces' account.

Deaths of Republican paramilitaries account for just under 10% of all deaths, and the largest share of these deaths (45.2%) have been internal – killings carried out by Republican paramilitaries themselves. By comparison, the security forces combined to kill just over 37% of that total, with the British Army alone responsible for just over 32% of Republican deaths. The deaths of Loyalist paramilitaries comprise just over 3% of total deaths; Loyalists have killed more Loyalists (just over 57%) than any other perpetrator. Some 19% of these killings (N = 23) were of UVF members killed by the members of their own organisation. Here, too, the pattern of paramilitary deaths points to the predominance of killings carried out by the paramilitaries of those within their own communities; either carried out as a method of disciplining or controlling rogue elements or informers, or as part of paramilitary feuding, which occurred amongst both Loyalist and Republican paramilitaries. Here too, using the data brings the focus onto the grievances between paramilitaries on the same side. Within these communities, families have lived with the shame of having a relative labelled as an informer, or the grievance of having a family member killed, and knowing that those who carried out these acts were or are their neighbours. Many of these grievances within communities have been suppressed and left unresolved, and have impacted on the fabric of the community's life.

In the overall pattern of deaths, just over 4% of deaths (N = 136) were carried out by unknown perpetrators, and in 64 cases (1.6%), the status of the victim is not known. Whilst a huge amount of documentation and information about the conflict exists (see, for example, McKittrick *et al.*, Sutton, Ardoyne Commemoration Project), there are a substantial number of killings about which little is known, no armed group or faction has ever claimed responsibility, and relatives are left with unanswered questions, and in a small number of cases without the bodies of their relative to bury. It is the relatives of these deceased that are most likely to be interested in recovering information and 'truth' about the death of their relatives.

Responsibility for suffering

How badly or well might the various armed factions emerge from a truth recovery exercise that is guided by the overall pattern of harm? In terms of their records of killings, there are some marked differences between the armed protagonists. The majority of deaths at the hands of the Republican paramilitaries were those of the security forces (52%), with the IRA accounting for over 94% of security forces deaths at the hands of Republicans, and 89% of all security forces' deaths. Loyalists' victims, on the other hand, were 87% civilians, and almost 7% were other Loyalists, with just over 3% of the Loyalist victims being Republican paramilitaries. The targeting of the Loyalist violence was influenced by their problem with the visibility of their enemy, the IRA. The emergence of Sinn Féin facilitated their targeting of political activists, but overall, the proportion of civilians killed by Loyalists reflects their policy of targeting civilians supposedly as a way of dissuading the Nationalists from supporting the IRA. The pattern of the Loyalist violence may also have been shaped by the alleged collaboration of the state with the Loyalist gangs and counter gangs.

The largest cohort of deaths caused by the security forces were of civilians (N = 211), comprising almost 55% of all deaths caused by them. The second largest category of deaths caused by the security forces were those of the Republican paramilitaries (N = 135) accounting for over a third (35%) of their total kill, and of these, the majority (87%) were deaths of IRA members.

Suffering in the two communities

The pattern of harm caused by the Troubles can be examined according to the damage done to the two communities in Northern Ireland. The material basis for the comprehensive and competitive sense of victimhood between the two communities can be challenged by examining the apportionment of deaths between the two communities, since the significance of these deaths in Northern Ireland is largely determined by the community identity of the victim. Whilst it would be naive to make claims for the effectiveness of such a challenge to alter entrenched views or achieve shifts in attitudes or behaviour, the exercise is valuable in providing some sort of benchmark or reality check against which perceptions of victimhood and claims to moral rectitude can be gauged. Table 2 disaggregates deaths by religion, using the categories Catholic which roughly corresponds to Nationalist, Protestant which roughly corresponds to Unionist, Non-Northern Ireland which contains those killed who were not from Northern Ireland, the bulk of whom were British soldiers, and there is a residual category for those who could not be attributed a politico-religious label.

This breakdown provides a glimpse of the material basis for understanding the wide divergence between the two communities in terms of their priorities in pursuing issues of truth and justice. On the one hand, Unionists and Loyalists have been energetic in their pursuit of the Provisional IRA and their political representatives, and have been enraged at the inclusion of members of the Sinn Féin government and their appointment as government ministers. The Provisional IRA has been responsible for over 47% of all deaths in the conflict and for 53% of all Protestant deaths. Republican paramilitaries in general have been responsible for almost 70% of all Protestant deaths, thus presenting the greatest threat in the past to Protestants and Unionists, and the greatest challenge in the present in terms of establishing trust and democratic relationships. Conversely, almost half (47.5% of Catholic deaths were due to the Loyalist paramilitaries), and yet the decommissioning of Loyalist weapons seems to have slipped from the agenda, and does not seem to be regarded as a priority by either the British or the Unionists and Loyalists. Similarly, over 20% of the Catholic deaths are due to the security forces, as opposed to 4% of the Protestant deaths, and 83% of all those killed by the security forces were Catholics, hence accounting for the priority given to state accountability, public inquires, confidence in the security forces and police reform by the Nationalists and Republicans.

Other factors, such as the overwhelming predominance of the Protestant community amongst the local security forces, some of whose former members of the security forces are now politicians in the Democratic Unionist Party or the Ulster Unionist Party, add fuel to the flames. Old suspicions, wrongs and grievances have not been left behind. They form the obstacles to sitting at the negotiating table, the barriers to trust and the veto on compromise. These are people who spent the best part of the last three decades trying to kill one another, or avoid being killed. It is not entirely surprising that, without some intervening process of formal addressing of grievances, they cannot cooperate with one another. Nor are the British or the Irish government neutral arbiters in this matter: as has been illustrated earlier, the British troops in particular are a part of this picture; they have lost young men on the streets of Northern Ireland.

Perceptions of suffering and subjective experiences of victimhood

These data both challenge and explain the excruciatingly predictable responses from all parties concerned with truth recovery in Northern Ireland. The response from Unionists and Loyalists is to attribute all responsibility for all violence to Republicans, the IRA in particular, and explain all state and Loyalist violence as simply a reaction. Republicans on the other hand, point to the special responsibility of the state as the upholder of law and justice, and the alleged impunity that has pertained over a number of controversial killings such as that of Pat Finucane, Rosemary Nelson and others, and highlight the revelations of alleged collusion between the security forces and Loyalist paramilitaries. Republicans argue that state security forces that still contain the personnel who participated in past collusion and breaches of the law cannot be trusted to uphold the rule of law in the present and the future.

Truth recovery, challenges and paradigm shifts

In this context, would a mechanism aimed at managing the legacy of Northern Ireland's troubled past, sponsored by the state and aimed at a coordinated, comprehensive and serious attempt to address Northern Ireland's past, such as a truth commission enable the political parties and civil society to address, if not resolve, issues related to the past? Could such an exercise facilitate the protagonists to move forward, and shake off at least some of the ghosts from the past that dog their footsteps? An awareness of the real as opposed to the imagined architecture of grievance might certainly inform the design of a process, and offer a mechanism for the apportionment of time and resources within such an exercise. Certainly a comprehensive process which reflected, in time and resource allocation the actual pattern of grievance, would offer a powerful challenge to the patterns of antagonism and victimhood that do much to drive the political impasse which has persisted since 2002 and before. Political actors in Northern Ireland have often been described as prisoners of the past. A truth process for Northern Ireland could potentially offer some prospect of release from this state, and containment for that past. Such an exercise would not be cost-free either in financial or political terms, and the political will to fund it is currently in doubt. Nonetheless, the cathartic potential of such a process might offer one of the few chances that Northern Ireland might have to make the paradigm shift referred to by Haass, one where the interdependence of the two communities is recognised and provides the basis for social and political progress. The potential and advisability of a truth recovery process for Northern Ireland is explored further in subsequent chapters. In a society where the force of sectarianism strives to deny that interdependence, the engineering of such a paradigm shift will indeed require seismic energy. Might a truth recovery process be just capable of unleashing such energy? Or could it trigger Northern Ireland into a downward spiral of greater instability and perhaps even violence. A more detailed examination of the evidence is necessary before any conclusion can be reached.

7 Readiness for truth
The Northern Ireland Affairs Committee Inquiry

Background and scope of Inquiry

In the context of increasing numbers of revelations about conflict-related events in the past, and a growing debate about how to manage the past, The House of Commons appointed the Northern Ireland Affairs Committee (NIAC) based at Westminster to enquire into 'ways of dealing with Northern Ireland's past' in November 2004. The terms of the Inquiry were to examine: 'The experience of efforts in other jurisdictions to move forward from a history of division and conflict, on a basis as widely acceptable as possible to affected communities and individuals who have suffered from violence.'[1]

It was intended that the Inquiry would conduct a comprehensive investigation over a lengthy period and this would assist 'the process on inter-community healing'. However, the work of the Inquiry was truncated by the calling of a general election, with the Committee recommending that this work be continued. The analysis presented here is of the work of the Committee to date, although there is no sign of the Committee's work resuming. However, this analysis may perhaps inform the work of future committees in evaluating the conclusions reached by the initial Committee and addressing some of the issues that arise out of this analysis.

Overall the operation of the Committee veered between operating as a mini truth commission, or a forum where outstanding issues could receive official attention, and an investigation, albeit a rather *ad hoc* one, into issues relating to past violence in Northern Ireland. The Committee invited and subsequently received submissions from a range of individuals and organisations, and heard 103 written submissions in 9 sessions spread over 8 days, interviewing 61 people from 29 organisations. For the purposes of this analysis, the published proceedings of this Inquiry, together with the government response to it, has been analysed in detail in order to examine the methods and rationale behind the current official position on truth recovery in Northern Ireland. This analysis involved a content analysis of the published material, both in terms of the deliberations on the substantive issues, and in terms of the composition, process and approach of the Committee itself. The published evidence to the Committee was also classified into several categories according to its source: Unionist; Nationalist; victim organisation; NGO, expert/academic and government. The volume of written and verbal evidence was then measured by a page count for the total evidence considered by the Committee from each source.

Composition of the Northern Ireland Affairs Committee

At the beginning of the Inquiry the NIAC was comprised of thirteen Members of Parliament (MPs), seven Labour, two Conservative, two Ulster Unionist Party (UUP), one Democratic Unionist Party (DUP) and one Social and Democratic Labour Party (SDLP). Of the four Northern Ireland MPs, three were Unionists – Roy Beggs, Martin Smyth from the Ulster Unionist Party and Gregory Campbell from the DUP – and one Nationalist, Eddie McGrady from the SDLP, who did not manage to attend any sessions (see Table 3). The Committee membership had changed by the time of the government response to the Inquiry, with only two MPs retained from the original Committee, Stephen Hepburn, Labour and Gregory Campbell, DUP. The political composition of the Committee also changed. In the original Committee, the Northern Ireland representation was one SDLP, one DUP and two Ulster Unionists, and in the new Committee the Unionists were now represented by two DUP (Gregory Campbell and Sammy Wilson) and one Ulster Unionist (Sylvia Hermon), with Alasdair McDonnell, SDLP, representing Nationalists. The new Committee also had three female members, Sylvia Hermon, Rosie Cooper (Labour) and Meg Hillier (Labour), perhaps as a response to the INCORE, University of Ulster criticism of the all-male composition of the original Committee. The levels of attendance are set out in Table 3.

Average attendance was almost 60% overall. As a result of the minimal representation of Nationalists on the Committee and the failure of that one

Table 3 NIAC members' participation in the Inquiry on Northern Ireland's past

Name	Party	Sessions attended
Hugo Swire	Cons	2
Gregory Campbell	DUP	5
Adrian Bailey	Lab	0
Tony Clarke	Lab	7
Stephen Hepburn	Lab	3
Iain Luke	Lab	6
Stephen Pound	Lab	6
Mark Tami	Lab	6
Bill Tynan	Lab	5
Eddie McGrady	SDLP	0
Roy Beggs	UUP	8
Martin Smyth	UUP	8
Michael Mates (Chair)	Cons	8

representative to attend any session, Nationalists were not represented at any stage. Approaches to Mr McGrady to ascertain the background to his absence have met with no response, so it is unclear whether he was not attending on principle or whether he merely prioritised other matters. Both UUP MPs, Roy Beggs and Martin Smyth, attended eight out of a possible nine sessions, their attendance only matched by the Chair, Michael Mates. There is no indication in the published record whether the Committee was aware that it is devoid of Nationalist representation, or whether they considered the impact of this factor on their ability to weigh evidence or to direct questions at witnesses. Given that Sinn Féin MPs do not take their seats in Westminster, Nationalist representation is perhaps not so easily secured. Nonetheless, there is no evidence that it was a matter considered by the Committee.

In the light of this, it is perhaps less surprising that the distribution of evidence heard by the Inquiry demonstrates a concentration on evidence from Unionist sources. Table 4 sets out the respective volumes of evidence, comprised of the total of both written evidence and transcribed verbal evidence from each source.

The largest volume of evidence came from Unionists (27%) followed by evidence from victims organisations (18%), with evidence from Nationalists accounting for 16%, and NGOs and experts each making up 14% of the total evidence. Of the victims represented, five came from cross-community victims groups, seven from victims groups in the Unionist community and six came from victim groups in the Nationalist community. The Committee could decide who to invite to give evidence and could seek additional evidence. It is clear from this analysis that the distribution of evidence favoured Unionists, that Nationalists had just under 60% of the time afforded by the Committee to Unionists, and victims from both communities and those from outside Northern Ireland were afforded only two thirds of the time afforded to Unionists. Yet it seems that the Committee may have been unaware of these trends within its own work. The Chair of the Committee, Michael Mates told witnesses on 23 February 2005: 'We spend most of our time listening to victims and victims' organisations.'[2]

Table 4 Distribution of evidence by political affiliation/status

Source of evidence	Number of pages
Unionists	37 (27%)
Victims/victims organisations	25 (18%)
Nationalists	22 (16%)
NGOs	19.5 (14%)
Academics/experts	19.5 (14%)
Government	16 (12%)
Total	139 (101%)

This raises questions about the level of awareness of the Committee of the balance of evidence they were hearing, which in turn will have influenced their conclusions and recommendations. Michael Mates was apparently unaware of this division of attention when he made this remark. Indeed, the issue of the representativeness of the evidence presented was raised at the beginning of an extensive and wide-ranging memorandum submitted to the Committee by the Northern Ireland Human Rights Commission:

> Although the Committee's announcement of the present inquiry refers to the Secretary of State "embarking on a programme of discussions" in May 2004, this does not seem to have been a very proactive effort: neither the Commission, nor several influential and representative victims' groups... were invited to contribute. When the Minister with responsibility for victims' issues recently conducted a consultation on the next phase of the victims' policy, the exercise was said to have "sought views and opinions from all interested parties," but we have no doubt that the dialogue needs to be more open and inclusive if the outcome is to command public confidence.[3]

In Northern Ireland, as in other divided societies, inclusiveness and proportional representation in such exercises is necessary in order to secure confidence in the outcome. Proactive strategies to ensure such representativeness are a regular feature of any policy work in Northern Ireland. The Committee, however, operated out of Westminster, where such sensitivities are perhaps not so acute, and none of the Northern Ireland MPs drew the issue to the Committee's attention.

Approach to witnesses

The NIAC heard evidence from victims, which made a deep impression on them. In giving evidence, WAVE's Witness B in Session 3, on 21 February 2005, talked about his family experience as the uncle of a man who had 'disappeared' and whose body had never been found. Other witnesses outlined similar family histories. This testimony obviously made a strong impact on the Committee as the plight of the families of the disappeared is an issue stressed in their conclusions.

There is also some evidence of a variation in the approach of the Committee to certain witnesses. For example, in terms of the process, the Committee heard the evidence from the Nationalist victims and prisoner organisations together. At the beginning of this session Michael Mates began: 'We are very pressed for time, I am afraid, but we just want to hear from you on some questions which I think you may have had indications of.'[4]

No other witnesses were cautioned about a shortage of time, and some sessions, such as that conducted with the author, were conducted in a leisurely manner.

At another juncture, Michael Mates said to Paul O'Connor from the Pat Finucane Centre: 'Please understand that I am not trying to put questions critically, because we are very grateful for your submission. Yes, it is controversial, but it is detailed and well argued whether we agree with it or not.'[5]

This comment from the Chair conveys a sense of unanimity within the Committee, from within which the Chair was able to label certain views as 'controversial' whilst others were simply heard and noted.

This raises the question of whether or not the Committee, albeit unconsciously, operated out of a pre-determined stance, in which certain views were not controversial, and certain witnesses entertained in a fashion distinct from others.

There are also patterns which emerge in the method of questioning of various witnesses. Evidence from Tom Roberts and William Smith from the Ex-Prisoner Interpretative Centre (EPIC), which, according to Tom Roberts serves: '...a certain constituency of those prisoners, namely ones with a Ulster Volunteer Force or Red Hand Commando background',[6] and

> We do not claim to speak for all of loyalism, we are talking about one particular element within loyalism, so being quite modest in what we can do we felt it was a starting point to look at our own constituency, given the fragmentation within loyalism and even unionism for that matter.[7]

No one on the Committee sought to ascertain Mr Roberts and Mr Smith's status, whether they are ex-prisoners or members or former members of the UVF, although it could be assumed that the Northern Ireland MPs might well have this information. Later in the session, Tom Roberts volunteers this information. In response to a question from Martin Smyth about the likelihood of arriving at the truth, Tom Roberts says:

> What came across in our deliberations was that there was an agreement that Republicans seem to be driving some sort of process towards truth, and people were asking the question, if you have the likes of Gerry Adams who, at this point in time, cannot even admit he was a member of the IRA, then what truth are they talking about.[8]

In response, the Chair confides to Mr Roberts and the Committee: 'I do not think he has gone as far as to say he was never a member of the IRA; I keep asking him when he left but he will not answer that question.'[9]

Here the Chair is joining Mr Roberts in his concern about Gerry Adams, yet Mr Roberts himself is or was a member of a paramilitary group. The consensual atmosphere in this session contrasts with the Chairman's incredulity in an exchange with Clara Reilly and Mark Thompson on the issue of killings by the security forces, where the Chairman suggests that there were few such killings:

Q162 CHAIRMAN: Bloody Sunday aside, that was a pretty rare occurrence, was it not?

MR THOMPSON: Three hundred and seventy six people were killed by the British Army and the RUC.
Q163 CHAIRMAN: I did say and I will leave this subject in a minute, I do not want to get into this. This is not what this inquiry is about. You just mentioned mothers and grandmothers who by implication had no part whatsoever in the argument but were just sort of killed on the way?
MS REILLY: Yes.
Q164 CHAIRMAN: There must be very few of those?
MS REILLY: Absolutely not.
Q165 CHAIRMAN: How many of them?
MR THOMPSON: One hundred and ninety-one civilians, 75 of them children, killed
Q166 CHAIRMAN: Has no one provided any explanation at all as to how those deaths occurred?
MR HOLLAND: I can give you an example... [gives the example of the killing of Elizabeth McGregor].[10]

This last exchange between the Chair, the Committee and the witnesses from the Nationalist side seem to indicate a disposition on the part of the Chair to minimise the concerns of the witnesses, 'that was a pretty rare occurrence', making the assumption that there has been very little violence on the part of the state. Second, the Chairman takes the view that such violence was not the concern of the Committee, yet the Committee's terms of reference sets out their remit as 'affected communities and individuals who have suffered violence'. Given that over 20% of deaths of Catholics were due to the security forces and of the 377 people killed by the security forces, 85% were Catholic, the Chairman's interpretation of the brief is puzzling. However, his interpretation of the brief, and resistance to discuss the experience of the witnesses, 'I do not want to get into this. This is not what this Inquiry is about' communicate to witnesses and to the reader little interest or understanding of this account emanating from the Catholic community's experience of violence. Rather, his remarks and questioning style associate him with a denial of the experience of that community, in which awareness of this pattern of victimhood and resultant suspicion of the security forces persists. It seems likely that the Chair at least, if not other members of the Committee, were operating on a 'two warring tribes' model of the conflict, where the role of the British and Irish governments is construed as that of neutral arbiters, in spite of the carefully crafted understanding on this issue that flowed from the Good Friday Agreement.

On other occasions, certain moral preoccupations of the Chair seem to emerge. In the first session with Tom Roberts, Michael Mates explores Tom Roberts' attitude to his past involvement in the UVF and the violence he was involved with, with a view to establishing if he had regrets.

Q51 CHAIRMAN: Please do not think I am in any way trying to be offensive or attacking you because I think this is one of the key points... but what I think you were saying is that now, in 2005, "I wish I had realised there was a better way then, although I thought what I was doing was right at the time."

MR ROBERTS: No, there is a better way now.

Q52 CHAIRMAN: But there was another way then.

MR ROBERTS: No, there was not, in my opinion. At the time I was involved in violence the legitimate security forces in Northern Ireland were overwhelmed and Republicans were killing our people with impunity; that is why I got involved.

Q53 CHAIRMAN: Okay. I am not trying to attack you or anything. I am just trying to get –

MR ROBERTS: I am sorry if my response was aggressive.

Q54 CHAIRMAN: I just want to get to the heart of what you are saying, Mr Roberts.[11]

Michael Mates seems unable to adopt an enquiring position in relation to politically motivated violence, nor does he seem open to the exploration of why paramilitary combatants might consider violence to be morally or politically justified. He appears not to be familiar with the discourses surrounding political motivation in Northern Ireland, but consistently seems to approach the matter of paramilitary violence from a stand of moral combat, seeking rather to bring combatants to see the error of their ways. Again, on 28 February, Mr Mates' opinion, rather than his desire to elicit information, is apparent in a question he put to Professor Tom Hadden:

What do you do in your so-called acknowledgment with those who do not acknowledge that murder is wrong? What do you do with the Brighton bomber who said, "Yes, I put the bomb there. I have done my time for it. I don't regret it because it was a legitimate act. I am very sorry about the women and children who fell by the way." What do you do about Mr Adams who says, yes, he regrets any mistakes, but has not issued one word of regret for any of the murders that the IRA had committed? If you have to have a blanket amnesty for those in the interests of getting the truth, have they not also got to say that what they did was wrong?[12]

Michael Mates has omitted to take the prior step of attempting to establish why they thought their acts of violence were right in the first place. Amongst those ex-prisoners, Loyalist and Republican, who participate in cross-community dialogue about such issues, and among observers who are party to such discussions, a sophisticated approach to such issues has emerged. This is based on a recognition that it is unlikely and unrealistic, even if some consider it to be desirable, to secure public statements of regret or recognition of the past error of their ways from former combatants. Michael Mates' approach is reminiscent of the pre-Good Friday Agreement days when the political motivation of prisoners was not recognised in official discourse. As such, this appears to be a retrograde step. It reveals a further shortcoming in the Committee processes. Members of parliament participating in the Inquiry, particularly those who are not from Northern Ireland, including the Chairman Michael Mates questioned witnesses on their submissions to the Inquiry and on any other matters they considered relevant. These questions do not often seem to be prepared, or based on any briefing or background knowledge of the conditions pertaining on the ground, the topic or the witness. The Committee might have been able to make better use of witnesses if a more structured approach, which included advance papers and briefings had been deployed.

To summarise, the analysis so far raises a number of concerns about the composition of the Committee, the lack of Nationalist input to it, the disposition of the Committee towards certain witnesses, an apparent unanimity amongst Committee members which is expressed by the Chairman at an early stage which indicates that the Committee had already formed its views, and the interpretation of the remit of the Committee as excluding state violence. Having identified these factors which may have influenced the Committee's weighing of evidence, further analysis of that part of their work and of the evidence itself was undertaken. Evidence was divided into that supporting a truth recovery process, evidence opposing, and evidence pertaining to methods and approaches to truth recovery.

Attitude to truth recovery

The attitudes represented to the NIAC Inquiry on the idea of a truth recovery mechanism within Northern Ireland were divided between those who favoured such an initiative, those who favoured it under certain conditions, those who would favour it in the future, and those who opposed it. Views were also expressed about the model that should be adopted and about the role of victims in any future scheme. Opposition to truth recovery came largely from the Unionist/Loyalist community and from those associated with the state security forces. Those supporting the institution of a truth recovery process largely came from within the Nationalist community, but were joined in this opinion by human rights and victims' organisations and a range of NGO representatives and expert witnesses. On this, as on many other issues in Northern Ireland opinion seems to divide largely along sectarian lines. However, not all witnesses to the Inquiry were asked directly about a truth recovery process or chose to express an opinion on the subject.

Support for truth recovery

Those who supported the idea of instituting a truth recovery process in Northern Ireland to the NIAC were: human rights and victims' organisations in the Nationalist community; Healing Through Remembering; a range of NGOs such as Democratic Dialogue and the Community Foundation; a human rights centre based in Queen's University; a psychiatrist and various expert witness.

Professor McClelland, a psychiatrist and Chairperson for Healing Through Remembering, a voluntary cross-community group devoted to the issue of managing the past, described the need for some form of truth recovery as 'an absence of broad civil recognition. Like acknowledgment, I do think we need a high level societal process that brings all this together.'[13] Colin Parry, who lost his son in the Omagh bomb referred to the feeling among British-based victims of the Northern Ireland conflict that they have been overlooked and did not have the opportunity to have their views considered. In his written submission, Colin Parry sets out his attitude to truth recovery: 'morally and emotionally, I support the creation of an Inquiry to examine how best to deal with N. Ireland's past. My support is subject to certain practical caveats....'[14] He spelt these out in his evidence to the NIAC.

> I suspect that a truth commission, if there was to be one, would only really have a chance of having any credibility if and when there is a declaration by all antagonists and protagonists that 'The war is over.' To even countenance a truth commission before then would be foolish and it would rapidly become a pointless exercise.[15]

> Without an end to the military campaign, the idea of a truth commission now would be a waste of people's time.[16]

It is significant that Parry's overall position is one of support for truth recovery, provided there is an end to the military campaign, whilst others who have definitively opposed truth recovery, cite continuing paramilitary activity and the absence of a declaration that 'the war is over' as their main reason. Clearly, Parry thinks that truth recovery could be of benefit, and such declarations could be elicited, in contrast to the pessimistic outlook of other witnesses to the NIAC. In the interim period since the NIAC hearings and report, it appears increasingly that the IRA's war is over, with further acts of decommissioning and the verification of these by the Independent Monitoring Commission, and the decision by Sinn Féin to participate in the governance systems of policing and to support the new policing structures.

Opposition was not unanimous, for example, the Disabled Police Officers Association, had also conducted survey of its membership, and in its memorandum to the NIAC, cited the survey carried out during August/September 2004 which revealed that whilst 70% were opposed to the idea of a truth and reconciliation commission, 30% supported the idea. Similarly the Northern Ireland Veterans' Association, representing British Army personnel who served in Northern Ireland, were not entirely unsympathetic to the idea, provided proper education and support were provided to them, and their problems of trusting the government could be overcome.

Other witnesses from the Republican community were optimistic about the level of cooperation that could be built within their community for truth recovery. In reply to Iain Luke's question about the Republican attitudes towards a truth recovery process, Mike Ritchie from a Republican ex-prisoners organisation stated:

> My guess is that if there was a real independent, probably international process to explore how it could happen, I think there would be a willingness on the Republican side to engage with that. It is important that people do have some input. It should not be a kind of finished product saying, "Here is the model. Either you participate or you don't."[17]

Tom Holland from Ardoyne Commemoration Project confirmed this assessment of Nationalist attitudes based on his work in Ardoyne. However, Paul O'Connor from the Pat Finucane Centre was less certain about the general enthusiasm for participation in truth recovery:

> I do not think at the moment there is any one of the groups that has been involved in the conflict, whether it is the IRA, the INLA, Loyalist groups or the state which is exactly jumping forward and saying, "I will take part in that. I am anxious to tell the story of what actually happened." I do not think anybody is.[18]

Nonetheless, there was a consensus amongst those from the Nationalist community about the importance and potential of truth recovery. Written evidence from Eolas (a coalition on truth and justice sponsored by Relatives for Justice) expressed their belief that while:

> the question of truth processes is fraught with difficulty... if sensitively handled, it could provide a real basis for moving forward in a way which respects victims' needs, allows appropriate lessons to be learned and provides a basis for improved relationships across Ireland.[19]

Memoranda from Relatives for Justice (a Nationalist victims group) and Firinne (a group representing victims of state violence), whilst supporting the idea of a truth recovery process, both stress their negative experiences of the British government and resultant lack of faith in its good intentions – something, paradoxically, these groups have in common with the Northern Ireland Veterans' Association amongst others. Reverend Rawding, speaking on behalf of the soldiers who had served in Northern Ireland, said, 'A lot of veterans would have issues with the government.'[20] Reverend Rawding saw the value in some form of truth recovery however:

> I think there needs to be an ongoing process of truth recovery where people volunteer to step into it and give information and other people

volunteer to step in and receive information. I think there should be an ongoing process.[21]

Other witnesses Jo Dover and Chris Gibson valued a storytelling approach. Trevor Ringland explained its value: 'Some people in particular need an opportunity to at least express to others what they have suffered'.[22] Brandon Hamber said that the main value of a truth commission was:

> that a truth commission gives official acknowledgement, and however one manages to achieve it there is some sort of consensus which is achieved about acknowledging what has happened in the past, and that comes from the highest levels – whether that is through apologies or statements of acknowledgement or even just all signing up to the final report, it gives that sense of officialness; you do not get that in other places. The second thing is that if they are run properly... there is a pooling of energies, pooling of resources, pooling of information and I think that that is more difficult if it is disparate.[23]

Defer truth recovery

A second cohort argued for a truth recovery process 'but not yet'. These included the Northern Ireland Human Rights Commission, the Community Relations Council and the Tim Parry/Jonathan Ball Trust. The NIAC itself also expressed a view on this issue. As Chair, Michael Mates seemed to indicate that even at a relatively early stage in the Committee's work, the second of nine hearings, the MPs had already decided some of its conclusions:

> We do not believe that there is any way in which you could start a formal process, which this is not – the Committee is formal, but it is not part of the process – until everybody in the community or most people in the community are ready for it. One of the echoes we are hearing from both sides is that there are some victims and victims' organisations who patently are not ready for that – and that is something which I think we are going to have to spell out in as moderate a way as we can find.[24]

Brice Dickson, Chief Commissioner of the Northern Ireland Human Rights Commission outlined the NIHRC's similar reservations about the timing of a truth process, although he was definitive about the need for such a process at some point:

> The Commission's view is that while some sort of truth recovery process must be put in place for Northern Ireland, the time is not right at the moment for that. We believe that there will have to be a lot more consultation with all the interested parties before such a mechanism could be put in place.[25]

Professor Dickson, whilst seeing the necessity for truth recovery expressed concern about the clarity of the NIAC brief, about the danger of confusing concepts of 'truth' and concepts of 'reconciliation', and of the need for these and other matters to be clarified and agreed before embarking on any truth recovery process. Oliver Wilkinson from Healing Through Remembering expressed concern about the political impact of a premature process without acknowledgement as a first stage:

> I am worried that it would be very divisive at this point in time. It would take a number of years, in my opinion, to get to a stage where the process you are hinting at might be of some use here... it would have to be set within the context of a number of initiatives that would complement what it is you are talking about.... The base on which all of this could have some meaning is... that we would begin by acknowledging as a society the contribution, to whatever extent admitted there has been to the pain and suffering of all and that all have experienced. On that base we can begin to have these other initiatives, but without it, I think it is going to fail.[26]

Andrew Robinson from the Haven Project, which works with victims in England, Scotland and Wales, was asked by Roy Beggs, 'Why are you opposed to a truth commission for Northern Ireland?' to which he replied:

> It is not so much that one is opposed to it, but the reality is that at this moment, due to the pain and suffering which people have and coming back to the roots, because the roots of the problems are still there and have not been addressed at this stage.... There has to be an element of trust, there has to be that element and ability of forgiveness and at this stage there is a tremendous lack of trust within communities within Northern Ireland. For there to be any form of truth and reconciliation commission, there has to be an absolute cessation of war. Whilst we have a military cessation, the reality is that the nature of the war has moved into a different arena, which is the political arena and the cultural arena.[27]

Robinson requires an 'absolute cessation' – an absence of political contests within the political and cultural arena, even of a peaceful kind? Only after such a cessation and becalming of society does truth recovery become possible, according to this view. It does, however, seem to set the bar impossibly high for truth recovery, laying out pre-conditions that many supposedly peaceful societies could not meet. Jo Dover of the Tim Parry/Jonathan Ball Trust took a similar view. In her memorandum to the Inquiry, she expressed the opinion that a truth recovery process could be of benefit to Northern Ireland at some point in the future when all sides were agreed that the conflict is fully over. Jo Dover also pointed to the issue of the lack of trust, and suggested that storytelling, specifically providing people with opportunities to hear stories from the other side, may be one way of remedying this deficit, a point to which other witnesses were to return.

Healing Through Remembering, the Belfast-based initiative on truth recovery conducted an audit of storytelling[28] initiatives throughout Northern Ireland, and found some twenty-nine projects or initiatives, motivated by a range of factors: to create a tool for advocacy; to promote healing to document what happened; to acknowledge or commemorate; to educate and to provide a conduit to other services. These initiatives adopted a range of approaches, such as 'talking circle workshops', discussion-based workshops, use of the creative arts and life history projects.

Certainly, storytelling has been used in highly structured therapeutic interventions[29] and in staff development and management.[30] Delgado's (1989)[31] 'plea for narrative' provides a useful analysis of the functions of storytelling. Delgado argues that storytelling and counter-storytelling can affirm identity, can be used to challenge dominant accounts, and 'can show that what we believe is ridiculous, self-serving or cruel'.[32] Delgado argues that

> stories humanize us. They emphasise our differences in ways that can ultimately bring us closer together. They allow us to see how the world looks from behind someone else's spectacles. They challenge us to wipe off our own lenses and ask, "Could I have been overlooking something all along?"[33]

Thus, it seems that evidence from elsewhere tends to confirm Jo Dover's assertion that storytelling can perform a useful function in broadening perspectives and could contribute to trust and confidence building.

It is perhaps unrealistic to expect absolute cessations of violence when communities such as those in South Africa and Northern Ireland have acquired the 'custom of violence' over several decades. Experience from elsewhere suggests that residual levels of violence continue even after the formal declaration of settlement. In South Africa, for example, political violence, particularly of a factional and internecine kind, morphed into gang conflict and continues to the present day. Similarly, internecine violence, particularly amongst Loyalists, proliferated after the Good Friday Agreement. Even in the face of substantial reductions in levels of violence and the declared cessations on the part of combatant groups, some, including victims, may be unable or unwilling to believe or trust in such developments. Thus, any truth recovery process is likely to have to contend with a significant minority who cannot believe the war is over, in spite of evidence to the contrary.

The memorandum submitted by the Community Relations Council states that 'the generic concept of dealing with the past is to be welcomed,' whilst acknowledging that 'truth telling without reparation and forgiveness may deepen resentment.'[34] Duncan Morrow, the Director of the CRC, had several reservations about the timing of a truth process.

> To pretend that this process can be done before there is agreement that we are going to be in a shared future leaves any process very open to being used by

any political actor on all sides to justify a past rather than to work towards anything which might be stabilising. (Q 126) A truth and reconciliation on the South African model, for my money, at the present moment is not the answer... it will not be done at this time. Please do not see this as dropping it, but as putting it off until it becomes more appropriate to be dealt with well into the future.[35]

The CRC recommended that the NIAC:

consider hosting or supporting the call for a series of public events to accompany further consultation. Such events would enable full and frank debate about the issue, facilitate public discussion and debate on possible processes and help identify key participants on the development of any initiatives forthcoming.[36]

The NIAC did not include this recommendation in its conclusions.

The Northern Ireland Veterans Association memorandum to the NIAC sets out the position of the British soldiers who served in Northern Ireland:

There are mixed feelings about a truth and recovery process among veterans. Veterans are suspicious that any such process would be for the political benefit of certain political parties, and would not benefit veterans at all. Other veterans wish to see senior commanders and politicians held to account for decisions that were made that appeared to show no regard for the lives of soldiers, or which seemed to worsen the situation in Northern Ireland. Some families of soldiers who have been killed feel that they required the truth to be able to move forward and leave the past behind.[37]

A concern raised in a number of the submissions is the timing of any truth initiative: that it should take place in the context of peace, since, if it were to proceed in the absence of peace, it would escalate conflict and make matters worse. The first people to appear before the Committee were Tom Roberts and William Smith from the Ex-Prisoners' Interpretative Centre (EPIC), a Loyalist ex-prisoners' project allied to the Ulster Volunteer Force. In their written evidence they quoted Brian Feeney to make a point which is reiterated by all those who are opposed to the idea of a truth recovery process and some who gave conditional support.

There have been about 40 truth and reconciliation processes around the world in places like South Africa and Peru. The only time they have worked is when the conflict has definitely come to an end. That is not the case here.[38]

In these circumstances, they contend in their memorandum: any truth process, runs the risk of indoctrinating a more 'militant' younger generation with hatred and providing justification for continuing conflict.[39]

Robin Wilson put it succinctly: 'One of the difficulties in this area... dealing with the past in Northern Ireland, history is it's not just the past and it is not even over yet.'[40]

However, it is far from clear what evidence or developments Wilson and others would require to satisfy them that the war was indeed over, and whether developments such as IRA decommissioning and rumours of its disbandment have subsequently satisfied them that moves towards peace are sufficient to warrant a re-examination of the past.

Some witnesses would only support a truth process if it benefited their constituency. When Janet Hunter from Families Achieving Change Together (FACT), a victims group in the Unionist community, was asked directly if she supported a truth commission, she replied:

> I could immediately say no, but if I saw the evidence and I saw how the outcome for victims was going to be, I might change my mind, if I saw that the victims were going to be taken care of, counselled, supported.[41]

However, in the absence of such guaranteed benefits, groups such as FACT remain dubious about the value of truth recovery. The Northern Ireland Veterans Association took a different view. Their opposition to truth recovery was based on the absence of consultation, support and education, and time was required for these to be put in place:

> **Rev. Rawding**: ... it is very difficult ... because there has been no consultation or education on truth processes among veterans. Secondly, it is problematic for us because we are seen to be perpetrators. We have people within our organisation who have killed people, so we are as likely to be dragged up in front of people and held up as the perpetrators and the offenders as others.... On the one hand we have the families saying, 'We cannot move on without truth'... on the other hand there needs to be a consultation and education process before we are dragged up as Soldier X or Soldier Y and put forward as the people who are part of the problem and who caused the problem. So it is far too early to be coming to quick decisions on the truth recovery process.[42]

Opposition to truth recovery

Those opposing the initiation of a truth recovery process included the Loyalist ex-prisoners, victim groups in the Protestant community, groups associated with the security forces and state forces, some of the other victim representatives and individual witnesses. EPIC explain their vulnerability in truth recovery arising from their lower levels of community support: 'Loyalist activists/ex-combatants/paramilitaries are particularly vulnerable to a "truth process" for they have never enjoyed the same level of legitimacy in their community as have Republicans'.[43]

Their suspicion about the concept of a truth recovery process was also increased by the Republican support for truth recovery and the political gains that they might make from it. Tom Roberts told the Inquiry:

> It became apparent to us pretty quickly that the view within our constituency was not unlike that within broader unionism and loyalism, in that there is a resistance to any sort of truth process because one of the primary reasons that we see is that Republicans are using this as a weapon to put the British Government and all its surrogates in the dock if you like, they seem to want to make everyone accountable for their role in the conflict except themselves.[44]

This deep distrust of Republican motives in supporting truth recovery and the lack of trust that they might participate fully in a process is a major factor in the Loyalist and Unionist opposition to truth recovery. The complete and utter lack of trust in Republican intentions is also to be found at many other points during the nine sessions.

William Smith from EPIC reports that the victims they have met also share his opposition to truth recovery: 'The vast majority of people we have met who are victims do not want it. A lot of people live with their own misery or their grief in their own way and they do not want these big inquiries.'[45]

The victims that William Smith is likely to have met, however, will probably have been drawn largely or exclusively from the Loyalist community. The sense of hopelessness and isolation is compounded by a fear of the consequences for their Loyalist constituency of the truth emerging. They expressed fears that, because Northern Ireland is a small and insular community, truth recovery could have potentially dangerous consequences for societal and family relationships. William Smith, citing unnamed authorities, told the Inquiry:

> There is a train of thought among some scholars etc that this type of recovery thing actually does more damage and opens up wounds. As I say, you could be living two streets away from a guy who gets up and says "I murdered your brother 20 years ago," it is only going to open up old wounds. In fact it will do more damage.[46]

> Put yourself in the position of an 18 year old or a 20 year old and your dad comes up and says "Yes, I murdered three people," how would he feel? Your total relationship would be affected. People are not going to do that.[47]

The EPIC delegation also claimed that a truth recovery process could widen the gap between victim and perpetrator – for example, if an apology or remorse were expected, none were forthcoming. Tom Roberts told the Inquiry:

> I would have preferred to have lived my life and caused no harm to anyone, but given the circumstances that I was brought up in and the political

conflict that raged at that time, I certainly was not sorry about what I was engaged in at that time. Certainly with hindsight there could have been better ways to do some things.... But to express remorse for something that happened 20 or 30 years ago, at that time I believed that what I was doing was right.[48]

Tom Roberts was unequivocal in response to Mark Tami's direct question, 'What do you see as the possible benefits of truth recovery for the Loyalist community as a whole?' Tom Roberts answered, 'I am not sure. None. None at all.'[49]

Disincentives within the Loyalist community are perceived to be that truth recovery would increase fears for personal safety, increase the isolation of Loyalists within and outside their own communities, since Loyalists enjoy less legitimacy than Republicans within their communities and result in further stigmatisation of Loyalists and their families. Many Loyalists wish to draw a line under the past, and fear that to do otherwise will harm relationships with younger people in their own communities should the truth about the past emerge. In the light of experience elsewhere, however, one has to wonder whether denial or avoidance of the past is the most productive and wise approach to this community dilemma.

The Director of one of the largest Non-Governmental Organisations in Northern Ireland, the Community Foundation, Avila Kilmurray, gave evidence which supported this picture of Loyalist anxieties about truth recovery. She referred to a survey carried out by her organisation in 2003 asking a number of groups about dealing with the past.

> Others, and I think particularly... on the Loyalist side were quite almost reluctant because they felt they were going to be stereotyped in terms of their role over the last 30 years and were quite resistant to looking at the past... there is a fear that the past will be used to justify positions rather than trying to share truths, albeit the truths may well differ, and there is a concern around that.[50]

Stephen Hepburn enquired how Ms Kilmurray thought that this Loyalist reluctance could be addressed. She responded: 'I think we can convince them by continuing to work with them at local community group level.... I think the main thing that will convince them, is that it is collective response rather than an individual response.'[51]

Indeed, Tom Roberts; evidence to the Inquiry backs up this analysis:

> The best case scenario that I could see... is some sort of blanket acknowledgement at an organisational level that they have caused great harm or whatever, but on an individual level... it would be very difficult in the society that we live in for anybody to voluntarily expose their role in the conflict, given the treatment of those who have involuntarily had their role exposed.'[52]

The idea of collective responsibility offers a possible place to start in terms of exploring any future truth recovery model. Indeed, collective acknowledgement of responsibility is not ruled out, and is indeed favoured by some in the Nationalist community also. Mark Thompson, for Relatives for Justice told the Inquiry:

> I think what we need to have is an exploration of dialogue about assuaging ideas, about the notion of truth and justice, the notion of "truth recovery," because I spoke to a Loyalist recently and he was of the opinion that it would mean individuals and of course our interpretations and concept of justice are very much different; and they are set in the context of moving society forward as opposed to taking us backward.[53]

Similarly, when probed about eliciting testimonies about individual responsibility for past events, Mark Thompson's answer was direct: 'We need to put the individual aspect of it completely out of the frame. It is not going to happen. We have got to be realistic. The only way it is going to happen is organisationally'.[54]

Trevor Ringland spoke against the establishment of a truth recovery mechanism, seeing it as impossible to establish the truth:

> I would not agree to a formal structure but what I would agree to is a template where you set down certain criteria that have to be met in any meetings that take place, that there has to be a cross-community element to it in the meetings. (Q571) I doubt if you will ever be able to create a structure whereby you will get everybody to get together and tell the truth. It will never happen.[55]

The arguments against a truth recovery process were that the conflict is not at an end, that there was a 'war by other means', and that there was nothing to gain from truth recovery. Loyalist paramilitaries viewed truth recovery as increasing their vulnerability because of lack of support in their communities, saw the process as a Republican project, and suspected Republican motives. Allied to this was the general Unionist lack of trust in Republican capacity to participate fully and honestly: the perception of Republicans as untrustworthy. This was compounded by a sense of hopelessness about their general situation, and helplessness and pessimism – 'you never get what you want.' Reconciliation was seen as impossible, and political movement was ruled out.

Concerns about models of truth recovery: imported versus tailor-made models

A number of witnesses to the NIAC Inquiry expressed anxieties of various kinds about the method of truth recovery that could be adopted in Northern Ireland, the wisdom of importing models from elsewhere, the amount of consultation and preparation for such a process, and the way decisions would be made. One of the major concerns was the over-reliance on the South African model, concern at the NIAC's seeming quest for an off-the-peg model, and the lack of appreciation of the need for a tailor-made model for Northern Ireland.

Speaking on behalf of Families Achieving Change Together (FACT), a victims' group in the Unionist community, Janet Hunter's rejection of truth recovery was framed in terms of the South African model: 'I think it would be a good idea to get all the groups to do something together to help people move on but I do not believe in the South African style of truth and reconciliation'.[56]

This concern was echoed by Avila Kilmurray, who made the point that in considering international precedents undue attention has been paid to the South African experience. Witness A from WAVE, a cross-community victims' group, also highlighted this tendency in evidence to the Inquiry: 'I would be a wee bit concerned about the associations that people draw between here and South Africa, almost as though the South African model of truth is the only model that existed.'[57]

The failings of the South African model, according to FAIR's analysis, are set out in their memorandum to the NIAC, and are described as, 'lack of independence and ownership; the disgrace of amnesty; bias against the state; politicisation of the project and recreation of history'.[58] In his testimony to the Inquiry, William Frazer outlines his sense of having been betrayed by the British state and stresses the importance of proper compensation for innocent victims.[59]

Later in session 9 of the proceedings, Northern Ireland Secretary Paul Murphy MP reported to the Inquiry the conclusion he drew from his experiences in South Africa, a conclusion that many of the local groups had already arrived at. His conclusion was that it was not possible to import a South African-style Truth and Reconciliation Commission to Northern Ireland. He made particular reference to Northern Ireland being so much smaller than South Africa and the difficulties this created in terms of the close-knit nature of the society.

However, in spite of these definitive rejections of an imported model, the NIAC chair posed a question to this panel, which indicates that he had not abandoned the quest for an off-the-peg model: 'Has anybody got examples of a country which has succeeded in designing an effective victim-centred approach to reconciliation? Can anyone drag anything out of their memories? We do not think we have found one.'[60]

Nor, in the report of the Inquiry to government is it clear that the NIAC have grasped the importance of a tailor-made process for Northern Ireland. The idea that the Committee could yet stumble upon a ready-made model for reconciliation for Northern Ireland does not seem to have been entirely abandoned.

Yet, in its memorandum to the Inquiry, the cross-community victims group, WAVE, emphasised that any truth recovery process must be tailored to the specific circumstances of the Northern Ireland conflict, and this point, too, emerged from many of the written and verbal submissions. In his evidence,

Brice Dickson pointed out that there are international standards which the Committee could use for guidance, should they come to design a process for Northern Ireland. Professor Hadden from the Human Rights Centre, Queen's University, raised another concern about the viability of a multi-purpose truth process, and he was doubtful whether 'a single process or a single commission can do all the jobs that need to be done.'[61]

Instead, he advocated a less-monolithic approach: 'divide it up into achievable objectives in respect of victims and in respect of state policy, in respect of paramilitary activity and in respect of individual perpetrators'.[62]

Others raised some of the very difficult issues, such as immunity from prosecution or amnesty for witnesses, and questioned the possibility of other kinds of processes running alongside a truth recovery mechanism. Some, like Robin Wilson, had very low expectations of any future truth process. He told the Inquiry:

> We are not in a situation where we have to talk about serious immunity anyway... because a lot of the perpetrators, even if they had immunity, still would not tell the truth in a way that would be recognised. So I think we should not assume that the only vehicle in all of this would be some kind of truth recovery process.[63]

Truth versus reconciliation

Others had concerns about the definition of terms that the NIAC and any future truth recovery process might operate under. In its substantial written memorandum, the Northern Ireland Human Rights Commission (NIHRC) stresses that the Committee should strive to avoid any conflation of the distinct ideas of reconciliation and truth. The memorandum expressed concern that the terms of reference of the Inquiry confused these two concepts. In his evidence to the Inquiry, the then NIHRC Chief Commissioner Brice Dickson also raised another definitional issue: 'We acknowledge that truth and justice are not necessarily the same thing, but the one should not be the enemy of the other'.[64]

Neutrality and the government's role

Andrew Rawding, on behalf of the Northern Ireland Veterans' Association explained the veterans' position, raising the issue of trust in the government's motivation and approach to truth recovery, and its ability to be neutral or fair:

> There is a real fear that the government is going to make a decision and say "We are going to do this." People will be very sceptical about whatever government as to why it is being done. Of course, some people have real issues

about the government, including veterans, so why should the government be controlling this?[65]

Others, unlikely allies, perhaps, of the Northern Ireland Veterans, shared the suspicion of government control and motivation. Speaking for Relatives for Justice (RFJ), a victims group in the Nationalist community, Mark Thompson's evidence to the Inquiry stressed the importance of independence of any process from government:

> A key thing – and this will be the test of your report – is whether you are able to say to the NIO, "You're not the people who should be leading this." There needs to be independence and there needs to be a recognition that the British state was a combatant in the same way that the IRA was a combatant and the Loyalists were combatants. If you want a real process, then you need to ask somebody else to do it.[66]

Thompson stressed his reservations on how this process has been handled by government to date.

> We think that they have failed to engage directly with the people who have been bereaved. They have announced the consultation yet failed to engage the sector. There is a view across the sector that the process needs to be a bottom up approach.[67]

Thompson then referred to the Patten Inquiry into policing as a positive example of how a process could be jointly owned and the need to ensure that no single participant to the conflict: 'whether they be Loyalists, Republican, or the British state, or the Irish Government for that matter, should be in the process of driving any initiative, but we welcome the exploration of finding collectively an agreed position.'[68]

Inclusivity

Paul O'Connor stressed the importance of any truth recovery process designed for Northern Ireland being totally inclusive: 'If it was established and it did not involve everyone then it will not work...if you have a truth recovery process that, for example, did not involve the IRA, it will not work'.[69]

Mike Ritchie from Coiste, the Republican ex-prisoners organisation, reflected on the importance of wide involvement in the design of any process:

> Experience around the world shows that you are never going to be able to design a process that everybody is happy with. You have to factor that in. If just Loyalists were not happy that would be bad, but in terms of individuals, there will always be individuals – I think Steve Biko's family in South Africa

were completely dissatisfied with the South African model tried to seek compensation and were turned down in the courts. So you cannot possibly come up with a process where everybody is happy, but at least if people are involved in the discussion and are part of designing the mechanism then that ensures maximum buy-in.[70]

Relative benefits and costs

Members of the NIAC revealed their own concerns and opinions about truth recovery by the tenor of their questions. Martin Smyth's concern for the balance of attention within a truth recovery process was clear when he prefaced a question to a witness as follows: 'Evidence has been given that sometimes there is more attention given to prisoners who were the perpetrators rather than victims who were completely innocent.'[71]

Ann Boal for the Disabled Police Officers' Association (DPOA) raised the experience of the Bloody Sunday Inquiry as an example of vast expense for limited returns, although the outcome at that time had not yet been announced:

> All you have to do is look at the Bloody Sunday Inquiry. How many millions of pounds are we going to spend? I listened to a statement made by Martin McGuinness during that time. He made it clear that the IRA take an oath of allegiance which forbids them from telling. Who are going to be the truth tellers and who the truth demanders?[72]

The issues of value for money, and the avoidance of spending large sums on legal fees (ensuring that the legal profession and few others profit from a truth recovery process) were clearly concerns for several witnesses. Mrs Boal's evidence implied that seeking truth, at least from the IRA, was a pointless exercise. Certainly, the vast amounts of distrust existing between the parties to the conflict raises the difficulty of the credibility of even *bone fide* disclosures.

The role of victims and victim centredness

The representatives from the Omagh Support and Help Group, representing victims of the Omagh bomb, were keen to use this opportunity to make the case for an inquiry into that event. Michael Gallagher made the point that storytelling can sometimes be used as a substitute for justice, and clearly they were more interested in justice than any other outcome. Nonetheless, Trevor Ringland and Chris Gibson each emphasised the importance and the redemptive power of storytelling and listening to other people's stories.

Others were more critical of the notion of victim-centred approaches. Chris Gibson from the One Small Step Campaign, which works on improving community relations, rejected the idea of reconciliation being victim-centred: 'A lot of things need reconciling here other than victims. Victimhood is a badge that people wear and it is a terribly comfortable badge to wear. That we have to get across.'[73]

Some victims, themselves, saw a wider role for a truth recovery mechanism. WAVE's Witness A pointed to the need to examine the role of the wider civil society:

> If you talk, for example, in terms of truth committees... essentially it should be victim centred but if you are going down that road, then obviously there are other aspects for society to take on board. We need to examine, for example, the role of the churches, the role of governments, the role of institutions like the Northern Ireland Housing Executive.[74]

This highlights the limited range of organisations, institutional representatives and individuals who appeared before the Committee, and is reminiscent of the point made by the youths cited by Krog (1999), that examination of complicity and failure to act should also be included in any truth process.

The memorandum submitted by FAIR is emotional, trenchant and occasionally biblical in cadence, emphasising their view that victims have been poorly treated in Northern Ireland: 'While we have visited a number of countries to see how they deal with their victims of terrorism and have found that they are treated like Royalty compared to the innocent victims of terrorism in Northern Ireland.'[75]

They see a central role for victims in matters relating to the truth, but fear that dealing with the past 'has the potential to re-traumatise victims, to raise then dash hopes, to create new victims and to add to rather than detract from the causes of conflict.'[76] They analyse the South African Truth and Reconciliation Commission, referring to the 'disgrace of amnesty' and its 'bias against the state' concluding that truth commissions 'trade truth for justice in a manner which excludes and abuses victims.'[77] The allegiances of FAIR emerge in such evidence, together with their preference for a purely retributive approach to issues of truth, and their suspicion and indeed scorn of restorative approaches.

Stephen Pound asked Janet Hunter from Families Achieving Change Together (FACT) (Session 3, 21/02/05), if she agreed that a victim-centred approach to reconciliation could sometimes put unbearable pressure on the individual. Ms Hunter expressed a general unspecified cynicism and lack of hope for the future, and sense of being less well catered for than perpetrators:

> As for truth and reconciliation, lot of things in Northern Ireland start off with the victim but it always ends up for the good of the perpetrator because it is easier and cheaper to change the perpetrator than it is to support the victim.[78]

Another witness, Mr Jameson from Omagh Support and Self Help Group, portrays the truth and reconciliation process as of benefit only to perpetrators:

> If I was an IRA man and I had done what they have done, and I go out here and tell all those people who are victims here, "Yes, I was a perpetrator." He

would go out of that door happy as Larry. He has cleared his belly, as they say here in Northern Ireland, yet we as the victims still have to live with it. The only man getting his conscience clear is the guy who perpetrated it.[79]

There is a sense of a zero-sum game, where one side loses because the other gains, a kind of intergroup security dilemma, with no vision of a future where truth and reconciliation is in the wider interests of all sections of society. The NIAC tended not to question or challenge such statements from victims, but rather seemed to accept them at face value. However, these views are by no means representative of all victims, a point made by Witness A from WAVE. In response to a question from Roy Beggs about whether the truth gave closure to victims, Witness A responded that it is very difficult to make such generalisations: 'People sometimes talk about victims as if they are talking about one person or one constituency that all think the same thing. That is not necessarily the case. Victims are like everyone else in life. They are all different.'[80]

This diversity of views and experiences amongst victims poses a challenge for those who would establish a 'victim-centred' approach to truth recovery. Indeed, there are scant models for such an approach elsewhere. Paul O'Connor of the Pat Finucane Centre questioned the extent to which the South African Truth and Reconciliation Commission was victim centred: '... one of the problems with the South African Commission is the perception that it is perpetrator-led, in other words, they made decisions, came forward and received an amnesty.'[81]

The Pat Finucane Centre argued that in order to deliver a viable truth recovery process, the essential elements were: factual clarification and truth recovery; justice and accountability; storytelling; acknowledgement and moral reparations were all required, and that: 'dealing with the past requires a broad strategy reflecting the reality that there are diverse needs within the victims' community and the needs of victims often change over time'.[82]

Marion Mitchell, who described herself as 'a victim from mainland Britain' advocated that more attention should be paid to those from England, Scotland and Wales who had been bereaved or injured.[83] Indeed, other victims echoed a sense of neglect, and of being 'used'. One of the witnesses from the WAVE spoke of this:

> We are very lost people. We are here now today talking to you but we are very lost people. We are like a book you take off the shelf and dust us and take us out now and again and it makes everybody feel good and we have coffee or we have a meal and it is all very nice and we go away and we do not hear a thing.[84]

None of the three witnesses from WAVE supported the idea of a truth recovery process. Others raised the issue of how representative the views of certain victims' organisations might be, and the role of other civil society organisations in supporting victims. Michael Potter from the Training for Women Network questioned the role of victims' organisation, as well as how representative they were:

> From a victim's perspective, there are a number of victims groups who see themselves as representatives of victims in Northern Ireland. The problem is that the victims' sector is very divided and those who are parts of groups are a tiny minority... What we have found from our research is that people seek help, guidance and support in a range of areas within society itself and not necessarily from victims' groups. Talking to victims' groups, therefore, will only reach a small proportion of people generally. Most ordinary human beings who do not feel themselves to be politically disposed one way or the other might seek help through the family, churches, other community organisations, but predominantly we have found that women's centres have sustained communities during the conflict.[85]

Potter pointed out the impact that a shortage of funding was having on the sector. In the same session, Professor Roy McClelland, a practising psychiatrist, from Healing Through Remembering argued for extra funding for the health service rather than the voluntary sector:

> 30 years of civil conflict has contributed to the mental health morbidity of this community... I do feel that a lot of the material needs of people can be met by adequate and proper resourcing of our health care system appropriate to the needs of the people of Northern Ireland, rather than a separate system to meet the needs.[86]

Whilst the statutory sector has latterly provided trauma services for those affected by the Troubles this is a relatively recent development, and those in the voluntary sector argue that voluntary and self-help provision which often filled the gaps in statutory services should continue to be supported.

Reparations

The awarding of compensation, usually of a financial nature, is another sensitive issue on which the Committee heard evidence. In spite of a variety of provisions for compensation of victims through various government agencies, schemes and funds, and a provision for compensation for members of the security forces and their families, negative comparisons are often drawn with public expenditure on other public sectors. Certain individual victims and victims' organisations complain of their treatment, and consider the amounts of financial compensation awarded to them as inadequate, complaining that, in comparison with the perpetrators, they have not been well treated. Whilst the actual monetary value of any reparations is undoubtedly important in its own right, Hamber and

Wilson (2003) hold that

> All reparations (including monetary compensation) are like tombstones – a way of materializing the dead...Reparations are, therefore, a material representation and fixation of memory work, recognition of the experience of liminality and its objectification in the external world...Reparations (and the processes of remembering and commemoration) stabilize ghosts, they domesticate and tame them by representing compensation for their death...genuine reparation, and the process of healing...does not occur through the delivery of the object (for example, a pension, a monument and so on) but through the process that takes place around the object.[87]

Since reparations perform this psychological and symbolic function, reparation that appears to be less valuable or significant than that provided for others, especially perpetrators, creates fresh grievance.

Reparation raises other difficult issues, as was discussed in Chapter 5. For some, the acceptance of any reparation is to relinquish hope of ever recovering what was lost. Thus the award of reparation requires a closure, a 'letting go', and as a result some find it more tolerable to live in faint hope or denial. For others, the acceptance of reparations is distasteful if it is not accompanied by a broader process of truth and reconciliation. As was pointed out in Chapter 5, some victims also see reparations as 'blood money'. The importance of engaging in truth recovery alongside reparations is pointed out by Hamber and Wilson (2003): 'Reparations without truth make survivors feel that reparations are being used to buy their silence and put a stop to their continuing quest for truth and justice'.[88]

Truth recovery processes that fail to deliver both of these functions alongside one another run the risk of further alienating victims.

Acknowledgement

A further function performed by truth recovery processes is that of acknowledgement of harm done, particularly by the armed parties to the conflict. Even in the absence of this, public acknowledgement of the suffering of victims, through testimonies, personal accounts and storytelling, offer participants their 'day in court' and an opportunity for acknowledgement. Their testimonies also lend depth to the picture of the conflict, and create opportunities for empathy to develop across deep societal divisions. Such testimony was a key part of the South African process. In Northern Ireland, in the absence of, or in advance of, a formal truth recovery process, many local groups have engaged in storytelling, and some have recorded, published or archived these stories, as a way of providing some form of acknowledgment. In the absence of a formal government-sponsored process, perhaps this is the best that can be achieved, or perhaps such work paves the way for a future formal truth recovery process.

Nonetheless, the writing of these accounts into some formal public and official account offers a formal acknowledgement that many victims would value and continue to seek.[89]

Reconciliation

The Inquiry was also charged with the responsibility to enquire into prospects for reconciliation in Northern Ireland. In written evidence the Community Foundation for Northern Ireland (CFNI) espoused the view that reconciliation might be an outcome of truth recovery, and that an inclusive Truth initiative may help to establish an informed basis for future reconciliation. In her testimony on behalf of CFNI, Avila Kilmurray questioned the goal of reconciliation:

> I think in terms of victims and survivors (and a lot would say this) talking about reconciliation is putting a bar too high...I think really we should be starting from the outside institutions and working inwards, rather than putting the pressure on the victims who suffered most acutely for the Troubles.[90]

The issue of who will provide leadership on such matters emerges. 'Outside institutions' according to Kilmurray, should provide the lead, implying the need for international involvement. This provides a broader context for Healing Through Remembering's recommendation that the two state parties, the British and Irish governments, together with the armed groups should lead the way in acknowledging the harm done on their respective behalves during the Troubles. The acceptance of such responsibility could provide a rare and valuable stimulus to others to move away from a blame culture into one where responsibility is acknowledged and shared. Such a process may well require an external 'witness', a disinterested international party. However, this issue is not pursued by the NIAC.

Mike Ritchie's evidence to the Inquiry on behalf of Eolas, a Republican ex-prisoners' group, was indicative that the reconciliation work was beginning at the community level:

> What we have been trying to do through the Eolas project that we are all involved in is to contribute to a more generous approach where we are saying that we recognise that our community has been involved in creating hurt. We would like other people to equally recognise that they have created hurt and we would like some meaningful discussion as to how we can take this forward.[91]

Ritchie's assertion occurs in a context in which the original motivation for and justification of violence is intact. His assertion signals a taking of responsibility for the consequences of past actions, not an admission that these actions were wrong or unjustified. Some Loyalists, and indeed some members of the security forces have taken a similar stance in encounters with their former enemies. There is undoubtedly some interest amongst former combatants – especially amongst former members of the security forces – in engaging their former enemies in discussion about the justification of past actions, and in some cases in bringing former enemies to see the error of their ways. Ritchie does not engage with this, but finds a method of engaging with the standpoint of the 'other' by focusing directly on the issue of the harm caused by past actions – whether justified or unjustified. A focus on harm caused does seem to be a productive avenue for exploration. Similar hopeful indications and signs of new developments were apparent in the evidence of other witnesses, such as Andrew Rawding, who spoke about his work with the Northern Ireland Veteran's Association.

> **Rev. Rawding:** We are participating in a form of reconciliation work specifically with IRA ex-prisoners and other ex-prisoner groups. This is essential to some of our veterans because the one way they might get to wholeness or to real reconciliation is to get to a point where they actually accept that they are no longer under threat and they no longer have an enemy. The only way they will get that is actually to come into physical contact with someone who they would perceive to be their enemy. We are proactively looking at this. Some of the veterans from the early seventies have tried every single therapy and psychiatric treatment. Some have actually insisted that they are not interested in the other agencies; they want to meet Republicans, they want to meet IRA or former IRA people.[92]

This desire to revisit or even confront the past was also apparent in the evidence from the Disabled Police Officers' Association. Mrs Grigg, Public Relations Officer for the Northern Ireland Veterans' Association told the Committee:

> While you have unfinished business, whatever it happens to be, to do with what happened, then you cannot have closure; you cannot completely move forward; you cannot take a second new life. There are people (veterans) who would like to go and visit where it happened but who have never had that opportunity. It would be helpful if that were to happen too.[93]

However other witnesses were less positive about the methods of taking forward the 'closure' or reconciliation agenda, the motivation for reconciliation, or the prospects of achieving it. On the topic of reconciliation, Celia Gourley, who lost both legs and part of a finger in an IRA bomb in 1991, told the Committee:

> The thesaurus says resolve, remedy, heal, cure, rectify. I feel that before we can do any of these things there is an enormous amount to be done by the people who perpetrated the sort of injury that I and Barbara and Maureen and many other people received. There is a great deal of hurt, there is a great deal of anger and there is a great deal that needs to be done, I am sorry to say, by those who perpetrated these events before these definitions of "reconciliation" can begin to happen.[94]

The three witnesses, Mrs Gourley, Mrs Mitchell and Mrs Deane all stressed the importance of perpetrators being remorseful and apologising, whilst casting doubt on the feasibility of achieving such a goal. Mrs Gourley said:

> I do think there need to be apologies right from the top down and from all political parties. I think we are doing the emperor's new clothes with Sinn Fein and have been for a long time. David Trimble's party has called Sinn Fen the IRA all along. We have been fooled, we have been accepting this façade and I think there needs to be honesty from them as well.[95]

Mrs Mitchell's evidence, given alongside that of Mrs Gourley's, conveyed a sense of powerlessness and hopelessness:

> I have actually met the perpetrators who did the things that happened and my opinion is that they will never give what Celia wants. They will never reconcile because the ones I have met and spoken to have never ever shown any remorse for the things they have done.[96]

> I would like to think it was not a hopeless cause, but my experience with the ones I have met I do feel at this point in time that it is.[97]

This hopelessness seems to be based on her assessment of the impossibility of eliciting remorse or apology from perpetrators. Other victims, also from a Unionist background were similarly pessimistic. Esther Andrews highlighted the grim reality of life in her border community. She describes a paramilitary presence she experiences as more oppressive than ever, and relations between the two communities as non-existent: 'I would say that the Protestant community in our area has no relationship at all with the Catholic community'.[98]

When asked what she feels about the whole peace and reconciliation process, she seems to indicate her lack of support for the peace process: 'I think the whole thing has been a farce. What have we gained? We are as far back now as we were then'.[99]

The sense that the 'war is not over' was apparent in other witnesses to the Inquiry. The chair of the Tullyvallen Community Association explained to the Committee that he was anxious that his identity should be protected because he was scared of paramilitary/Nationalist violence against him, even though he had already identified himself as the Master of Tullyvallen Orange Hall. His evidence revealed similar sentiments:

> I cannot see anybody in our immediate community in the foreseeable future, even if there was an agreement in a year's time, coming down for reconcili.ation. Reconciliation is to me where you go on the ground and meet with your neighbours and talk about it. They are not going to do that in the foreseeable future.[100]

This man does not say that he would refuse to go and meet with his neighbours – instead it is others in his community who would refuse to do so. Nor is this the failure of leadership unique to the Unionist community, although it is particularly acute there. He recounts how his attempts to reach out to the other community failed:

> I had approached a Republican community organisation to come here today. They had agreed to do it but then when they went and thought about it they did not want to stick their heads out and have to take recrimination maybe from Sinn Fein or the wider community.[101]

In the matter of gestures of conciliation, risk-takers and leaders in both communities are constrained by the attitudes of their constituent community. These attitudes restrict how far they can go and what they can do. To offer leadership out of such entrenched positions is to risk ostracism. The alternative, to accept negative attitudes as a more or less unchangeable fact, is a safer option. For leaders to live within this sad status quo and to accept that fear is predominant, and movement or change is not possible, is a more secure position for them as leaders.

These issues were also apparent in the questions from some of the Northern Ireland Members sitting on the NIAC. Gregory Campbell MP's question to Michael Gallagher reveals much of the insecurity felt by some Loyalists about cross-community work:

> Just on the issue of cross-community work... you will appreciate that the committee have been speaking to a range of people – that they are concerned or fearful about engaging in cross-community work. When I ask this question I am talking about genuine cross-community work and I was pleased to hear you in an earlier part making it very clear that you would distinguish between perpetrators and victims, because at the outset of the Committee's deliberations, we made precisely the same point. So it is genuine cross-community work that I am talking about, not being expected to get in with perpetrators. Have... you knowledge of people who are concerned because of security

implications or if there are other concerns that they might have regarding cross-community work among victims?[102]

In reply, Mr Gallagher stated that 'People would be encouraged to mix with one another because there are a lot of good people on both sides.'[103] Gregory Campbell went on to ask William Frazer, '[Do] you think that now is the right time or will there ever be a right time to embark on that kind of issue [an official truth and reconciliation process]?'.[104] Mr Frazer replied:

> Truth and reconciliation will never be acceptable to the victims, because we know the truth. I know every man who was involved in the murder of my family and my family members. I know every one of them, so what more truth do I need to know?[105]

The strong negativity emanating from some of the testimonies is not challenged by any of the questions. Perhaps the MPs were so daunted by the physical suffering and hopelessness of witnesses that they were reluctant to question them too closely. Indeed, Gregory Campbell's questions to some of the witnesses indicated that he was in agreement with the suspicions and cynicism expressed by them, and so had no motivation to challenge them. The evidence from those witnesses who expressed doubts and fears about reconciliation, and who failed to see any benefit in a truth and reconciliation process in Northern Ireland seems to have weighed heavily on the Committee.

Rituals of reconciliation

Albie Sachs, a prominent South African lawyer, now head of South Africa's constitutional court, suffered a violent attack, clandestinely perpetrated by the South African security forces during the *apartheid* era. He lost an arm and the sight of one eye, and sustained multiple injuries. He described[106] how, during the political transition whilst the TRC was still at hearing, he agreed to meet the policeman responsible for planting the bomb that injured him. The policeman introduced himself to Sachs, who felt unable to shake his hand after the encounter. Sachs advised his attacker to give evidence to the TRC. On a second meeting, the policeman reported that he had given evidence to the TRC, and described to them his role in the attack on Sachs. At that point, because of the policeman's participation in the TRC, Sachs felt able to shake his hand. The policeman experienced some form of emotional release, and wept for a period of weeks after this encounter. In this case, the TRC offered a public, official mechanism to both Sachs and the policeman, whereby the earlier transaction between them could be exposed, explored, adjudicated and disposed of. This provided a new basis for the relationship between them, in which past events and deeds were present, but had been processed in a way that allowed them to be negotiated openly on the basis of a shared public discourse and acceptance of responsibility.

Not all victims are able, as Sachs was, to reconcile with their attackers, nor are all perpetrators willing to face their victims. However, public truth recovery processes at least offer potential mechanisms for such reconciliation for those who seek it, or are able to avail themselves of it. That such encounters, however few, occur at all, begins to send signals to the wider society about a shift in intergroup relations. In the description and discussion of such encounters, new ideas about old grievances are circulated in the public sphere, thus contributing to a wider process of societal change.

The Northern Ireland Affairs Committee's conclusions

Having heard the evidence and the statement from the Minister, the Inquiry concluded that the establishment of a truth recovery process in Northern Ireland was 'virtually impossible', citing a range of reasons in support of this conclusion. These can be summarised as follows:

1　lack of a consensus on the subject of truth recovery
2　lack of political progress in Northern Ireland
3　the chances of large sections of the population refusing to cooperate with such a venture and the negative consequences of this
4　lack of clarity about how a truth recovery mechanism would dovetail with the existing judicial processes
5　the lack of consensus on amnesty for perpetrators
6　the lack of conviction amongst some that violence is at an end
7　lack of readiness in communities to accept an 'official' version of history, which would be the output of a truth recovery process
8　Truth recovery could exacerbate political tensions.

All of these reasons refer to the conditions in the polity, and amongst the key participants in any future official truth process, emphasising their lack of 'readiness' for truth recovery. Yet the Committee recognises the need for some form of truth recovery and calls on government to encourage and publicise creative methods of local truth telling. Their conclusion, that the time for an official process was not right, thus differentiates between the official and unofficial processes. The time is not right for an official process, but local processes should proceed. The Committee does not specify how these local processes should proceed, how if at all they might contribute to a more comprehensive process, or to what extent they should be supported to clarify the issues and address the fears surrounding the issue of truth recovery. Nor is it clear whether government sees any potential connection between informal and formal processes, a point that will be taken up in the Conclusions.

Indeed, it is not clear that the need for a firm political will to engage in the hard work of moving the issue of truth recovery forward is understood at either government or community level. The lack of engagement of the political parties, with the possible exception of Sinn Féin, is also symptomatic of the tendency to lapse into rehearsing old grievances and demands rather than attempting to create new understandings or address the suspicions that proliferate in relation to this issue. Yet, even if political progress is made, it is unlikely that any rough consensus about truth recovery will develop without significant dialogue and groundwork in order to clarify the issues and to address fears. It seems that the Northern Ireland political parties find political progress hard to come by and consensus on truth recovery even harder. It remains to be seen, in the light of the slightly more positive political developments since the NIAC Inquiry report was published, whether these difficulties will persist.

The government position

In various parts of the evidence to the Inquiry and the Inquiry's response to that evidence, the lack of enthusiasm on the part of government for a formal truth recovery process for Northern Ireland becomes apparent. In an exchange with Paul O'Connor in which O'Connor asserts the government's reluctance to sponsor truth recovery, Michael Mates indicates what he considers to be the government position.

> MR O'CONNOR: ...Clearly we are coming out with a very different perspective from yourself in that we do not believe that the state to date has shown a great willingness to participate in any kind of truth recovery exercise, whether that be in an official inquiry or through a different type of mechanism.
> Q382 CHAIRMAN: If we were to conclude, and I am choosing my words very carefully, that there was some move forward, I think that would be quite a push for the government today.... you say in your submission... that this must be an international body and there are few who would differ from that... What would you say to an international body that was chaired by someone from the United Kingdom? The difficulties of putting a foreign person in charge of it would be a very difficult matter for any government, let us put it that way....[107]

Bernice Swift from Firinne, elucidates the position of those affected by state violence, raising the question of the future role of the British state:

> The main question of the families themselves is how might the British Government acknowledge their role within the conflict in the North of Ireland. That is the big question and the families actually wonder where the spirit of generosity might be to lead that process forward.[108]

Later, Paul Murphy's comments to the Inquiry seem to preclude any initiative on the part of the government, in advance of the Inquiry's deliberations: 'We could not embark on the sorts of things we would like to have embarked on until we are making greater progress.'[109]

> I am simply saying I did not think that this was the time for it (TRC) and if anything it could be counterproductive. The idea of being able to set up quite an extensive and indeed elaborate consultation system on the whole question of dealing with the past at a time of really deep political uncertainty I thought would do damage to such a process rather than help it, hinder it rather than help it. In a sense, if you like, for the time being we have shelved the wider consultation until such time as we think the people of Northern Ireland a) would be ready for it by a consensus and b) when we get further political progress.[110]

Murphy's statement seems to indicate that the government had already established its position on this issue, a factor of which the Committee was very respectful and to which it paid due heed in the course of its deliberations. The statement appears to suggest a curious dichotomy in government thinking. In one sense it is the people of Northern Ireland who are somehow not ready for mature and considered reflection on their past; yet, on the other hand, there is no sense that those governing this unready population might have a responsibility to lead them towards a position where such reflection was possible. Instead the option of storytelling – which might cynically be represented as the 'talk among yourselves' option – is the only one which Mr Murphy recommends to the people of Northern Ireland. Whilst the value of storytelling and other local initiatives has been clearly established by the work of, for example, Healing Through Remembering, such work cannot deliver the official acknowledgement and definitive outcomes of a formal truth process. But it seems a key official sponsor, the British government, is less than keen to proceed.

When the Minister was challenged by Iain Luke MP that several witnesses had indicated that they believe that the time is right for Northern Ireland to start engaging in wide-ranging public consultations about a process for dealing with the past, he insisted that the government was not trying to close down such a process, merely putting it on hold until times were perceived to be more auspicious. However, he subsequently indicated that the Government was simply daunted by the prospect of what any such process might involve:

> We knew how sensitive that was... can you imagine trying to deal with these issues when everybody is in turmoil. It is hard enough trying to cope with the political situation at the moment without having it come down to these difficult issues.[111]

Thus, it seems that the government position was clear from an early stage. There was never any appetite on the part of government for an official truth recovery process, and three factors – the lack of general political progress; the lack of consensus on the issue of truth; and the contests between advocates of retributive and restorative approaches to the past losses – provide sufficient justification for placing truth recovery on a very long finger. The work of the Police Ombudsman's Office on issues such as collusion between the security forces and Loyalist paramilitaries, and the outcomes of similar inquiries that have been initiated since the publication of the NIAC report, are likely to increase government reluctance to embark on a comprehensive truth recovery process for Northern Ireland.

8 Is Northern Ireland ready for truth?

The deliberations of the Northern Ireland Affairs Committee (NIAC) on the feasibility of a truth recovery process for Northern Ireland articulated and formalised the dominant view that Northern Ireland is 'not ready' for such a process. Yet, in societies emerging out of a conflict, it is arguably important that the grievances of the past be put to rest in order to ensure that peace and stability can be secured and that unresolved past grievances do not jeopardise such security. Sometimes, a mechanism for managing the past has formed part of the peace agreement, as in El Salvador and Guatemala. No mention of truth recovery, however, was made in the Good Friday Agreement, and successive accusations and disclosures about spying, dirty tricks and collusion have proved to be, at least, political irritants stimulating renewed rounds of accusation and denial, and, at worst, destabilising influences on the peace process. The allegations of spying by Republicans in the Northern Ireland Assembly and the subsequent police raid on the Sinn Féin offices at Stormont contributed to the downfall of the Assembly. (It emerged later that the manager of the office, Sinn Féin member Denis Donaldson, was a British agent.) The murder of Robert McCartney, allegedly by members of the IRA, and the campaign by his sisters has highlighted the shifting power dynamics at community level. Later disclosures about the infiltration of the Republican organisations by the security forces has led, *inter alia*, to the death of Denis Donaldson, and similar revelations on the Loyalist side have resulted in the death of William Stobie, also a British agent and allegedly implicated in the death of Pat Finucane.

The publication of the Stephens and Cory reports have increased the appetite for truth amongst Nationalists, and the delay in establishing a public inquiry into the death of Pat Finucane alongside the new legislation circumscribing the powers of such inquiries has further eroded Nationalist confidence in the intentions of the British government. It seems unlikely that this steady stream of disclosures, destabilising though they may be, will dry up soon, unless it is tackled at source. That source is the dark pool of undisclosed business of the past, the clandestine deeds and secret pacts, the hatreds and rivalries which provided, and for some still provide, the motivation for conflict. Attempts at burying the past by any or all of the participants seem singularly unsuccessful.

Public opinion in Northern Ireland on the issue of truth recovery has undoubtedly been influenced by The Bloody Sunday Inquiry. On the one hand, the Inquiry has attracted much interest, and, in advance of the findings, criticism has been directed at the enormous cost of the proceedings and the huge fees paid to the lawyers which contrast sharply with the financial circumstances of many of the bereaved families. On the other hand, the attitude of the British government to the Inquiry, and, depending on your view, its lack of enthusiasm for participation or failure to cooperate with aspects of the Inquiry, have been perhaps indicative of government's disposition to such delving into the past.

Yet, through the response to the NIAC Inquiry into truth and reconciliation, the government has concluded that it is Northern Ireland, not it, that is not ready for a process of truth recovery, and that to embark on such a process – rather than its absence – might be destabilising to the delicate political balance in Northern Ireland. This raises several questions. Is the political balance really that delicate? Will Northern Ireland ever be ready for truth recovery? How will we know if and when Northern Ireland is ready for such a process? Who will be the judge of this, and what indicators will this judge take into account? In order to elucidate some of these questions, some light might be shed by the literature on readiness or 'ripeness' during peace processes where there has been a debate about detecting readiness.

The notion of readiness or 'ripeness' (Zartman, 1985) has been used to describe the condition of the societies who are ready – or not – to embark on peace processes. Is it possible to discern whether or not a society is 'ripe' for peace – or, in this case, truth recovery? Two aspects of how this literature engages with the question of 'ripeness' or readiness are of interest here. It addresses first the issue of whether or not it is possible to discern if a conflicted society is ready to make peace; and second, if this is possible to detect, the question of how it is to be done, what indicators should be used.

Detecting 'ripeness'

Zartman (1985), and later Stedman (1991) and Haass (1990), have argued that 'ripeness' for peace has occurred in societies in conflict when a number of identifiable conditions arose. The first of these is that the parties to the conflict must experience a 'Hurting Stalemate' or 'deadlock' where the parties are locked into a situation where each recognises that no gains can be made by either of them. Zartman (1999), in later work, went on to link the concept to the 'Imminent Mutual Catastrophe' or 'deadline' which combines with the stalemate, according to him, to produce a situation where the conflict is 'ripe for resolution'.

Edmead (1971) described the concept of 'entrapment', where political leaders become trapped in a continuous quest for 'victory' in spite of the unbearable costs of such a quest. These costs then come to be regarded as 'investments' in the conflict, making it impossible to settle for anything less than complete victory. The damage sustained thus becomes a reason for continuing the conflict. The anticipated future costs of continuing the conflict cannot outweigh the past costs, so the conflict continues. The turning point is when a major re-assessment of strategy occurs, and leaders shift from justifying past sacrifices to salvaging what they can in the present. Outsiders, according to Edmead, play a key role in creating the conditions under which this reassessment takes place.

Mitchell (1989) and Crocker (1992) describe an alternative model, the 'Enticing Opportunity Model', whereby leaders find themselves presented with new options which offer the opportunity to achieve their goals at less cost. Crocker has described this as 'the planets in conjunction' (quoted in Mitchell, 1995, p. 44),[1] where a number of key factors are in place, like a railway track with the points all switched to a setting that allows the train to reach its destination. The factors involved can include a change in leadership, or the emergence of new resources. Both leaders and followers see the gains to be achieved by making a deal.

All of these approaches depend on the identification of certain conditions under which conflict can be resolved. These conditions are variously listed by the range of authors, but contain certain recurring themes – stalemate, a deadline, a shared perception of the desirability of an agreement, the ability of leaders to agree, agreements that are saleable to both constituencies, agreed procedures for dealing with conflict in the future or new opportunities such as new resources or changes in leadership. Kleiboer (1994), however, is less than sanguine about the methodological aspects of, particularly, Zartman's and Haass' work, which she says: '...leave the reader puzzled about the conceptual and empirical basis of their theoretical ideas. Their prerequisites for ripeness appear out of the blue. In both books, the notion of ripeness itself is not questioned'[2] (Kleiboer, 1994, p. 113).

Stedman's (1991) approach appears to be methodologically more robust, analysing old and new ideas about ripeness across four attempts, three unsuccessful and one successful, to resolve conflict in Rhodesia. Concentrating on one society holds constant many of the external factors, thus facilitating analysis; and Stedman uses a structured, focused, comparative method developed by George (1989). As a result, Stedman concludes that none of his examples complies with Zartman's criteria for 'ripeness'. However, he points to two factors, as two characteristics emerging from the Rhodesian analysis: that at least some of the parties must fear a deterioration in the situation if it is not resolved; and that there needs to be a change in power relations. For Stedman, however, three other factors – *internal politics of conflicting parties*, changes in the *mediation effort* and the *ability of mediators to learn* from the past – are the definitive aspects of ripeness. We will return to these factors later in relation to the readiness for truth recovery in Northern Ireland.

Whatever the criteria used to detect 'ripeness', Mitchell (1995) has convincingly argued that it is the *meaning* attached to these conditions by leaders that is the crucial factor:

> writers using all four models...acknowledge that, fundamentally, whatever the apparent imperatives of the structural conditions facing leaders in conflict, *it is ultimately the interpretation of these conditions by those leaders* that determines whether the time is ripe.[3]

According to these approaches, even if the material conditions for settlement are in place, unless it is the subjective assessment of the leaders that conditions are right, then the moment is not 'ripe'. Kleiboer's (1994) analysis raises similar issues in her critique of the 'ripeness' approach, and Lederach (1997)[4] makes a similar point, arguing that diagnosing ripeness can only be done in a rear-view mirror, with hindsight. Discussing the process and measures by which ripeness can be brought about, Kleiboer concludes that: 'Ultimately, this quest to get at the roots of ripeness leads to a reduction ad absurdum, an elusive quest for the "holy grail of ripeness."'[5]

Ripeness, Kleiboer concludes, is a subjective phenomenon, composed of the willingness of parties to find a peaceful solution:

> Ripeness then comes to equal what one might call "complete willingness": a certain moment when *all* the important parties are willing to search for a peaceful settlement. Willingness is thus a *minimal* requirement for a settlement or a resolution to come about – however, even when all parties are willing it is not a *sine qua non* that this indeed will happen.[6]

Kleiboer concludes that ripeness can best be defined as Justice Potter Stewart once described pornography: 'I know it when I see it' (quoted in Stedman, 1991, p. 240).

Indicators of 'ripeness' for truth recovery in Northern Ireland

The 'ripeness' model for truth recovery has been applied by the Northern Ireland Affairs Committee to Northern Ireland, and ripeness was not detected; but, setting aside concepts about the representativeness of the inquiry, how viable was this model of ripeness or readiness? In detecting ripeness for embarkation on peace processes, Zartman, Stedman, Haass, Crocker and others have pointed to factors such as the mutually hurting stalemate, the imminent mutual catastrophe, the entrapment model and the enticing opportunity in relation to ripeness for peace settlements. However, in the light of Mitchell's critique of this work, and Kleiboer's points about the lack of methodological robustness and the role of subjectivity, it might be worth subjecting these criteria to greater scrutiny.

Kleiboer's work suggests two questions in relation to readiness for truth recovery in Northern Ireland:

a   What external factors influence the levels of willingness amongst the parties?
b   What can be done by the parties and/or third parties to achieve what Kleiboer calls 'complete willingness'?

Stedman's (1991) analysis directs us to three factors which determine readiness:

a   the internal politics of conflicting parties;
b   changes in the mediation effort and
c   the ability of mediators to learn from the past about moments of ripeness.

These five factors can be considered under two broad headings: *external factors*, including third-party roles and changes in these, and the *ability of third parties to intervene effectively* in relation to truth recovery and *internal factors*, namely the *internal politics and position of the parties vis-à-vis* potential truth recovery.

External factors and ability of third parties to intervene

To date, third-party intervention in relation to the issue of truth recovery has been limited. Exhortations to the British government by the Irish government about public inquiries to investigate specific controversial cases cannot be seen as third-party interventions since the Irish government is a party to the Good Friday Agreement and has its own agenda in relation to truth recovery. At the time when the United States remained seized of developments in the Irish peace process, truth recovery was not one of the priority issues on the agenda. Therefore, the influence of the State Department's Northern Ireland points-person on truth recovery has not been felt, although The United States State Department, alongside the Irish government, criticised the British government for dragging its feet in relation to the issue of public inquiries in the matter of four murders investigated by retired Canadian judge Peter Cory, who found evidence of collusion between the security forces (*The Guardian*, Tuesday, 6 April 2004).

There have been judicial interventions from various international sources in relation to matters of state responsibility such as human rights, killings by the security forces and allegations of torture. The various rulings by the European Court of Human Rights have found Britain guilty, *inter alia*, of violating Article 2, the right to life, and the court was critical of domestic investigative practices, processes and institutions such as the civil courts, the inquest system and the Director of Public Prosecutions.[7] There has been involvement of the United Nations Special Rapporteur on Summary and Arbitrary Executions. Also, in 2001, in relation to the British government's responsibility in Northern Ireland, the United Nations Human Rights Committee recorded:

> The Committee is deeply disturbed that, a considerable time after the murders of persons (including human rights defenders) in Northern Ireland have occurred, a significant number of such instances have yet to receive fully independent and comprehensive investigations, and the persons responsible to be prosecuted. This phenomenon is doubly troubling where persistent

allegations of involvement and collusion by members of the State party's security forces, including the Force Research Unit, remain unresolved.... The State party should implement, as a matter of particular urgency given the passage of time, the measures required to ensure a full, transparent and credible accounting of the circumstances surrounding violations of the right to life in Northern Ireland in these and other cases.[8]

It does not appear that the British government is particularly responsive to the findings of either the UN Human Rights Committee or the European Court; however, in any case, neither of these bodies can or would recommend the institution of a comprehensive truth recovery mechanism. The report of the Committee on International Human Rights of The Association of the Bar of the City of New York (ABCNY), which examined, *inter alia*, progress on the investigations into the murders of Pat Finucane and Rosemary Nelson, did make such a recommendation in its conclusions:

> One of the great challenges facing the Northern Ireland criminal justice system in the aftermath of political conflict is the need to address the unsolved deaths of hundreds of people on both sides of the community. While we continue to call for public inquiries into the murders of Patrick Finucane and Rosemary Nelson... we recognize that many others in Northern Ireland lost family members during political conflict, including members of the police force. There is a need for accountability, but we recognize that traditional criminal investigations many years after deaths present difficulties in terms of cost, delay and preservation of evidence, and may not be realistic options. We call upon the Law Society and the Bar Council to help propose alternatives that might help bring a sense of justice and closure to these many unsolved cases. Other societies have struggled with alternatives and none offer a perfect solution.[9]

There have been more recent external inquiries. One, in October 2006 by the Independent International Panel on Alleged Collusion in Sectarian Killings in Northern Ireland, based at the Center for Civil and Human Rights, Notre Dame Law School, USA, found:

> significant and credible evidence of involvement of police and military agents of the United Kingdom, both directly and in collusion with loyalist extremists, in a pattern and practice of sectarian murders of members of the Catholic community in Northern Ireland in the 1970s.... The panel has also found that at least some police superiors in Northern Ireland knew of and expressed approval of instances of this conduct, and that senior officials in London had information sufficient to put them on notice of the serious risk of such conduct.[10]

Perhaps the attritional effect of successive external reporting from the outside world might eventually persuade the British government to reconsider the issue of truth recovery. However, overwhelming though this body of findings might appear, it is difficult to foresee there being a sufficient volume of such cases to stimulate the level of outside influence necessary in order to convince the British government of the desirability of a truth recovery mechanism. Nonetheless, the cases are not insignificant in this matter, bringing some of the unresolved issues to local and international attention, and might perhaps stimulate outside parties to bring influence to bear on the British government.

It has largely been those from the Nationalist community who have brought such cases, and the findings against the British government have reinforced the sense of injustice and lack of redress felt by them, and validated their grievances. Thus, external influence acts on the perceptions and confidence of the aggrieved to encourage them to continue to pursue their grievances. Also, outside influence in the matter of truth recovery is largely concentrated on the issue of alleged or actual state misdemeanours, yet state violence accounts for a relatively small proportion of the deaths and injuries sustained in the Troubles. Nevertheless, the state's unique claim to the legitimate use of force must place allegations of misdeeds made against the state in a special category of concern, especially in a period of reconstruction when efforts are focused on increasingly the legitimacy of the state's operations, particularly in criminal justice and policing. However, levels or directions of external influence to date have not been sufficient to move the British government in particular towards a more favourable attitude to truth recovery. Rather, it seems that the government has in the past largely set aside the findings of international bodies, and proceeded with business as usual.

External influences on Loyalists and Republicans

Republicans are influenced by their supporters in the diaspora, particularly in the United States, although the nature of this support has shifted since the advent of both the Good Friday Agreement and the War on Terror. Although, for example, the campaign on the killing of Pat Finucane is widespread, the issue of truth recovery had largely been discussed internally by Republicans rather than with external supporters until late into the peace process. Certain United States politicians maintain links with the various parties over a range of issues, and latterly Unionists, too, have established political links in Washington. However, in none of these cases has truth recovery featured largely until after 2003. Indeed, the overall level of United States' interest in the Northern Ireland situation has diminished with the advent of a Republican administration on Capitol Hill, the instigation of the War on Terror, and the relative pacification of the conflict in Northern Ireland.

Ability of third parties to intervene

In the light of the response to the findings of various external bodies, and to the censure of external governments, it is difficult to anticipate a third-party intervention that would persuade the British government to institute a comprehensive truth recovery process. However, it is possible that a succession of third-party interventions over a period of time might act on government opinion. On the other hand, interventions by prominent individuals such as Archbishop Desmond Tutu[11] (BBC Television: Facing Northern Ireland's Troubled Past; 3 March 2006), while serving to highlight the issues of truth recovery, have divided opinion rather than strengthening the case for such a process.

Internal politics and position of the parties

If ripeness is simply the willingness of the various factions to make a deal, what then of the 'ripeness' of the various parties to the Northern Ireland conflict for a comprehensive process of truth recovery? Are they willing to embrace the concept of truth recovery? If a truth process were to be instituted, would they participate and what would be the likely nature of that participation? If they are resistant, on what is their unwillingness based?

Before reviewing each of the potential participants in turn, it might be useful to note that if the level of participation of each of the parties is commensurate with

a   their burden of responsibility for a quantum of deaths, and
b   their overall level of authority and responsibility then clearly some participants can be expected to play larger roles than others.

Parties' burden of responsibility for deaths

Clearly, the greater the share of killings carried out by a party,[12] the more crucial their participation and cooperation with any truth process. If we rank the parties according to their respective shares of responsibility for deaths, then the ranking is as follows:

Republicans carry the largest share of responsibility; they were responsible for 56% of all deaths in the Troubles, and just under 10% of all deaths were those of Republican paramilitaries – 45% of whom were killed by other Republicans and 37% were killed by the security forces.

Loyalists were responsible for 28% of all deaths in the Troubles, and just over 3% of all deaths were those of Loyalists, 57% of whom were killed by other Loyalists.

The state was responsible for 11% of all deaths in the Troubles, and 31% of all victims were members of the security forces, with British soldiers making up 14% of total deaths. Ninety-five per cent of these deaths were due to the actions of Republicans, and IRA alone was responsible for 90% of these.

Other or unknown perpetrators were responsible for 6% of all deaths and in 1.6% of all deaths the status of the victim is unknown.

Parties' overall level of authority and responsibility

However, if we rank the parties according to their degree of formal authority and legitimacy, the ranking is reversed.

State parties to truth recovery clearly carry responsibilities and levels of accountability that non-state actors do not. Even though the state's share of responsibility for deaths in the conflict is markedly lower than for any of the paramilitary parties, the danger of impunity in relation to the state is of particular concern in a way that it cannot be for non-state actors. This is compounded by incomplete lustration within the security services, whereby it is not clear that all those who have been involved in criminal activities or human rights violations have been removed from the police and army.

Non-state actors operate outside the law, with no regard for the legality of their actions, and in resistance to the state's attempts to control their activities. The state, on the other hand, has claims to legitimate authority and monopoly on the use of force. The state's continued claim to legitimacy depends on such force being exercised – and being seen by citizens to be exercised – within legal limits. Since non-state actors have no formal legitimacy in the first instance, and their use of force is a challenge to the state's right to the monopoly on the use of force, their use of violence is either explicitly (when they are caught, convicted and punished) or implicitly (when their actions go unpunished) illegal. In some instances, non-state actors' use of violence is facilitated or tolerated by the state, as is allegedly the case with some periods of Loyalist violence.

Thus if we rank the parties according to their level of authority and responsibility, the British and then the Irish government would top the list, followed by Loyalist paramilitary groups some of whose violence was condoned by the state, and Republicans ranking last. This would suggest that the cooperation of the state parties in any truth recovery process is the top priority. There is a tendency to think of the dispensation of government as deriving from victims' views, but as we have seen in Chapters 5 and 7, there is a diversity of views and many disagreements amongst victims. Furthermore, as is evident from the proceedings of the Northern Ireland Affairs Committee, analysed in Chapter 7, the government tends to weigh the various cohorts of victims' views differently, so that some views are more influential than others. As we have seen in the previous chapter, the British government has relied heavily on an analysis of victims' views. However, no robust canvas of the totality of these views has been conducted, and any such canvas would be likely to confirm the divergence of views amongst the victim population. Furthermore, whilst there is clearly a need to place victims' wishes at the centre of any consideration, there are also good arguments against basing any decision about truth recovery entirely on victims' views.

The disposition of the various parties towards the prospect of a truth recovery process for Northern Ireland, and the degree of unanimity within each will now be examined.

British government

The British government view, informed by the deliberations of the NIAC is that the time is not yet right for truth recovery. The Committee's deliberations on the subject concluded:

> While we agree that the 'few' should not be able to hold up progress for the 'many' in seeking a truth recovery process, where large sections of the population withhold co-operation from such a process the outcome is likely to be circumscribed and its value reduced correspondingly. In addition, many uncertainties remain to be resolved over the way in which such a process would work alongside the normal judicial process. Finally, it is clear that many in Northern Ireland remain unconvinced that the campaign of violence is truly at an end.[13]

The government view is that the general public would not cooperate with a truth recovery process, and that there is no clear idea of the method of truth recovery suitable for Northern Ireland. Although models of truth recovery and recommendations on models, have been put forward by some in Northern Ireland (see Eolas/Relatives for Justice, 2003; Healing Through Remembering, 2002; 2006), the government has not considered methods of truth recovery, generally restricting itself to general comments on the feasibility of the entire project. In the absence of any more concrete discussions about the form and method of truth recovery that might be applied in Northern Ireland, it is inevitable that 'many uncertainties remain to be resolved' which can only be rendered certain by an engagement with the details of constructing a model, yet there seems to be no impetus to move towards this resolution. In the absence of any clue about the way truth recovery is to be conducted, even the firmest advocate of truth recovery is likely to remain wary. Certainly, it is unlikely that cooperation with truth recovery processes will be obtained until the nature of those processes is spelled out. The lack of a discussion regarding a concrete model in itself gives rise to an inability to subscribe to the process.

It is clear from the evidence of successive witnesses to the NIAC that the arrival at a model for truth recovery for Northern Ireland will require a process of consultation and negotiation with all the key stakeholders. Beginning this process, which is likely to be protracted, will be a first step towards diminishing the uncertainty surrounding the subject.

Another reason given for reluctance about truth recovery is that some people in Northern Ireland do not believe that the Troubles are over. This refers to the Unionist and Loyalist fears about the IRA intentions,[14] and it is significant that these fears are singled out as an obstacle to progress. The NIAC makes no reference to the objective evidence on the levels of political violence, which had drastically diminished by the time of the NIAC Inquiry, or the main source of any residual political violence, which has been conducted by Loyalists largely involved in internecine attacks. The fear of renewed IRA violence must be related to the actual risk of such violence, which has been officially assessed as low, an assessment supported by acts of decommissioning by the IRA subsequent to the NIAC process. If the government is unwilling to act on truth recovery until certain Unionists' and Loyalists' suspicion of Republicans diminishes, then the wait may well be a very long one.

Public opinion is cited by the NIAC as a reason for its reluctance to advocate a truth recovery mechanism for Northern Ireland. Based on the evidence presented to them, they concluded:

> We accept the view of those who have told us of the importance of an 'official' version of history and truth which might be a key feature of any truth recovery commission. But the Northern Ireland communities must be fully ready and able to accept and share that official version of historical truth, and it is our view, based on the evidence we have been given, that this stage has yet to be reached.[15]

The Inquiry's conclusions also run contrary to the evidence on public opinion on the issue of truth recovery. A poll carried out in July 2005 by the Northern Ireland Life and Times team found that

- 52% of respondents felt a truth commission is important for the future with 28% declaring it would be unimportant.
- 60% of Catholics supported a truth commission with 21% expressing disapproval and 44% of Protestants expressed broad approval with 34% being against the process.
- 69% of 18–24-year-olds thought a truth commission was important.
- When asked who they would trust to run a truth commission 92% (95% of Catholics and 89% of Protestants) said they would not trust the British Government. Similar levels of suspicion were directed at the Northern Ireland Assembly (89%), the Irish Government (97%) and Republican and Loyalist groups (99%). Judges (95%), churches (88%) and victims (92%) also fared badly.
- 48% felt that international organisations like the United Nations should run any truth commission and 76% said ordinary people should decide who runs a commission.
- 82% felt a truth commission should be held in public with 83% saying commission members should travel around and talk to members of the public (http://www.ulster.ac.uk/news/releases/2005/1776.html).

Dr Patricia Lundy from the Life and Times team in the University of Ulster concluded:

> What we can take from all this is that there appears to be broad, if cautious, approval that a truth commission would be a good idea, even if people are not sure it will deliver the truth....There is clear opposition to any of the major political actors involved in the conflict overseeing such a process. It is difficult not to draw the conclusion that, if people do not think a truth commission will get to the truth, then it is because they lack confidence in the governments, parties, groups and bodies most likely to be involved in the running of a truth commission to do so.[16]

The NIAC Inquiry, based on their less-than-scientific assessment, concluded that rather than risk failure, truth recovery in Northern Ireland should not proceed:

> In these circumstances, and with considerable regret, it seems to us appropriate to wait until the probability of success for any Northern Ireland-wide truth process is realistically high, rather than press ahead with the likelihood of failure, or partial success at best.[17]

It is not clear what the measure of success is to be, or who should be the judge of it. There is also circularity to this argument. The people are not ready for some unspecified truth recovery process, and it is unclear if they will ever be ready, or indeed if they do become ready, by what process this state will be arrived at.

Internal politics within the British state

The official attitude to truth recovery is, however, by no means unanimous. There are those in public office and within government roles who take a different view. In early 2004, Professor Desmond Rea and Denis Bradley, Chair and Vice Chair of the Policing Board for Northern Ireland called for consideration to be given to a truth commission. Subsequently, Sir Hugh Orde, Chief Constable of the Police Service of Northern Ireland backed the call. It seems likely that the new blood with the reformed Police Service of Northern Ireland would welcome a mechanism to expunge the ghosts of the past, and neutralise the power of successive disclosures of involvement of the police in 'dirty deeds'.

Peter Cory, the retired Canadian judge, who was commissioned by the Chief Constable to investigate four murders, found evidence of collusion between the security forces and paramilitaries, and criticised the government for dragging its feet in relation to the issue of public inquiries into such matters. Cory's work points to another dimension to government reluctance to embark on a process of truth recovery. Since any truth recovery process would include in its remit security forces, activities as well as those of paramilitaries, the government reluctance on truth recovery might well be the same reluctance they show in relation to other investigations in the past. These include European Court judgements on the use of inhumane and degrading treatment,[18] and more recently the killing of lawyer Pat Finucane and several other controversial killings carried out by the security forces.

The 2007 Statement by the Police Ombudsman for Northern Ireland on the circumstances surrounding the death of Raymond McCord Junior described how her investigations of allegations of collusion met with resistance from some serving and retired police officers. The investigation found that police informers had been killing people, with no attempt being made by police or army handlers to stop them, and indeed the investigation found evidence that some police handlers obstructed investigations into the killings concerned.[19] In March 2007, the Police Ombudsman announced another inquiry into allegations of collusion in the case of police informer Freddie Scapaticci, who was the IRA enforcer for many years, so at least one more such report of this kind – and one suspects that there will be more than one – has yet to emerge.

The attritional effect of such disclosures about the past behaviour of the security forces, the effect on contemporary police morale and the difficulties posed for those who would build confidence in the police and criminal justice system might explain why those within the Northern Ireland policing world might welcome some form of comprehensive truth recovery process. Some in official positions can see value in disposing of past grievances by some mechanism such as a truth commission, so that the slate can be cleared and the new dispensation can be free of the Damocles' sword of the past. Part of the government's reluctance is likely to be based on fears about opening the floodgates for enormous amounts of compensation having to be paid by them to victims' beneficiaries where they – the government – are found culpable in any truth process. This reluctance is also related to the government's desire to avoid the shame that would attach itself to some of the misdeeds of their agents in the past. Yet, as discussed in Chapter 4, powerful agents can be the most successful at shame-avoidance, since their very power affords them the opportunity to shut down or avoid shaming experiences.

It seems that, although the stated reasons in the NIAC Inquiry are based on assessments of the state of public opinion in Northern Ireland, government reluctance might well be based on a wish to avoid revealing secret aspects of security forces operations during the conflict and to incur heavy costs if and when unsavoury events are revealed. In the light of this, the impossibility of the British government being cast in the role of neutral arbiter on matters of truth recovery becomes apparent. This points to the absolute necessity of international involvement by a neutral third party in the deliberations about the feasibility of truth recovery, in the design of any truth process and the implementation of that process.

Irish government

The position of the Irish government on the issue of truth recovery is somewhat equivocal, in that it has taken the British government to the European court over its conduct in Northern Ireland, and is seen to urge the British government to carry out public independent inquiries into controversial cases. An Irish Government inquiry, which reported in 2006 on a range of events including the bombing of Kay's Tavern in Dundalk, left the Irish government Sub-Committee 'in no doubt that collusion between British forces and terrorists was behind many if not all the atrocities that are considered in this report'[20] (Irish Government, 2006, p. 61).

Yet the Irish government seems reluctant to follow its own advice, especially in relation to cases such as that of Seamus Ludlow, killed by four members of the Red Hand Commando, two of whom were allegedly also serving members of the British Army's Ulster Defence Regiment at the time. Questions have been raised about the ability of the killers to strike over the Irish border, and about a lack of transparency by the police on both sides of the border in relation to the nce on the Ludlow case. The Irish government decided to hold a private ·y into the case, much against the wishes of the relatives. Similarly, the nment decided on a private rather than a public inquiry for the Dublin and Monaghan bombings on 17 May, 1974 which killed thirty-three people (twenty-eight died in the Omagh bomb). Again, relatives of those killed raised concerns about the operation of the security forces on both sides of the border on that day, and they took a civil action as a result of their dissatisfaction with the response of the state. Finally, the case of John Morris, an INLA man shot in Dublin in 1997 led to a judicial review which overturned the state's intention to hear police witnesses from behind screens and to withhold information on the weapon used. The Morris case led to allegations of a shoot-to-kill policy in Ireland, and again there has been illustrative of a less-than-transparent approach on the part of the Irish state.

Given the involvement of the Irish government in controversial cases of its own, and its attitude in those cases, it hardly leads by example in relation to influencing the British government in the matter of truth recovery. It is likely that the Irish government shares some of the reservations felt by the British about revealing sensitive security matters and escalating compensation to victims. However, the Irish government lobbied for a Bloody Sunday Inquiry, and continues to lobby in the matter of other individual cases. The level of support for a comprehensive truth recovery process amongst the Irish government that would focus on the activities of the British government and the paramilitaries is likely to be reasonably high, but less enthusiasm will likely be forthcoming for the Irish state's own participation in truth recovery.

Internal politics within the Irish state

The electoral successes of Sinn Féin within the Irish Republic has challenged the main parties there, and led to the development of an intense political rivalry between them and the other parties, including the party in government. Thus, the internal politics within the Irish state might, in the context of truth recovery, lead to a tendency to capitalise on aspects of Republicans' pasts that could potentially damage their political fortunes in present-day Ireland.

Republicans and Nationalists

The position of the Social Democratic and Labour Party (SDLP) and that of Sinn Féin in relation to truth recovery has consistently been that the British government should be held accountable for its actions, such as Bloody Sunday, and other controversial killings such as that of Pat Finucane. In early February 2005, Patricia Lewsley formerly of the SDLP (appointed Children's Commissioner for Northern Ireland in 2006) stated:

> The SDLP believes the time is right for an inclusive and comprehensive truth recovery process. A truth process that will work best for all would have all

the following elements: The creation of a Victims Forum...; The creation of a truth recovery, public process, whereby the IRA, UDA, other paramilitaries and elements of the state acknowledge and account for their actions; Statements of apology and exoneration in cases of miscarriage of justice; A powerful Commissioner for Victims, with the resources, money and role to promote victims needs; The right model and sufficient finance for the PSNI review of around 2600 unsolved killings.[21]

Much of the legal energy which went into challenging the British government in the European Court and elsewhere came from within Nationalism, since the majority of those killed in controversial circumstances by the security forces directly or indirectly, were Nationalists. Both the SDLP and Sinn Féin campaigned for the British state to make itself publicly accountable. However, as distinct from Sinn Féin, the SDLP can afford to take a straightforward attitude to the issue of truth recovery, given that they are unencumbered with a military past and do not have an armed organisation associated with them. Their line is a straightforward one, that all armed groups should be made accountable for their actions. Mark Durkan, leader of the SDLP prioritised victims' rights in the matter of truth recovery: 'The time has come to put all victims' rights to truth and closure ahead of the victim-makers' desire to avoid embarrassment and discomfort.'[22]

Sinn Féin however face the reality that their Republican constituency contains the armed groups that carried out the largest share – over half – of all the killings during the Troubles. As with other matters, the issue of truth recovery has been thoroughly discussed within Republican circles, significantly through a process of workshops and discussions sponsored by Eolas, an umbrella body that includes victims and ex-prisoners' organisations, which culminated in the production of a consultation document[23] which sets out the position of Republicans on truth recovery:

> The debate within our own community is, as is the case in the unionist community, uncertain about dealing with the past. Despite the fact that we are mostly suspicious of the intentions of the British state, we believe that it is imperative that we do deal with the past... The purpose of this document is to develop...[the] discussion on truth and justice by examining the case for an official truth process, and presenting some models...it does not represent a final position of those involved...but rather a 'brainstorming' exercise to imagine how a formal mechanism might look which would address some of the concerns within our community.[24]

The document sets out three models for truth recovery, which contain a number of common elements: an international dimension to any truth recovery process in order to assure its independence; a bottom-up, victim-centred and community-oriented approach with NGOs' participation; a balance between the individual and the institution, a balance between 'micro' truth including individual victims' concerns and the role of institutions in the past ('macro' truth), including combatant groups and the state, with the emphasis on collective rather than individual responsibility and acknowledgement; an investigative dimension; non-punitive and non-judicial outcomes; and public acknowledgement of suffering and wrongdoing. There was no consensus on the issue of amnesty for witnesses to any truth process, or whether evidence gathered in a truth process should be used in future litigation. One group thought that a truth process could expunge criminal records acquired for politically motivated activity.

This level of detail, and the proposal of three models indicates a constituency with a good grasp of the issues, and a positive attitude to the prospect of public truth recovery. This is in spite of the fact that Republicans stand to be confronted in such a process with the scale of the harm that their activities inflicted on all sides including their own.

In October 2006, Republican ex-prisoner and former hunger striker Jackie Mc Mullan, a man with considerable clout in Republican circles, published an article in the Sinn Féin organ, An Phoblact/ Republican News in the wake of an internal seminar which addressed the issue of attitudes within Republicanism to the issue of truth recovery.

> Some suggested that Sinn Féin should campaign for an independent truth process while others felt that this would be making a rod to beat ourselves with.... If our opponents want to make political capital out of it, then let's deal with that as a separate issue. It's too easy to lash out at others when we need to be taking a hard look at ourselves.... But working to expose Britain's dirty war doesn't absolve us from our own responsibilities. And, twelve years on from the first cessation the question facing us is, do we have the moral courage to confront the ghosts form our own past? ... Republicans have to set the standard in acknowledging and addressing the suffering of all those we hurt during the conflict. We cannot undo the past or bring an end to their suffering, but by demonstrating courage and moral leadership we can engender hope for the future.... If we bring courage and honesty to how we deal with victims and Truth Recovery it might cut through some of the bitterness and anger which infects politics on this island and transform the way the past is accepted and understood. It might also help build bridges between the unionist community and ourselves. And it might help some people achieve some healing. None of those outcomes are guaranteed but we should not be seeking to reap political advantage. As republicans we should do it because it is the right thing to do.[25]

Why should there be an appetite for such a risk? A number of factors influence Republican attitudes. First, in spite of the Unionist misgivings, a solid core of Republicans believe that their war is over and that democratic politics is the way forward. Yet their acceptability in democratic circles is impaired by their past paramilitary activity. A truth recovery mechanism that offers the possibility of drawing a line between such a past and the present offers a potential solution to this difficulty, a rite of passage from combatant to civilian status, from guerrilla to politician. The level of Republican support for truth recovery is remarkable, given the degree to which they are likely to be held accountable in such a process. Yet it seems that Republicans, for the most part, have adopted that stance that if the price to be paid is some uncovering of Republican paramilitary deeds of the past, then the cost–benefit analysis comes out in favour of truth recovery, in Republicans' assessment. McMullan's article also calls upon Republican ideals, and indeed relies to some extent on the idea of 'warrior's honour' (see Chapter 4) in his call upon an ideology which contains ideas of selflessness, discipline and morality which he deploys in the argument for truth recovery, even if there are costs.

This is to take a generous interpretation of Republican motivation, with an emphasis on their support for the peace process. Those cynical of Republican motives suspect that truth recovery appeals to Republicans because it offers the prospect of uncovering the dark deeds of the British state and this holds great appeal for Republicans, and this is undoubtedly a factor. However, Loyalists, too, have a score or two to settle with the British state, so Republicans are not unique in this, yet Loyalist have not to date, championed truth recovery in this manner. It seems that the Republican assessment has come down in favour of truth recovery, concluding that it is a pain worth bearing, given the possible rewards.

Internal Nationalist and Republican politics

Three internal factors are significant in relation to the Nationalist and Republican disposition towards truth recovery. First, whilst both Sinn Féin and the SDLP support the idea of truth recovery, there is no love lost between them, and inter-party rivalries may mean that opportunities for point scoring are not passed over. Second, whilst the broad consensus within Republicanism is in support of truth recovery, there are those who are less than convinced, either because of scepticism about public processes, or because of a persistent adherence to the 'warrior's honour described in Chapter 4, and the resultant lack of willingness to disclose details of past involvements. Third, a small but significant cohort of Republican dissidents do not support the peace process, and are outside the consensus on truth recovery as they are on other issues. However, none of these internal factors significantly dilute the broad support for truth recovery within Nationalism and Republicanism.

Unionists and Loyalists

One of the earliest Unionist pronouncements on the issue of truth recovery was made by the Democratic Unionist Party in their document, 'A Voice for Victims; The Democratic Unionist Party's policy on Innocent Victims of terrorism' (Belfast, Democratic Unionist Party, 2003). The document addresses the issue of justice for victims, and the need for active investigations of unsolved killings.

The document expressed the suspicion that these killings were not being investigated for reasons of political expediency related to the peace process. There was the fear that prosecutions would be compromised by the proposed 'On the Run' legislation, whereby those who fled during the Troubles could return without fear of prosecution. 'A Voice for Victims; The Democratic Unionist Party's policy on Innocent Victims of terrorism.'[26] The document points out that the Bloody Sunday Inquiry and other investigations where nationalists 'have been the perceived victims' have been the result of political pressure and campaigning and calls for some balance in such inquiries, since: 'unionists feel that an enquiry has been granted mainly in cases in which nationalists feel that their community has suffered.'[27]

The document dismisses the idea of a truth commission, arguing that Northern Ireland is too small for such a venture, and that

> while the state would have to be fully accountable and would be required to co-operate fully and to disclose all information fully to such a Commission, the terrorist groups would have full control over their level, or lack, of participation. [A Truth Commission] would serve only to hold those who served in the Crown Forces to account for their actions while terrorists can hide behind the cloak of anonymity.[28]

The state is implicitly cast as a powerless actor, with less-than-full control over their level of participation, and the truth commission as a witch-hunt against the security forces. This resistance to the accountability of the security forces to anyone but themselves is illustrated in the experience of the Police Ombudsman's Inquiry into the death of Raymond McCord, where she found some members of the security forces to be less than totally cooperative.

In response to the call in 2004 from Professor Desmond Rea and Denis Bradley of the Policing Board for consideration to be given to a truth commission, the DUP's Arlene Foster made an unequivocal statement (Democratic Unionist Party, 19 February 2004) – a truth commission and amnesty was 'the last thing Northern Ireland needs'. Foster went on to characterise any truth commission as 'nothing more than a "Brit bashing session"', and to express doubts about the ability of the IRA to tell the truth: 'Are we expected to take the word of the IRA even in the format of a truth commission? They have made lying and deceit an art form.'[29]

Foster was joined in her condemnation of the prospects of a truth commission by Alderman George Ennis, DUP, who objected on the same grounds as Foster, stating that: 'New victims are being created all the time. The line is yet to be drawn under terrorism in Northern Ireland,' and he, too, expressed fears that whilst the security forces would be held to account, 'there would be no such compulsion on terrorists.' Ennis also raises the issue of the costs of such an exercise, referring to the £150 million cost of the Bloody Sunday Inquiry. Ennis concludes by reiterating the DUP proposal for the establishment of a victim's commission as an alternative.[30]

David Burnside, then Ulster Unionist Member of Parliament for South Antrim raised the issue of a truth commission in the House on 1 April 2004. In the wake of the Secretary of State's response to the Cory report into collusion between the security forces and Loyalist paramilitaries, Burnside[31] asked Paul Murphy why, from the point of view of the families of those killed in the security forces there was not a truth commission aimed at eliciting truth from the IRA. The Secretary of State's response acknowledged the suffering of the security forces and their families:

> They suffer, too, and there are no public inquiries into their deaths. Obviously, it is important to try to find out who committed the murders, but we must not in any sense undervalue the significance of the grief and pain that those families have undergone. As far as the Truth – or whatever one wants to call it – Commission is concerned, it is right that all parties in Northern Ireland should consider what their attitude to such a Commission should be.[32]

Later in April, the debate on a truth commission continued to arise in the context of the Cory report. Clearly, this focus on collusion between the security forces and Loyalist paramilitaries shifted the focus away from Republican misdeeds, a shift that Ulster Unionist Assembly Member for Mid-Ulster Billy Armstrong was keen to correct. Pointing to the 'trails of destruction' left by the Republican movement, their lack of remorse and the prominent public positions now occupied by Republicans with a track record of political violence, Mr Armstrong set out his objections to a truth commission:

> The Government must remind themselves that Adams and McGuinness do not feel a requirement to tell the truth – one is bound by an IRA code of honour and the other bound by a concern that the statesman persona he has carved for himself in certain quarters could be irreparably damaged by an admission of; "yes I was a member of the Provisional IRA." Government must ask themselves, whose truth they are proposing to establish? If the Government were to proceed with the ill thought out plans of a truth commission, they would be merely serving up a carvery for the Republican Movement for which they would feast. The Republican Movement would actively seek to rewrite the history of the troubles of the past 30 plus years.... If they were genuinely committed to addressing the wrongs of the past they would for example; let families of the disappeared know where their loved ones remains lie so that they could give them a Christian burial.[33]

For Armstrong, the prospect of a Republican input to rewriting the history of Northern Ireland is intolerable. Only one group of people, victims of Republican violence, is qualified, according to Armstrong, to decide how the past should be managed:

> Those whose loved ones were murdered or maimed whilst attempting to uphold law and order or those whose loved ones were killed purely because

they fitted a particular religious background grouping. They are the victims, not those who condemned them to that suffering via their direct actions or those who acquiesced with those actions.[34]

Armstrong's resistance to a broader definition of victimhood, and his desire to avoid public exploration of Republican or Nationalist grievances or perspectives is a leitmotif within general Unionist discourse on truth recovery.

An exception, and among the most considered statements on truth recovery emanating from a Unionist source came almost two years later in March 2006. The Unionist Group, an informal 'coming together' within the Ulster Unionist Party produced a document, 'Drawing a Line Under The Past' which was based on their discussions with the political parties, a range of Republican, Nationalist and Loyalist groups and aimed to suggest ways of dealing with the past. The document emphasised the importance of contact between all parts of society, including cross-border work, and suggested that truth recovery could be carried out in a low-key manner at a local level, an exercise that 'needs to be in the hands of communities all over Northern Ireland and led by local people'.[35] On the question of a formal truth commission, they were equivocal. Initially they saw the benefits, and argued for a tailor-made Northern Ireland process:

> When considering mechanisms to help draw a line under the past, we gave prior consideration to the idea of a truth commission. The core of such an endeavour, as in the South African model, is laudable and has clearly brought benefits to that country. However, in order to attain success and healing in Northern Ireland...the model needs to be adapted to our particular circumstances.[36]

They saw the need for some mechanism for truth recovery, but worry that in a divided society such a process would offer 'opportunities that could be exploited to rake over the coals of past grievance'. They fear that

> A semi-judicial commission, if not established in the right way, could even stimulate rivalry and discord based on conflicting perceptions. It might cause wounds to fester and extend hurt into future generations. We understand why the Presbyterian Church, the largest Protestant church in Northern Ireland, was unable to endorse such a Truth Commission...there are well founded fears that this could, like the Bloody Sunday Inquiry, gather a mass of information at tremendous cost, but shed limited light on the matter under investigation.... The Agencies of the State would be expected to tell the whole truth but neither the British or Irish governments nor the IRA and Loyalist paramilitaries or others are likely to do this...more harm than good might result.[37]

Yet they recognised the importance of seeking the truth, but conclude that 'any search for a singular agreed historical narrative will...prove illusory.'[38]

Is Northern Ireland ready for truth? 163

The document predictably met with a scathing response from Jim Allister of the Democratic Unionist Party who described it as 'utterly vapid and insulting to victims' and 'a telling insight into the shallow attitude of some within the Ulster Unionist Party towards the innocent victims of terrorism'.[39] Allister's complaints focus on the Group's assertion that the truth is subjective, and the fact that they

> sought out Coiste na n-Iarchimi, a Republican prisoners group, at Clonard Monastery, an Official Republican Group and the IRSP, but they ignored groups like Saver/Naver, West Tyrone Voice and FAIR. Little wonder their document is so out of touch with genuine victims and their needs.[40]

Allister further complains about the Group's suggestion for a joint ceremony by the 'Sovereign and the President' on the grounds that 'the President of the Republic of Ireland...gratuitously insulted the entire Protestant population.' Of the various gestures of tree planting suggested in the document, Allister retorts:

> Is that all the sacrifice of the innocent means to these Ulster Unionists? I am appalled. Such cliché-ridden stunts might pander to the extreme liberal agenda of the authors of this document, but they do nothing to heal the hurt of the innocent, particularly since its proponents do not even make an adequate distinction between innocent victims and perpetrators.[41]

Allister's attack on the Unionist Group document signals the competition between the DUP and the UUP for the role of the champion of victims in the Unionist community. This is a competition that the DUP has comprehensively won, certainly in relation to those victim groups who question the entitlement of other groups to the status of victimhood by calling themselves the 'innocent' victims.

From the mainstream of the Ulster Unionist Party, Lady Sylvia Hermon indicated a rather different attitude to those of the Unionist group in her response to the subsequently ill-fated draft legislation clearing the path for the return of those from the paramilitary groups that are 'on the run' (OTR). Hermon proposed amendments to the bill requiring OTRs to

> disclose all the crimes in which they have been involved so that the whole process becomes one of volunteering the truth.... Justice can only be served when those responsible for the most heinous of crimes appear before a court of law.[42]

This is because, according to Hermon, 'victims deserve justice and truth,' (UUP Press release, 2/12/05).

For mainstream Unionists, the concessions granted to Republican prisoners and the proposed concession to those 'on the run' are transgressions of victims' rights to justice, and to their day in court.

An interview given by Reg Empey to the Irish News (Monday, 12 June 2006) seemed to mark a new line of thinking within the UUP. The interview, conducted in the wake of the UUP deal with the late David Ervine of the Progressive Unionist Party, the political wing of the Ulster Volunteer Force, marked a new discourse on the relationship between armed Loyalism and Unionism. Empey argued that mainstream Unionism used Loyalist paramilitaries, and whilst laying the bulk of the blame at the door of Ian Paisley, concluded that '...while our responsibility may be less than his, I don't think it is something you can cast aside' (Irish News, 12/06/06, p. 14). On the topic of state involvement with 'dirty tricks' and with Loyalist paramilitaries, Empey describes such operations as:

> clearly [is] a breach of the state's obligation to its citizens. I just don't know how to reconcile that. But a lot of unionists don't believe this. That's the truth. And I don't think people have really got their heads around it.[43]

On the relationship between loyalists and the security forces, Empey takes a novel line:

> First of all, there are cases, and there clearly are, where these relationships exist; they clearly shouldn't have existed and they have to be dealt with.... And of course we have to put it in the context of a huge republican assault which was merciless.... And all people wanted was for it to stop and the government to stop it. That in turn incentivised loyalist paramilitaries and they took it out on people – some of whom were merely bystanders.... I think it is a bit early to say where all of unionism will settle on this.... But the more factually based evidence that emerges could change opinion. I think it is too early to say where it will end up.[44]

As the leader of the – albeit waning – Ulster Unionists, Empey is offering a fresh perspective on the issues of unionist and loyalist responsibility for some of the wrongs of the past, and crediting new and emerging evidence with the power to change opinion. Empey is appealing to middle-ground Unionists to countenance the idea that Unionism, too, has been implicated in some of the wrongs of the past. The significance of this however must be read in the context of the overall fortunes of the UUP, whose vote went down by 7.7% in the Assembly elections of March 2007, culminating in their losing nine seats, compared to the 4.4% and six-seat gain of the DUP.

Finally, in 2004, in response to Paul Murphy's announced consultation[45] on the topic, EPIC, an ex-prisoners organisation aligned with the UVF, produced a consultation document *Truth Recovery: A Contribution from Loyalism*.[46] The position set out in the document was later elaborated in the Memorandum by EPIC to the NIAC, and discussed in their evidence to that Committee. It's significance lies in the fact that it is a positive engagement with the issues, arrived at as a result of a consultation process within the Loyalist community, albeit one part of the community, and that this is the considered view of those close to one faction of armed Loyalism. Their position can be summarised as follows:

1 They wish to be 'involved' in a genuine process of conflict transformation that helps to improve the quality of life of ordinary people.
2 They repeatedly acknowledge their responsibility for inflicting suffering on others, and refer to the Combined Loyalist Military Command statement in 1994 after the Loyalist ceasefire, where the Loyalist paramilitary groups offered 'to the loved ones of all innocent victims over the past 25 years abject and true remorse. No words of ours will compensate for the intolerable suffering they have undergone during the conflict.'[47]
3 They acknowledge that their reflections on truth recovery as 'inward looking and self-reflective', but this reflects the conditions in their constituency.
4 Significantly, the document sets out their 'intent is not to alienate others; our intent is to encourage honest and challenging thinking within a constituency and to allow others to respond critically to that thinking.'
5 They recognise the need for a 'fresh start' and for healing at community level.
6 Truth recovery is not possible until there is a 'a clear, final political/constitutional settlement'.
7 The conflict has not definitively come to an end. Loyalists 'feel their culture and future to be under threat by a "Republican war" carried out by politics and propaganda' – a war by other means.
8 Sectarianism is worse that it was a decade ago, and optimism of the Good Friday Agreement has 'all but evaporated in Loyalist areas'.
9 In what they see as an unstable political environment, embarking on a truth recovery process 'that attempts to open up old wounds runs a real risk of re-igniting violent conflict instead of helping society to move beyond the Troubles. Many wounds are still too raw for a "truth process" to have a realistic chance of succeeding.'
10 A 'truth process' conducted in such an unstable environment risks 'indoctrinating a more "militant" younger generation with hatred and providing justification for continuing conflict'.
11 Northern Ireland is too small and the conflict too localised in for example North and West Belfast for participants to make public disclosures 'about his or her past activities there will be no place to hide. Not only will that person face high risks in terms of personal safety, but his or her family will also be endangered.'
12 Since Loyalists have never experienced the equivalent level of support enjoyed by Republicans in the nationalist community, nor have the ideological justification of a 'liberation struggle' used by Republicans, Loyalists are vulnerable to criminalisation within a truth process in a way that Republicans are not.
13 Loyalists are also vulnerable as a result of their '... carrying their campaign to the community that they regarded as the real enemy'[48] because '[t]hat

nationalist community was, for many young loyalists, as responsible for their armed groups as Germany or Japan was for their armies of aggression.'[49]

14 Loyalists concerns are also focussed on the impact of truth recovery on the integration of Loyalist ex-prisoners in the Protestant community. The 'stigmatisation, criminalisation and even demonisation of Loyalist ex-prisoners' by what EPIC refers to as 'middle-Unionism' leads them to the conclusion that 'it would be foolish for any loyalists who have not been successfully prosecuted to expose any of their actions before a truth commission.' Any gains in terms of growing acceptability of ex-prisoners within the Protestant community could be reversed. '[I]f new "dirty details" were to be exposed, the door would certainly be slammed in the face of ex-prisoners.... Many people who are now prepared to work with some of these ex-prisoners may no longer be prepared to do so.'[50]

15 Loyalists do not perceive any benefit for themselves out of a public truth recovery process, therefore 'there is very little chance that they will co-operate/participate.'

16 Loyalists are concerned about the impact on the families of ex-prisoners and combatants of revisiting the suffering of their families, because: 'People have found ways of dealing with the hardships of partners and fathers in prison, including undeserved guilt by association. However, they want those difficulties to remain buried in the past now; ...they are not prepared to revisit those bad days.'[51]

17 Loyalists are concerned about the impact of disclosures about the past on intergenerational relationships within the Loyalist community. 'Children today will probably find it difficult to imagine the threats and fears that inspired their fathers to take up arms. Once their fathers became involved in the "dirty war" a certain hardening often took place, which will be difficult to understand unless one has been in the same situation and political context.'[52]

18 There are ideological obstacles to Loyalists apologising for their past, since they continue to feel justified in taking up arms to defend Ulster in the past and would do so in the future. The collective apology delivered in 1994 must not be misunderstood as a rejection of the political cause for which loyalists fought.'[53]

19 This lack of Loyalist remorse 'might be experienced as salt rubbed into the victims' wounds, which is unlikely to contribute to healing' and combatants who did not participate 'might be portrayed as callous, or less than human, or insensitive to the needs of victims'.[54]

20 Loyalists are suspicious that a truth recovery process would play into the Republican hands, because of their perceived skill in propaganda, and the bulk of the blame would be allocated to the British state and its surrogates, namely Loyalists, whilst Republicans are let off the hook. There is no confidence in the Republican intent to honestly explore their own past misdeeds. Similarly, Loyalists are suspicious of British intentions, they fear that the government will use a truth process as a cynical public relations

exercise without any real commitment to uncovering the truth, as a pragmatic way of avoiding numerous expensive public inquiries.
21 Finally, the EPIC document expresses concern about the ability of any truth process to ensure that 'other groups and institutions, such as government, media, churches, business and non-combatants, accept responsibility for their role in the conflict?'[55]

EPIC did see some potential benefits in a truth recovery process, although they mention these benefits only in passing. They see having submitted to a truth process as a potential rite of passage for Loyalist ex-prisoners and paramilitaries from their present stigmatised state to a more acceptable status. They also see the benefit of one process 'mopping up' the issues that currently have led to the prospects of a series of public inquiries, all perceived to serve a Republican agenda and undermine Loyalism. They also refer to a desire to 'tell the story/stories of our community, warts and all' and to 'get the truth out as we see it' in order to counterbalance the Republican advantage with regard to 'the past'. EPIC concludes, however, that a truth recovery process has little chance of success unless the benefits for Loyalism are clear, and presumably substantial.

At the launch of the EPIC document in November 2004, Dawn Purvis, subsequently appointed leader of the Progressive Unionist Party on the death of David Ervine, said: 'It is the start of a process. I think it challenges and debates all the issues but it is by no means complete.' Tom Roberts from EPIC said although there was a lot of fear within the Loyalist community about a truth process, loyalists were not dismissing the possibility.[56]

Internal Unionist and Loyalist politics

The increasing fragmentation of Unionism since the Good Friday Agreement has been demarcated, according to Farrington (2006) by their various divergent attitudes to the Belfast Agreement. In spite of a degree of Unionist agreement over the political environment, Farrington argues that there are four divergent Unionist responses to the Agreement: a principled-yes position; a pragmatic-yes position; a principled-no position; and a pragmatic-no position.[57] This has been accompanied by a dramatic shift in party politics within Unionism, with an overall reduction in the number of political parties returned by Unionists to a situation where the two main parties, the UUP and the DUP are the only substantial rivals for Unionist votes. The outcome of this rivalry has been that the DUP has overtaken the Ulster Unionists to become the main party of Unionism. The competition between the various positions on the Good Friday Agreement within the Unionists, together with the electoral battles between the parties has been fierce and vociferous, with each faction ever vigilant for evidence of any softening of the hard line on Republicanism on the part of their rivals, since such evidence is valuable ammunition to be used against them. Latterly, this battle has culminated in the heavy losses described above for the UUP.

The second dynamic, already alluded to by EPIC is the attitude of the two main Unionist parties to the paramilitary groups and their (at least public) disavowal of any sympathy or links with them, a situation which has two main outcomes, Reg Empey's latter-day pronouncements notwithstanding. First, it ensures continued Unionist occupation of the moral high ground, since they can claim to have no links with 'terrorism' or private armies. Second, it marginalises the Loyalist paramilitaries, alienates them from mainstream politics, particularly given the inability of either the Ulster Democratic Party when it existed, or the Progressive Unionist Party to secure substantial political representation of their own. This leaves Loyalist paramilitaries with few political channels, and a sense of stigmatisation by what EPIC referred to as 'middle Unionism'. However, recent moves by Empey and the UUP may mark a shift in their position on these issues, in an attempt to appeal to more moderate Unionist opinion, leaving the hard liners to the DUP. The electoral rivalry between these two parties is another dimension of the dynamic within Unionism, with the DUP's fortunes rising whilst the UUP's are on the wane.

The third dynamic is the sporadically violent and often-fatal rivalry between the two main Loyalist paramilitaries. Bruce (2004) argues that the UVF's rather more enthusiastic support of the Agreement compared with the reluctance of the UDA is one factor in the rivalry between the two groups. Alongside this, he points to difficulties for Loyalist paramilitaries in relinquishing paramilitary roles, given the comparatively narrow opportunities for peaceful roles in Loyalist communities, in comparison to their Republican equivalents, where a vibrant community sector offers more openings for Republicans.[58] Bruce also points to differences in structure and history between the two organisations, and to the attritional blighting of Loyalist communities, and their steady decline in morale. He also charts the personal ambition and rivalry between various Loyalist leaders as a factor in inciting violence between the two groups. Most significantly, Bruce accounts for the intensification of rivalry by contests over control of territory and competition for the spoils of racketeering and drug dealing as: 'the rewards of contemporary terrorism, and hence the rivalry over their control, [became] far greater than they were at the start of the Troubles.[59]

Given the overall low morale in the Unionist camp, the intensity of internal conflicts outstrips those on the Nationalist side. This internal dynamic within Unionism and Loyalism is undoubtedly a challenge in terms of creating political movement and willingness on issues such as truth recovery, although the UUP may be showing early signs of movement on this.

Resistance to truth recovery

A commitment to a truth recovery process can be part of a peace settlement, as was the case with the peace agreement in Guatemala. There, truth recovery was included in the agreement, and the relatively weak position of the National Guatemalan Revolutionary Unity (URNG), the political elite were subservient to the army in the early 1990s, the army considered themselves to be victorious.

Furthermore, the army still enjoyed the confidence of substantial sections of the population, unlike the situation in El Salvador or Argentina. The peace agreements were consequently much weaker in their provision for demilitarisation than the comparable agreement in El Salvador. Initially, the army were resistant to any form of accountability for past human rights violations, and attempted to block UN, Catholic Church and civil society initiatives to have a truth commission included in the agreements. Finally, after two years in which the army opposed such a development, the creation of the UN-sponsored Historical Clarification Commission/Comisión de Esclarectimiento Histórico (CEH) was agreed. The limitation on the operation of the CEH was that its recommendations would not have 'legal objectives or effects' and in spite of opposition from human rights organisations, a new amnesty law was passed which prevented prosecution of perpetrators unless they had been involved in torture, genocide or forced disappearances.[60] Significantly, grass-roots initiatives in dealing with the past played a significant role in Guatemalan truth recovery.

In other situations, such as Honduras, the truth recovery process arose out of the gradual process of demilitarisation and pressure from human rights organisations to secure accountability, combined with a lack of confidence in the military, who were regarded as corrupt and involved in criminal behaviour. This combined with a reduction in the United States' funding of the military provided the incentive for some method of reforming relations between the military and civil society. The creation of an office of the National Commissioner for Human Rights, together with the establishment of a commission for police and judicial reform led to the civilianisation of the criminal justice system, and ultimately this began to investigate past violations alongside the Human Rights Commissioner, who investigated the situation of the disappeared. In none of these cases has any army enthusiastically embraced the idea of investigating the deeds of the past.

In Northern Ireland, a commitment to engage in a truth recovery process did not form part of the Good Friday Agreement. As time passes since the Agreement was signed, and difficulties in its implementation continue, the initial optimism about that Agreement has waned as the difficulty in eliciting such a commitment from all the parties in Northern Ireland has waxed. Yet, as in the case of Honduras and elsewhere, human rights activists and relatives of victims succeeded in sustaining pressure in order for some mechanism for establishing accountability for past violations to be established. Not all of these have been comprehensive or have had wide-ranging powers.

Such accountability mechanisms are invariably established in the face of opposition from various quarters. In Guatemala, the army consistently opposed the establishment of a truth commission (Sieder, 2001, p. 168) and even, apparently successful processes, such as the South African TRC had to deal with resistance, both during its establishment and operation. In retrospect, the South African Chair of the TRC, Archbishop Desmond Tutu, reflected ten years after the Truth Commission began its work, that it had failed to sufficiently engage the white community. Moreover it failed to persuade prominent leaders from the old regime, such as PW Botha, who presided over the government operation of death squads and the use of torture, to take part. Botha's failure to cooperate merely earned him a suspended prison sentence, even though it seriously undermined the establishment of accountability for the crimes of Apartheid.[61] Tutu told the BBC journalist Peter Biles:

> people usually speak about how we got only the foot soldiers, and the big fish tended to slip away.... I went to see Mr Botha because we didn't want him to think that we wanted to humiliate him. We could have just subpoenaed him, and if he ignored the subpoena, it would have been a criminal offence. But we didn't really want that. We didn't want to be abrasive. We were supposed to be helping the country to heal. And yes, he remained the intransigent, very difficult old man.[62]

In the South African case, the combination of the extraordinary magnanimity of *ubuntu* combined with the premium placed on forgiveness and healing by the Christian ethos of the TRC, contributed to Tutu's and others' unwillingness to energetically challenge the resistance to participation in truth recovery and culminated in several of the 'big fish' escaping more or less scot-free. However, the dynamic in the South African case was a contributory factor, with the former state president suddenly in the role of a war criminal. No such inversions have taken place in the Northern Ireland case, nor are they likely to do so. In spite of the successive revelations about the state security forces there, these tend to be seen as 'bad apples' rather than as part of a discredited regime. The management of resistance to truth recovery is a matter of balancing the rigorous pursuit of wrong-doers with the imperative to reconcile antagonistic interests and elements. But there are more substantial worries about a less than totally rigorous approach to truth recovery. Tutu and his colleagues attracted the anger of many of the victims of Apartheid by his seemingly placatory stance in relation to Botha and others. Brandon Hamber outlines how critics of the South African process have interpreted this approach:

> reconciliation – with the TRC as its champion – has become a euphemism for the so-called compromises made during the political negotiations, i.e. the maintenance of white control of the economy with some black elite economic advancement at the expense of radical structural change. From this perspective racialised structural violence as the bedrock of *apartheid* oppression was sidelined in favour of an individualized violation-driven analysis... a cynical view is that the rapprochement between the old and new governments was primarily about consolidating a new black elite under the banner of reconciliation.[63]

Hamber has usefully pointed out that the South African TRC itself was a contested space. This contest is manifest by, for example, the unsuccessful legal challenge to the TRC's granting of amnesty as a denial of victims' rights to access to the law mounted by the families of the murdered Steve Biko, Griffiths Mxenge and Fabian Ribiero. The judgment in these cases held that amnesty was a necessity in the project of building democracy in South Africa; that domestic law was of greater significance than international law; and that prosecutions were not possible given the limitations of the legal system (Hamber, 2004, p. 1087).

These patterns of resistance in South Africa are instructive in relation to the Northern Ireland case, where it seems the same broad categories of resistance can be observed. First, there are those who resist because of their own past involvement and their unwillingness to have that involvement exposed and/or problematised and its moral or legal status undermined. Second, there are those who resist because they fear that a truth recovery mechanism will undermine or remove their access to retributive justice. However, this is not the way resistance is manifest in Northern Ireland.

Resistance in Northern Ireland

Resistance to establishing a truth recovery mechanism for Northern Ireland has been articulated in a number of ways. First, there are those who oppose truth recovery on the grounds that the time is not right for whatever reason. This, indeed is the government position, set out in several adamant passages in the NIAC report which, whilst not dismissing the issue of truth recovery entirely, postpones it indefinitely to some vague and unspecified point in the future when the conditions might be ready. Even setting aside worries explored in Chapter 7 about the robustness of the process by which the government has reached this conclusion, the government position raises more questions than it answers. Under what conditions will the time be right? How will we know when the time is right? Who will be the judge of that? What pre-conditions do we wish to set for truth recovery to be embarked upon? By whose agency will these pre-conditions be achieved? If the pre-conditions are set so that, for example, there must be a consensus about truth recovery, then the prospects for the 'time ever being right' according to this approach are bleak.

There is another perspective on the government stance on truth recovery. The lack of government enthusiasm for cooperation and participation in the various public inquiries into controversial killings in Northern Ireland, in which the security forces were allegedly implicated, provides a clue about another, unarticulated motivation for the government's unwillingness to champion truth recovery in Northern Ireland. It is likely that this unwillingness is related to the challenge that such a process, if credible, would pose to that government's own past involvement in clandestine and irregular military activities in Northern Ireland, also to its own breaches of international standards and the liability (and shame) that all of this would create.

Second, are those like Willie Frazer, and others who oppose truth recovery because if conducted along the lines of the South African model, it would interfere with processes of retributive justice, even though full access to retributive justice for victims may be difficult if not impossible to achieve, and may not be in the interests of settlement. According to this view, perpetrators should face the full rigour of the law, and the punishment that this determines for their past deeds. For some who hold this view, their attitude to perpetrators is personally and politically uncompromising, and their interest in truth and reconciliation minimal or non-existent. In the NIAC Inquiry, Gregory Campbell asked William Frazer if he thought that '...now is the right time or will there ever be a right time to embark on that kind of issue [truth recovery]?' Mr Frazer replied:

> Truth and reconciliation will never be acceptable to the victims, because we know the truth. I know every man who was involved in the murder of my family and my family members. I know every one of them, so what more truth do I need to know?[64]

Mr Frazer and others of similar opinion, see no prospect of change in the disposition between victims and perpetrators. They see no value in engagement, they know all they need to know, and they do not share a vision of a reconciled community in a post-conflict period. For them, the war must go on, until those who wronged them are caught and punished, or till the death. Their focus is on their own victimhood, the sense of which is constantly stimulated by the success of Sinn Féin as a political party, and their increasing and unproblematic inclusion in democratic politics. This must be a deeply distressing and hopeless position to occupy, particularly, as is the case, that access to formal justice processes and prosecution is unlikely to be achieved in many cases. The work of the Historic Enquiries Team within the police force may achieve results for some, but bearing in mind the lapse of time in some cases, results may prove difficult to achieve.

Third, there are those who oppose truth recovery because they resist being held accountable for their past deeds, fearing such impact on their current position. This is the position articulated most clearly by Loyalists, specifically EPIC. However, it is unlikely that those associated with the UVF are unique in this fear, even though they are its most lucid articulators. Indeed, this resistance to accountability can be detected in the government's own response to the prospect of truth recovery, and even in Mr Fraser's resistance to diverting attention from the wrongs done to his family and community to a broader and more-inclusive consideration of wrongs committed by all parties.

The government's disposition at the time of writing is to acquiesce to those who resist truth recovery and resist those who champion it. This avoidance or postponement of engagement with truth recovery raises a number of political questions. These questions are as follows:

1   Is the level of denial in and about Northern Ireland serving the interests of peace and stability as opposed to fuelling debate and stalemate?
2   To what extent is the opposition to truth recovery in Northern Ireland a product of political hopelessness as a result of the protracted political stalemate?

3   To what extent is the opposition to truth recovery in Northern
    that can be accommodated without jeopardising political prog
4   Could truth recovery in Northern Ireland create a moral climate o
    ambiguity, exposure, self questioning that could ultimately co
    new politics of fraternity?

These issues will be taken up in the concluding chapter, Chapter 9.

9 Conclusions

This final chapter draws together the arguments presented in the preceding chapters in relation to truth recovery, and points to a set of questions and dilemmas for further consideration and research. The chapter also attempts to draw some tentative conclusions on the Northern Ireland case in relation to the way forward for truth recovery there.

Truth recovery

This book has examined the role of truth recovery in the context of societies coming out of a conflict. Truth recovery becomes a sub-project within a larger enterprise of what has come to be called post-conflict reconstruction. The reader is cautioned in Chapter 1, that this book leaves largely un-interrogated the idea of a 'peace process' and is alerted to the possibility of seeing a peace process as entirely constructed by the imposition of an external framework of meaning on an armed conflict rather than by any quality inherent in the conflict itself. Defining when a conflict tilts from being a conflict into a post-conflict situation, and the imposition of such a framework, is the prerogative of powerful political actors. As is evident in the Iraq of 2007, a nominally post-conflict situation may be virtually indistinguishable, in terms of levels of hostility and instability, from war.

Certainly, the goal of post-conflict reconstruction is, *inter alia*, the underpinning of moves towards the reduction and ending of hostilities and the consolidation of non-violent relationships. Since the publication in 1993 of the UN report on the Truth for El Salvador, there has been a proliferation of truth recovery processes, as part of post-conflict reconstruction efforts. Ambitious claims are made about the benefits of such processes, and these range from their ability to rehabilitate the rule of law and end of impunity to their capacity to achieve societal reconciliation. Although there is little systematic evidence of the benefits and outputs of truth commissions and other truth recovery mechanisms, it seems clear that they may serve some useful purposes. For example, truth recovery can assist with rewriting the history of the past, or can offer acknowledgement of victims' suffering. However, they also have limitations, and present dilemmas, such as the desirability of trading truth for justice, should amnesty be used as an incentive for perpetrators to give evidence, as in the South African case. Nonetheless it is difficult to resist the logic, even if it is based on hunch rather than evidence, that some revisiting of the terrible deeds of the past is required if the past is to be put to rest, society enabled to move forward and the lessons of the past learned.

Chapter 3 examined the nature of truth and the tendency for legal and religious approaches to define truth as singular and absolute, a definition which tends to reinforce the dualistic 'black and white' cultures of violence which persist into the post-conflict period. Such bifurcation is compounded by the adoption in several truth recovery processes of a partial or wholesale retributive justice model, with strict demarcations between the innocent victim and the guilty perpetrator. The retributive model replicates the bifurcated dynamic of the conflict itself, and thus can emphasise division. Whatever model of truth recovery is adopted, the prevalence of disinformation, secrecy and specific forms of identity management during conflict indicates the importance of some form of 'factual truth' to challenge the 'cultures of organised lying' and 'normalised lying' that have supported political violence. As violence diminishes, these cultures of lying are less necessary or feasible and as they begin to fall apart, and their true nature tends to be exposed. Politics is the resolution of contests between competing versions of truth, and such contests are particularly intense during conflict, in propaganda wars, and in the aftermath of conflict where they compose the 'war by other means'. Truth-tellers, then, are a threat to politicians, because they have the power to disrupt hegemonic versions of truth, which are often implicated in the 'war by other means'. Arguably, truth telling can perform an important function in unsettling the bifurcated but fixed versions of truth associated with polarisation and disidentification (De Swaan, 1997), which might, in turn, make way for the establishment of a new societal solidarity, where new emotional identifications can bridge former divisions. Narrative and dialogical forms of truth offer the possibility of truth being arrived at through a process of storytelling, interaction and negotiation, which can serve to underpin the emergence of more-inclusive accounts of the past, and perhaps eventually new forms of societal solidarity.

For Elias (1994) shame is a 'master emotion' significant in its power to control violence through the creation of inhibitions at the individual level, located in a 'civilising process'. The distribution of shame during and after political violence, it is argued in Chapter 4, is significant in both supporting the conditions under which violence is considered honourable, and conversely in rendering identification with the 'other' shameful during the post-conflict period. It is argued that the emergence of a 'new economy' of shame, through the dismantling of codes of 'warrior's honour' and instituting internalised codes of *civilité* (Elias, 1994) can be facilitated by the process of truth recovery. Indeed, the whole post-conflict reconstruction process, or the certainty that part of it concerned with social and political relations, can be seen as an Eliasian 're-civilising process', where war has been a 'de-civilising' one. Some form of public truth recovery can act as the mirror to society in order to encourage critical reflection on the past, to contribute to the creation of a 'new economy of shame', and the dispensing with warrior codes of honour, all of which will tend to inhibit violence.

It is commonplace within discussions on truth recovery to argue that they must be victim-centred and victim-led, and indeed some victims strongly advocate truth recovery as a means of meeting their needs. Yet the diversity of experience of victims, the pathologising of their condition, their expressed needs for justice and reparations are unlikely to be comprehensively and totally satisfied in any truth process. In Chapter 5, the feasibility of the victim stereotype of innocence, suffering, dependence, helplessness, powerlessness and passivity and the role of victims as 'moral beacons' is deconstructed through an examination of the work of Arendt and Levi. Such stereotypes are further undermined by an examination of the complex nature of identity during conflict, where victims can simultaneously be perpetrators, and perpetrators explain their actions with reference to their prior experience of victimisation. Contests over who qualifies as a victim and the political appropriation of victims' suffering becomes part of the substance of the 'war by other means'. Furthermore, since cultures of victimhood are deployed in the legitimisation of violence, they are antithetical to the consolidation of a culture of peace. Such a deployment is at the expense of concerns with healing and meeting victims' needs. According to Arendt, leaving intact the bifurcated ingroup–outgroup dynamic and ideology of past conflict contributes to the facilitation of racialised and divided politics in the post-conflict period, and poses major problems for the project of nation building. With the establishment of a more complex perception of victim identity, where victimhood does not become an all-encompassing identity, those who have been victimised can retain their complexity and diversity as both agents and subjects.

Within truth processes, victims are ascribed the role of having the power to grant or withhold forgiveness, and in some processes, such as the South African TRC, huge importance was placed on forgiveness. Yet forgiveness, for a victim whose suffering has come to symbolically represent the suffering of their entire community, is not a merely personal, individual matter, but is configured into the politics of the situation. Furthermore, the Christian approach to forgiveness reinforces the good – evil split between victim and perpetrator, a reinforcement which is arguably not desirable in the context of encouraging a less-dualistic culture in the post-conflict period. A restorative approach too, would predicate forgiveness and the (re)establishment of relationship with the perpetrator taking full responsibility. However, if responsibility is, for example, collectively owned (an approach favoured by several key actors in Northern Ireland) then arguably, one must look also to the collective, as well as to the individual victim, for forgiveness.

Truth recovery is also often held to be an agent of societal reconciliation. This seems to run counter to the fears expressed by some that truth recovery might in fact increase tensions, rather than reconcile the two communities. There are increasing doubts, in any case, about the positing of reconciliation as a realisable goal in societies such as Northern Ireland, where divisions run deep, segregation continues and opportunistic violence continues, albeit at a much reduced level. In any case, reconciliation may well be setting the bar too high in such circumstances. At least to begin with, non-violent co-existence might be more realisable, with the more ambitious goals of some form of mutual identification and ultimately new, even partial forms of societal solidarity to follow, as later stages in a process which may well be required over a generation or more.

Truth processes are often posed as being a service primarily for victims. However, it would appear from evidence of several such processes, that the truth recovery is, rather, a service performed by victims for the benefit of the broader society, often at some emotional cost to themselves. Victims' testimonies, painful to give and also to hear, inscribe new accounts of the past into the history, thus acting to diversify and broaden understandings of the past. Whilst victims may derive important public acknowledgement of their suffering from such testimonies, their own goals – perhaps of stimulating an admission of guilt or remorse, or of recovering the body of a loved one – may often go unsatisfied. Depending on the manner in which it is framed and the model adopted, truth recovery may perform valuable services to the society as a whole, rendering complex that which was previously seen to be simple, whilst retaining a recognition of the societal moral duty to victims.

The Northern Ireland case

Northern Ireland is the subject of the case study in Chapters 6–8. In the light of the caution that peace processes may not be entirely peaceful interludes, it is necessary to clarify that Northern Ireland is substantially pacified, with marked and sustained reductions in the levels of political violence. Chapter 6 sets out the political dynamic between the parties, much of which is characterised by an Eliasian 'double bind problem', a kind of societal security dilemma, whereby the pursuit by one party of their increased security increases the insecurity of the other. There has been significant progress since 1994, although obstacles still remain, and prospects for the introduction of democratic government there have improved.

In Chapter 7, a detailed examination of the deliberations of Westminster's Northern Ireland Affairs Committee (NIAC) on 'Ways of Dealing with Northern Ireland's Past' were analysed in detail, both as a method of gaining insight into the views of the various parties on the prospects for truth recovery in Northern Ireland, and as an interrogation of the government's process for arriving at the conclusion that Northern Ireland was 'not ready' for a process of truth recovery. The lack of any Nationalist involvement on the NIAC did not inhibit the Committee from its deliberations, although an analysis of the evidence sought by the Committee and heard by it showed a distinct bias in favour of the Unionist witnesses, at the expense not only of Nationalists but also of victims. The Committee seems to have been unaware of this, and their perception of their work was that they listened mainly to victims.

Analysis of this evidence also afforded an overview of how the various groupings in Northern Ireland were disposed to truth recovery. Generally, there was more support for embarking on some kind of truth recovery process amongst Nationalist and Republicans than amongst unionists and loyalists, who largely expressed resistance to the idea. Some others expressed caution, too, on the question of truth recovery, with, for example, the Northern Ireland Human Rights Commission raising questions about the timing and parameters of such a project. Generally, resistance to truth recovery in Northern Ireland was based on three main objections:

- First, it will serve an exclusively Republican agenda, resulting in political gains for Republicans, and consequent inevitable political losses for Unionists and Loyalists as the result of the opportunity for 'Brit-bashing' that truth recovery would present to Republicans.
- Second, that by opening the 'can of worms' that the past represents for many in Northern Ireland, a fresh area of battleground will open up, tensions will be exacerbated, and this will lead to an escalation of conflict, possibly even violence.
- Third, a major Loyalists fear about truth recovery is that any truth that emerges is likely to be profoundly disruptive of relationships within the Loyalist community. If the nature and extent of the past Loyalist violence and personal involvements in it are revealed, family relationships will be damaged, and an incentive to further violence provided for a younger generation of Loyalists.

It is important to locate resistance to truth recovery as emanating not only from the Unionist and Loyalist quarters, but also from the British government, since it was implicit in their construction of the Inquiry, the outcome of which was largely a foregone conclusion. Other observers, too, expressed doubts about the advisability of embarking on a truth recovery process, and these doubts were often based on a lack of clarity about the model of truth recovery to be deployed, concerns that the South African model would be imported wholesale, and fears of making community tensions worse.

In Chapter 8 the concept of 'readiness' for truth recovery was examined, using Zartman's (1985) notion of 'ripeness', which was originally devised for use in determining when and under what conditions conflicts are 'ripe' for resolution. In order to determine Northern Ireland's state of readiness according to this model, certain conditions would be in place in order to render the situation 'ripe' for truth recovery. However, one cannot be sure exactly what those conditions might be, or who would be qualified to judge their presence or absence. Furthermore, Lederach's (1997) has pointed out that ripeness can only be definitively identified in hindsight, since only at the end of a process will it be possible to gauge its success.

Kleiboer's (1994) alterative model, that of detecting 'willingness' on the part of protagonists to engage, seems to offer a more viable analytic frame, whilst also offering a more dynamic sense of the conditions under which truth recovery might occur. 'Readiness' seems static; they are either ready or they are not, with little sense of how political actors might intervene to change this state, whilst 'willingness' is more fluid. 'Willingness' can be supported and encouraged with inducements provided to increase it, or conversely, political or other developments can act to diminish it. Therefore, the prospects for truth recovery in Northern Ireland, it is argued, are dependent on the *willingness* of the various parties to not only engage in such a process, but *to act to increase the willingness* of other parties. The work of projects such as Healing Through Remembering and various human rights and victims' groups in Northern Ireland can be seen to fulfil this function.

Other internal and external factors which affect or even determine the disposition of the various parties towards peace recovery were examined. Since shortly after the signing of the Belfast Agreement in Northern Ireland, there has been a steady stream of disclosures about the past, about spying, double agents, the location of the disappeared, collusion and so on. This stream shows, if anything, a propensity to increase in volume as mechanisms, such as the Office of the Police Ombudsman and the Historic Enquiries Team, engage with the task of reinvestigating the past or addressing grievances. The seemingly relentless flow of such disclosures may well provide an incentive to establish some kind of truth process which could contain and dispose of these disclosures once and for all. Certainly, there is support amongst those charged with such investigation of past events, namely the newly reformed police force, to provide some form of 'wrapping up' the past in the interests of freeing up energy and resources which could be deployed in the present and in planning for the future. What, then, are the considerations in approaching the issue of truth recovery in Northern Ireland? There are a number of key issues.

In Northern Ireland, as elsewhere, the choice of a method and a model of truth recovery will determine not only the outcome of such a process, but the degree of support it will attract. Fears of a 'one-size-fits-all' mentality are exacerbated, for example, when Ministers make visits to South Africa to learn about truth recovery. The South African model, a mixture of retributive and restorative approaches with a Christian ethos and emphasis on forgiveness, is judged by many, including the author, to be inappropriate for Northern Ireland.

Certain points of agreement seem to have emerged about truth recovery in Northern Ireland, for example, the necessity of placing emphasis on collective rather than individual responsibility. This reinforces the importance of designing a model for Northern Ireland that takes into account such emerging consensus and integrates the individual and the collective responsibility in a manner that maximises the willingness of parties to engage in the process, thus increasing the chances of participation. Designing a process that reflects the interconnectedness of the individual and the collective posited by Elias and others, maximises the chances of it making a contribution to political, social (and personal) reconstruction.

A number of factors have led to a reconsideration of retributive models of truth recovery. Concern about the scale and costs associated with the Bloody Sunday Inquiry, and the fact that the expenditure was largely on lawyers fees have led some to question the feasibility of judicial, adversarial processes as the way forward in dealing with Northern Ireland's past. Concern about the adversarial approach, and its culture which is largely antithetical to negotiation, compromise or resolution have led some towards favouring a restorative over a retributive model. Others favour a more interactive, dialogical approach, where the history is rewritten by participation at all levels of society through a narrative process. In this way, aspects of the past that have been omitted from existing accounts are placed on the record, and actors are brought into a closer alignment with one another through an exchange of narratives about the past.

However, this movement towards restorative, narrative and dialogic approaches has implications for the possibility of obtaining justice, which is at the forefront of some victims' minds. The central dilemma of truth recovery is about trading truth for justice. Clearly, the establishment of any truth recovery mechanism will require the creation of a legislative environment in which it can operate. Will the pursuit of a restorative or a narrative approach entail the provision of immunity from prosecution or amnesty in order to make it feasible for perpetrators to participate?

What is abundantly clear is that the resolution to this and other tough questions about truth recovery must be obtained through a process of negotiation between the potential participants to such a process, and crucially those victims who have long argued for truth recovery. No ideal solution is possible, but it does seem that Northern Ireland is uniquely placed to design a process that dovetails creatively with the ongoing efforts by the Historic Enquiries Team, the Police Ombudsman's Office and various other inquiries and processes. The very existence of more retributive efforts at dealing with the past allows more emphasis in any newly initiated process to be placed on restorative and narrative approaches. Whilst the goal of justice, the aim of retributive approaches is crucial to long-term stability, so, too, are the goals of the creation of a more-inclusive version of history, and the acknowledgement of the suffering that was inflicted in the past.

But why even consider truth recovery in Northern Ireland, when there are fears about the impact of such a process on existing tensions and stability? The prospect of truth recovery raises for some observers the spectre of exacerbating division and conflict. Yet one has to question the basis of such fears. Certainly, internecine violence has continued, particularly amongst Loyalists, throughout the peace process, but otherwise, levels of violence have remained low, and the processes of demilitarisation and decommissioning of weapons have decreased the risk of violence. Further political progress in the form of a stable devolved government will further reduce such risks, as indeed will the establishment and consolidation of non-violent methods of dealing with difference at all levels in society. Embarking on any society-wide project such as truth recovery involves risk. One concern is that, aversion to taking such a risk is driven by a perhaps exaggerated desire to avoid escalating conflict. Those who have lived through terrible times are often fearful of their return.

However, as the democratic path in Northern Ireland becomes more well-trodden, such fears must be put in their place, and the importance of taking risks in order to make progress can be recognised as one of the lessons of the Northern Ireland peace process. Indeed, there would be no peace process in Northern Ireland were it not for the risk-takers in all camps.

Perhaps, then, risk taking in the matter of truth recove_ Such a reconsideration will entail the identification resistance to truth recovery and efforts to create and engage in it. Although the prospect of establishing a truth for Northern Ireland is profoundly politically challenging, the prospect of continuing to manage the regular disclosure 'leak' into and pollute the present. The maintenance of an progress, whilst excluding the truth about the past, is no less search for truth and the activities of those who seek it can be prot threatening to any regime relying on an even partial exclusion c ... it seems that politicians must choose whether or not Northern Ireland will have a comprehensive, contained and relatively orderly process of managing the truth. The format of such a process must be negotiated between the participating parties, and time limits and parameters for the process agreed. The alternative is that Northern Ireland will continue in a situation where political and personal life is regularly punctuated by a series of new disclosures about the tragedies of the past.

There are a series of questions which might inform such deliberations:

1 Does the lack of a comprehensive mechanism for managing the past serve the interests of peace and stability in Northern Ireland?
2 To what extent is the attitude to truth recovery in Northern Ireland a product of political hopelessness as a result of the protracted political stalemate?
3 Will a failure to put in place a comprehensive truth recovery process in Northern Ireland jeopardise long-term political stability?
4 Could truth recovery in Northern Ireland create a moral climate of greater questioning and the openness that could ultimately contribute to dismantling, or at least eroding the cultures of division that have fuelled the violence of the past?

These are questions that demand a critical appraisal of the assumptions made about truth recovery. One might hope that civil society actors and responsible politicians would engage in such an appraisal, irrespective of their vested interests in either burying or uncovering the past.

1 Introduction

1 Phillip Appleman, 'Waiting for the Fire' in *New and Selected Poems 1956–1996*, Fayetteville: University of Arkansas Press, 1997.

2 The function of truth recovery in transitional societies

1. See Breen Smyth, Marie 'Truth recovery, and the Role of Victims' Voices: Observations from the Northern Ireland and South African experiences', Occasional Paper: Centre for Democracy and Security, Euro-Balkan Institute, Skopje, 2005.
2. Elias, N., *The Civilising Process*, London: Blackwell, 2000, p. 160.
3. Elias, N., *The Society of Individuals*, edited by Michael Schröter, translated by Edmund Jephcott. Cambridge, MA: Basil Blackwell, 1991.
4. Habermas, J., *Communication and the Evolution of Society*, Toronto: Beacon Press, 1979, p. 3.
5. Ibid.
6. Habermas, J., *Moral Consciousness and Communicative Action*, Cambridge: Polity Press, 1990.
7. Krog, A., *Country of My Skull*, London: Vintage, p. 42.
8. Alex Boraine, *A Country Unmasked: Inside South Africa's Truth and Reconciliation Commission*, Oxford: Oxford University Press, 2000, p. 339.
9. Alex Boraine, *A Country Unmasked*, p. 440.
10. Michael Stone conducted a gun and grenade attack on the parliament buildings some months later, giving rise, in retrospect, to some doubt about his commitment to peaceful dialogue.
11. Alex Boraine, *A Country Unmasked*, p. 441.
12. Hannah Arendt, *The Human Condition: A Study of the Central Conditions Facing Modern Man*, New York: Doubleday Anchor Books, 1959.
13. Joyce Mtimkulu interview with Michael Ignatieff, 'Getting Away with Murder', Special Correspondent Programme, BBC 2. Cited in Hamber and Wilson, ibid., p. 160.
14. Levi, P., *The Drowned and the Saved*, London: Penguin, 1988.

3 Truth and cultures of organised and normalised lying

1. Troelsch, E. (1972 trans.), *The Absoluteness of Christianity*, London: John Knox Press.
2. Hillyard, P., *Suspect Community*, London: Pluto, pp. 257–258.
3. *Mail on Sunday*, 23 September 1990, cited in Hillyard, p. 259.
4. Healing Through Remembering, 2005.
5. Deane, S., *Reading in the Dark*, London: Vintage, 1996, pp. 42–43.
6. An Phoblacht/Republican News, Thursday 31 January 2002 available at http://republican-news.org/archive/2002/November21/21new2.html, accessed 2 February 2007.

7 Jenkins, R. 'Review: Ardoyne; The Untold Truth', *The Global Review of Ethnopolitics*, 2003, 3(1): 108.
8 See, for example, Rayner, E. (1999). 'Some Functions of Being Fair and Just', *International Journal of Psycho-analysis*, 80: 477–492.
9 See, for example, Zeitlin, S. B., McNally R. J. and Cassiday, K. L. 'Alexithymia in Victims of Sexual Assault: An Effect of Repeated Traumatization?' *American Journal of Psychiatry*, 1993; 150: 661–663; and Perry, B. 'Incubated in Terror: Neurodevelopmental Factors in the "Cycle of Violence" ', in Osofsky, J. D., *Children in a Violent Society*, New York: Guildford, 1997, pp. 124–148.
10 Arendt, H. 'Between Past and Future', *The New Yorker*, 25 February 1967 reprinted in Peter Baehr (ed.) *The Portable Hannah Arendt*, London, Penguin, 2000.
11 Ibid., p. 549.
12 Hobbes, Leviathan, chapter 46.
13 Spinoza, B., quoted in Arendt, H. 'Truth and Politics', In Peter Baehr (ed.) *The Portable Hannah Arendt*, London: Penguin, 2003, p. 550.
14 Kant, I., ' "What is enlightenment?" and "Was heisst sich im Denken orientieren?" ', quoted in Arendt, H. 'Truth and Politics', in Peter Baehr (ed.) *The Portable Hannah Arendt*, London: Penguin, 2003, p. 550.
15 Arendt, 1967, p. 554.
16 Levi, P., 'A Conversation with Primo Levi', in P. Levi, *Survival in Auschwitz*, Touchstone: New York, 1996, pp. 175–191.
17 Ibid., p. 181.
18 Levi, P., 'The Side of Good and Evil' in Primo Levi, *Survival in Auschwitz*, Touchstone: New York, 1996, pp. 77–86.
19 Ibid., p. 88.
20 Arendt, 'Between Past and Future', p. 554.
21 See also http: transcripts.cnn.com/TRANSCRIPTS/0611/04/i_if.01.html, accessed 29 August 2007.
22 Police Ombudsman for Northern Ireland, Statement by the Police Ombudsman for Northern Ireland on her investigation into the circumstances surrounding the death of Raymond McCord Junior and related matters, Belfast, Police Ombudsman's Office, 2007.
23 Arendt, 1967: p. 556.
24 Ibid., p. 564.
25 See, for example, Sanders, J., *Apartheid's Friends: The Rise and Fall of South Africa's Secret Service*, London: John Murray, 2006.
26 Elias, N., *The Civilising Process*, Oxford: Blackwell, 1994.
27 See Turner, B. S., 'Weber and Elias on Religion and Violence: Warrior Charisma and the Civilising Process', in Steven Loyal and Stephen Quilley, *The Sociology of Norbert Elias*, Cambridge: Cambridge University Press, 2004, pp. 245–264, for a more detailed discussion of these points.
28 New Yorker, 23 May 2005, cited in Sanders, 2006, p. 395.
29 See Fay, M. T. and Smyth, M., *Personal Accounts of Northern Ireland's Troubles: Public Chaos, Private Loss*, London: Pluto, 2000 and Smyth, M., Morrissey, M. and Fay, M. T. *Northern Ireland's Troubles: The Human Costs*, London: Pluto, 1999.
30 Arendt, 1967, p. 570.
31 Ibid.

4 Shame, honour and cultures of violence and peace

1 An Afrikaans term which translates as the 'black threat', a term used during Apartheid for the security threat that the black African population posed to the white government.
2 Violations carried out by opponents of Apartheid were also examined by the TRC.
3 See Winer, S., 'South Africa, the High Price of Appeasement', ZNet, 2003, available at http://www.zmag.org/content/showarticle.cfm?ItemID=2984, accessed 28 January 2007.

184 *Notes*

4 China Daily, 'German leader: We Bow in Shame' (2 August 2004), available at http://www2.chinadaily.com.cn/english/doc/2004-08/02/content_356754.htm, accessed 27 January 2007.
5 Rothschild, M. (2000), 'Transforming Our Legacies: Heroic Journeys for Children of Holocaust Survivors and Nazi Perpetrators', *Journal of Humanistic Psychology*, 40(3): 43–55.
6 Elias, 1994, p. 493.
7 Williams, 1994, p. 220.
8 Cooley, 1992, pp. 184–5.
9 Pattison, 2000, following Goffman, 197, pp. 63–64.
10 Ibid., p. 147
11 Balkin, J. M. 'How Mass Media Simulate Political Transparency', *Cultural Values*, October 1999, 3(4): 393–413(21).
12 House of Commons Hansard: February 1996: column 616.
13 See Tangney J. P. and Dearing R. L., *Shame and Guilt*, New York: Guilford, 2003.
14 Levi, P., 'The Last One', in Primo Levi, *Survival in Auschwitz*, Touchstone: New York, 1996, p. 150.
15 Ibid., p. 150.
16 Levi, 1989, pp. 57–8.
17 Ibid., pp. 56–7.
18 Levi, P., 'The Drowned and the Saved', in Primo Levi, *Survival in Auschwitz*, Touchstone: New York, 1996, p. 88.
19 Levi, 1989, pp. 56–7.
20 Ibid., p. 66.
21 Levi, P., 'Shame', in P. Levi, 'The Drowned and the Saved', London: Abacus, 1989.
22 Levi, 1989, p. 65.
23 See http://news.bbc.co.uk/1/hi/uk/209093.stm, accessed 24 August 2007.
24 See Shorter, E., *A History of Psychiatry: From the Era of the Asylum to the Age of Prozac*, New York: John Wiley, 1998.
25 See http://www.shotatdawn.org.uk/, accessed 24 August 2007.
26 See full details at http://cain.ulst.ac.uk/viggiani/south_memorial.html, accessed 24 August 2007.
27 Pirabakaran, cited at http://www.eelamweb.com/leader/quotes/, accessed 2 February 2007.
28 Fischer, 1989, p. 765. Cited in Cohen *et al.* 1998.
29 See Ignatieff, M. *The Warrior's Honour: Ethnic War and the Modern Consciousness*, New York: Henry Holt, 1998.
30 Wacquant, L. 'Decivilising and demonizing; the remaking of the black American ghetto' in Steven Loyal and Stephen Quilley, *The Sociology of Norbert Elias*, Cambridge: Cambridge University Press, 2004, pp. 95–121.
31 Levi, P., 'The Story of Ten Days', in P. Levi, *Survival in Auschwitz*, Touchstone: New York, 1996, p. 160.
32 Levi, 1989, p. 160.
33 Habermas, J. trans. T. Burger and F. Lawrence, *Structural Transformation of the Public Sphere*, Cambridge, MA: MIT Press, 1989 [1962].
34 Pattison, 2000, p. 135.
35 John Darby and Roger McGinty, *The Management of Peace Processes: Coming Out of Violence Project*, London: Macmillan, 2000, p. 260.
36 Darby and McGinty, p. 260.

5 Victims, healing, forgiveness and truth

1 Fay, M. T., Morrissey, M. and Smyth, M., *Northern Ireland's Troubles: The Human Costs*, London: Pluto, 1999.
2 Ibid.

3 Northern Ireland Office estimates.
4 SIPRI Yearbook (1999) *Armaments, Disarmaments and International Security*, Oxford: Oxford University Press.
5 Fay, M. T., Morrissey, M. and Smyth, M. *Northern Ireland's Troubles*.
6 Ibid.
7 Emirbayer, M. and Goldberg, C., 'Pragmatism, Bourdieu, and Collective Emotions in Contentious Politics', *Theory and Society*, December 2005, 34(5–6): 469–518(50).
8 Gabriel, A. H., 'Grief and Rage: Collective Emotions in the Politics of Peace and the Politics of Gender in Israel', *Culture, Medicine and Psychiatry*, September 1992, 16(3): 311–335.
9 Patočka, J. (1996), 'Heretical Essays in the Philosophy of History', trans. Erazim Kohák, ed. James Dodd, Chicago, IL: Open Court, 125ff.
10 http://www.ukzn.ac.za/ccs/default.asp?6,37,14,52 Khulumani and the Apartheid Debt Campaign v. Barclays National Bank, *et al.* Case No. 02-CV5952 (S.D.N.Y. 2002) was an action taken by Khulumani against Barclay's Bank in which they sought to hold those businesses that aided and abetted the apartheid regime. For example, the Plaintiffs allege that the mining industry was involved in helping to design and implement apartheid policies. Plaintiffs also allege that IBM and ICL provided the computers that enabled South Africa to create the pass-book system used to control the black South African population, and so on. Plaintiffs allege that the Banks provided the funding for South Africa to expand its police and security apparatus, and were instrumental to the furtherance of the abuses and so integral to the abuses that apartheid would not have lasted without their participation. http://www.laborrights.org/projects/corporate/ATCA%20summaries.htm, accessed 28 August 2007.
11 http://www.madres.org/, accessed 28 August 2007.
12 http://www.victims.org.uk/, accessed 28 August 2007.
13 Smyth, M., Hayes, E. and Hayes, P. (1994), 'Post Traumatic Stress and Victims of Violence in Northern Ireland: The case of the Families of the Bloody Sunday Victims', Centre for the Study of Conflict/N.I. Association for Mental Health Conference on Violence and Mental Health, Queen's University, September 1994.
14 Hayes, P. J. and Campbell, J., *Bloody Sunday: Trauma, Pain and Politics*, London: Pluto, 2005.
15 Edkins, 2003, p. 34.
16 See for example Hadden, W. A. Rutherford, W. H. and Merrit J. D. 'The Injuries of Terrorist Bombing: A Study of 1532 Consecutive Patients', *British Journal of Surgery*, 1978 (65): 525–531.
17 See, for example, Shorter E., *A History of Psychiatry*, New York: Wiley, 1997.
18 Giddens, A., *The Transformation of Intimacy: Love, Sexuality and Eroticism in Modern Societies*, London: Polity, 1993.
19 Young, A., *The Harmony of Illusions: Inventing Post-traumatic Stress Disorder*, Princeton, NJ: Princeton University Press, 1995.
20 See McHugh, P. R. and Treisman, G., 'PTSD: A Problematic Diagnostic Category', *Journal of Anxiety Disorders*, 2007, 21(2): 211–222. Epub 2006.
21 Hunter, H. D., 'The Work of a Corps Psychiatrist in the Italian Campaign', *Journal of the Royal Army Medical Corps*, 1946 (96): 127–130. Quoted in Garland, C. 'The Traumatised Group', in C. Garland (1998) *Understanding Trauma: A Psychoanalytic Approach*, London: Duckworth/Tavistock. 1998.
22 Barker, P. *Regeneration*, London: Penguin, 1992.
23 Straker, G. and the Sanctuaries Team (1987) 'The Continuous Traumatic Stress Syndrome: The Single Therapeutic Interview', *Psychology and Society*, 1987 (8): 48.
24 Smyth, M., Fay, M. T., Morrissey, M. and Wong, T. 'Report on the Northern Ireland Survey: The Experience and Impact of the Troubles', Derry Londonderry, INCORE/the United Nations University and the University of Ulster, 1999.

25 Thomas, L. M. 'Suffering as a Moral Beacon: Blacks and Jews' in H. Flanzbaum (ed.) *The Americanization of the Holocaust*, Baltimore, MD: Johns Hopkins, 1999.
26 Ibid., p. 204.
27 De Swaan, A. (1995) 'Widening Circles of Identification: Emotional Concerns in Sociogenetic Perspective', *Theory Culture Society*, 1995, 12: 25–39.
28 Smyth, M., Hamilton, J. and Thomson, K., *Caring through the Troubles: Health and Social Services in North and West Belfast*, Belfast: Eastern Health and Social Services Board/North and West Health and Social Services Trust 2001.
29 De Swaan, A., 'Widening Circles of Disidentification: On the Psycho- and Sociogenesis of the Hatred of Distant Strangers; Reflections on Rwanda', *Theory, Culture and Society*, 1997, 14(2): 105–122.
30 Borer, 2003, pp. 1088–1089, cited in Bouris, 2007.
31 Northern Ireland Office (NIO) Research and Statistical Series: No. 7 – Who are the Victims? Self-assessed victimhood and the Northern Irish conflict, Belfast, The Sationery Office, June 2003.
32 Smyth, M. 'Remembering in Northern Ireland: Victims, Perpetrators and Hierarchies of Pain and Responsibility', in B. Hamber (ed.), *Past Imperfect: Dealing with the Past in Northern Ireland and Societies in Transition*, Derry Londonderry INCORE, 1998.
33 Bouris, 2007, p. 49.
34 Arendt, H., *The Jew as Pariah*, Ron Feldman (ed.) New York: Grove Press, 1978, p. 417.
35 Enloe, C., 'Margins, Silences and Bottom Rungs: How to Overcome the Underestimation of Power in the Study of International Relations', in C. Enloe, *The Curious Feminist: Searching for Women in a New Age of Empire*, Berkeley, CA: University of California Press, 2004, p. 24.
36 Arendt, 1987, pp. 235–236, cited in Bouris, p. 70.
37 Hamber, Kulle and Wilson, 2001, pp. 216–217.
38 Gobodo-Madikizela, 2004, p. 117, cited in Bouris, p. 44.
39 A Review of Criminal Injuries Compensation in Northern Ireland. A report to the Secretary of State for Northern Ireland by the review team – Sir Kenneth Bloomfield, Mrs Marion Gibson and Professor Desmond Greer (June 1999). Available at http://www.ofmdfmni.gov.uk/report_of_the_review_of_criminal_injuries_compensation_in_ni.pdf, accessed 28 August 2007.
40 The UDR was later disbanded, and allegations of its subversion by Loyalist paramilitaries and dual membership of the UDR and Loyalist militias are discussed in Chapter 11.
41 Williams, P. and Scharf, M., *Peace with Justice: War Crimes and Accountability in the Former Yugoslavia*, New York: Rowman and Littlefield, 2002.
42 Holbrooke, R., Senate Confirmation Hearing, testimony 6/24/1999, quoted in Bouris, E., *Complex Political Victims*, Bloomfield: Kumarian, 2007.
43 Bouris, 2007, p. 16.

6 Framing the grievances of the past: Northern Ireland since the Belfast Agreement

1 Herz. J., *Political Realism and Political Idealism*, Chicago, IL: University of Chicago Press, 1951, p. 231.
2 Butterfield, H., *Christianity, Diplomacy and War*, London: Epworth Press, 1953, p. 43.
3 Buzan, B., 'Societal Security, State Security and Internationalisation', in Waever, O., B. Buzan, M. Kelstrup and P. Lemaitre, *Identity, Migration and the New Security Agenda in Europe*, London: Pinter, pp. 41–58.
4 Waever, O., 'Insecurity and Identity Unlimited' COPRI Working Paper, no. 14, p. 19.
5 See Christopher Farringdon, 'Unionism and the Peace Process in Northern Ireland.' *British Journal of Politics and International Relations*, 2006, 8(2): 277–294.

6 'David Trimble once commented that Northern Ireland was a co
More recently, the UK Secretary of State for Northern Ireland
' "Northern Ireland must not become a cold place for Protestants
needed is a house that is warm for all those who live there.' Ric
to the National Committee on American Foreign Policy, New
http://www.state.gov/s/p/rem/7300.htm, accessed 1 March 20
'Even official statistics indicate two thirds of violent attacks i
work of loyalists. That if it is a "cold place" for unionists it mu
nationalists goes unnoticed by the British State.' Joe Craig,
Belfast: A Cold Place for Unionism', 14th January 2002 is at http://www. socia...
democracy.org/News&AnalysisIreland/News&AnalysisIreTheViolenceInNorthBelfast.
htm, accessed 1 March 2006.
7 Evans and Duffy, 1997, p. 47.
8 Richard Haass, Address to the Foreign Affairs Committee, 7 January 2002, at http://www.state.gov/s/p/rem/7300.htm, accessed 1 March 2006.
9 The Eighth Report of the Independent Monitoring Commission, 1 February 2006 concluded that 'We have no doubt that the PIRA, uniquely among paramilitary organisations, has taken the strategic decision to eschew terrorism and pursue a political path. There are a number of signs that the organisation is moving in the way it indicated in its statement of 28 July 2005. But in the light of some of the activities we refer to, a real question remains of whether this will involve purely conventional politics conducted with a culture of lawfulness. Loyalist groups, which are violent as well as responsible for a wide range of other crimes, have not made the strategic choice which the PIRA have made. However there are some early signs of change amongst loyalists which we hope to see taken much further. The one paramilitary murder was by members of the UDA of one of the organisation's senior leaders. Loyalists were responsible for all the other reported shootings and assaults, bar one of the latter which was the responsibility of a dissident republican group' (p. 35).
10 Anderson, Benedict, *Imagined Communities: Reflections on the Origin and Spread of Nationalism*, London, Verso, 2006.
11 See Fay, M. T., Morrissey, M. and Marie Smyth, *Northern Ireland's Troubles: The Human Costs*, London, Pluto, 1999.

7 Readiness for truth: the Northern Ireland Affairs Committee Inquiry

1 House of Commons Northern Ireland Affairs Committee, (2005) 'Ways of Dealing with Northern Ireland's Past: Interim Report – Victims and Survivors; Tenth Report of Session 2004–5 Volume 1', London; The Stationery Office. p. 7 para 1. (Henceforth NIAC).
2 NIAC: Ev 131, Q 586.
3 NIAC: Ev 145, para 6.
4 NIAC: Ev 47, Q 140.
5 NIAC: Ev 93, Q 371.
6 NIAC: Ev 5, Q 2.
7 NIAC: Ev 7, Q 23.
8 NIAC, Ev 8, Q 31.
9 NIAC, Ev 8, Q 32.
10 NIAC: Ev 52, Q 162–166.
11 NIAC: Ev 10 Q 51–54.
12 NIAC: Ev 169, Q 668.
13 NIAC: Ev 211, Q 749.
14 NIAC: Ev 214, Memorandum submitted by Mr Colin Perry.
15 NIAC: Ev 216, Q 760.
16 NIAC: Ev 217, Q 769.
17 NIAC: Ev 56, Q 186.

NIAC: Ev 94, Q 375.
   NIAC: Ev 43.
20 NIAC: Ev 141, Q 653.
21 NIAC: Ev 141, Q 653.
22 NIAC: Ev 120, Q 568.
23 NIAC: Ev 211, Q 749.
24 NIAC: Ev 50, Q 154.
25 NIAC: Ev 170, Q 672.
26 NICA: Ev 212, Q 750.
27 NIAC: Ev 234, Q 834.
28 Healing Through Remembering, Storytelling Audit. Healing Through Remembering, Belfast, July 2005.
29 See, for example. Besley, A. C., 'Foucault and the Turn to Narrative Therapy', *British Journal of Guidance and Counselling*, May 2002, 30(2): 125–143. or Carr, A., 'Michael White's Narrative Therapy', *Contemporary Family Therapy*, December 1998, 20(4): 485–503. Weingarten, K. 'The Small and the Ordinary: The Daily Practice of a Postmodern Narrative Therapy', *Family Process*, 1998, 37: 3–15.
30 Swap, W., Leonard, D., Shields, M. and Abrams, L., 'Using Mentoring and Storytelling to Transfer Knowledge in the Workplace', *Journal of Management Information Systems*, Summer 2001, 18(1): 95–114.
31 Delgado, R. 'Storytelling for Oppositionists and Others: A Plea for Narrative', *Michigan Law Review*, 87(8): 2411–2441, Legal Storytelling August 1989.
32 Ibid.
33 Ibid.
34 NIAC: Ev 34.
35 NIAC: Ev 41, Q 136.
36 NIAC: Ev 34.
37 NIAC: Ev 130.
38 NIAC: Ev 2.
39 NIAC: Ev 3.
40 NIAC: Ev 209, Q 742.
41 NIAC: Ev 67, Q 245.
42 NIAC: Ev 141, Q 652.
43 NIAC: Ev 3.
44 NIAC: Ev 7, Q 24.
45 NIAC: Ev 8, Q 30.
46 NIAC: Ev 9, Q 37.
47 NIAC: Ev 9, Q 39.
48 NIAC: Ev 10, Q 48.
49 NIAC: Ev 10, Q 56.
50 NIAC: Ev 39, Q 125.
51 NIAC: Ev 41, Q 137.
52 NIAC: Ev 8, Q 36.
53 NIAC: Ev 50, Q 153.
54 NIAC: Ev 59, Q 210.
55 NIAC: Ev 120, Q 573.
56 NIAC: Ev 65,Q 238.
57 NIAC: Ev 79, Q 327.
58 NIAC: Ev 178.
59 NIAC: Ev 186, Q 691 ff.
60 NIAC: Ev 206, Q 731.
61 NIAC: Ev 170, Q 672.
62 NIAC: Ev 170, Q 672.

63 NIAC: Ev 210, Q 747.
64 NIAC: Ev 167, Q 662.
65 NIAC: Ev 141, Q 653.
66 NIAC: Ev 50, Q 153.
67 NIAC: Ev 48, Q 141.
68 NIAC: Ev 48, Q 142.
69 NIAC: Ev 94, Q 376.
70 NIAC: Ev 61, Q 216.
71 NIAC: Ev 75, Q 284.
72 NIAC: Ev 141, Q 654.
73 NIAC: Ev 120, Q 569.
74 NIAC: Ev 77, Q 319.
75 NIAC: Ev 174.
76 NIAC: Ev 174.
77 NIAC: Ev 174.
78 NIAC: Ev 67, Q 246.
79 NIAC: Ev Q 728.
80 NIAC: Ev 78, Q 320.
81 NIAC: Ev 93, Q 371.
82 NIAC: Ev 81.
83 NIAC: Ev Q 437.
84 NIAC: Ev 112, Q 505.
85 NIAC: Ev 207, Q 734.
86 NIAC: Ev 209, Q 741.
87 Brandon Hamber and Richard A Wilson, 'Symbolic Closure through Memory, Reparation and Revenge in Post-Conflict Societies' in Ed Cairns and Mícheál D. Roe, *The Role of Memory in Ethnic Conflict*, Basingstoke: Palgrave Macmillan, 2003, p. 157.
88 Ibid., p. 160.
89 See for example the work of the Ardoyne Commemoration Committee, and their published report, Ardoyne Commemoration Project (2002), *Ardoyne: The Untold Truth*, Belfast: Beyond the Pale.
90 NIAC: Ev 37, Q 114.
91 NIAC: Ev 57, Q 194.
92 NIAC: Ev 140, Q 647.
93 NIAC: Ev 141, Q 654.
94 NIAC: Ev 013, Q 438.
95 NIAC: Ev 106, Q 461.
96 NIAC: Ev 104, Q 441.
97 NIAC: Ev 104, Q 442.
98 NIAC: Ev 110, Q 484.
99 NIAC: Ev 110, Q 485.
100 NIAC: Ev 111, Q 490.
101 NIAC: 110, Q 488.
102 NIAC: Ev 192–3 Q 727.
103 NIAC: Ev 193 Q 727.
104 NIAC: Ev 193 Q 728.
105 NIAC: Ev 193 Q 729.
106 Interview with Albie Sachs, Radio 4, 19 October 2005.
107 NIAC: Ev 95, Q 382.
108 NIAC: Ev 48, Q 144.
109 NIAC: Ev 242, Q 837.
110 NIAC: Ev 242, Q 838.
111 NIAC: Ev 247, Q 851.

8 Is Northern Ireland ready for truth?

1. Cited in Mitchell, Christopher, 'The Right Moment: Notes on Four Models of Ripeness', *Paradigms*, Winter 1995, 9(2): 44.
2. Kleiboer, M. (1994) 'Ripeness of Conflict: A Fruitful Notion?' *Journal of Peace Research*, 31(1): 109–116 and 113.
3. Mitchell, 1995, p. 48 (my emphasis).
4. John Paul Lederach, *Building Peace: Sustainable Reconciliation in Divided Societies*, Washington DC, United States Institute of Peace, 1997.
5. Kleiboer, M. (1994) 'Ripeness of Conflict: A Fruitful Notion?' *Journal of Peace Research*, 31(1): 109–116 and 113.
6. Ibid., p. 114.
7. Finucane, 2003, App No 2978/95; Kelly V. United Kingdom, App No 30054/96; Jordan v United Kingdom, App No 24746/94 (2001); Shanaghan v United Kingdom, App No 37715/97 (2001); McKerr v United Kingdom, 34 Eur.Ct.H.R. 20 (2002); McShane v United Kingdom, 35, Eur. Ct. H.R. 23, (2002).
8. United Nations Human Rights Committee, 73rd Session, Concluding Observations of the Human Rights Committee: United Kingdom of Great Britain and Northern Ireland. CCPR/CO/73/UK;CCPR/CO/73/UKOT. Geneva: Office of the United Nations High Commissioner for Human Rights, 06/12/2001.
9. Association of the Bar of the City of New York (ABCNY) (2004) Northern Ireland: A Report to the Association of the Bar of the City of New York from a Mission of the Committee on International Human Rights. New York: ABCNY, p. 45.
10. Center for Civil and Human Rights (2006) Report of the Independent International Panel on Alleged Collusion in Sectarian Killings in Northern Ireland, Chicago, IL: Notre Dame Law School, p. 83.
11. BBC Television: 'Facing Northern Ireland's Troubled Past', 3 March 2006.
12. Statistics presented here were collected in a earlier study, The Cost of the Troubles Study, see Fay, M. T., Morrissey, M. and Smyth, M. (1999) *Northern Ireland's Troubles: The Human Costs*, London: Pluto.
13. NIAC (2005), 1, para 28, p. 13.
14. See EPIC (2004), *Truth Recovery: A Contribution from Within Loyalism*, Belfast: EPIC.
15. NIAC (2005) 1, para 29, p. 14.
16. Northern Ireland Life and Times/ Patricia Lundy (2006) 'Cautious Support for an Irish Truth Commission,' Coleraine: University of Ulster, press release, 11 July 2005. Available http://www.ulster.ac.uk/news/releases/2005/1776.html, accessed May 20.
17. NIAC (2005) 'Ways of Dealing with Northern Ireland's Past: Interim Report – Victims and Survivors Volume 1', London: The Stationery Office, para 29, p. 14.
18. European Commission of Human Rights, 25 January 1976. App No 5310/71 Ireland v The United Kingdom of Great Britain and Northern Ireland; Report of the Commission The European Court of Human Rights 18 January 1978, 'Case of Ireland v The United Kingdom Judgement, Council of Europe, Strasbourg.
19. Police Ombudsman for Northern Ireland, statement by the Police Ombudsman for Northern Ireland on her investigation into the circumstances surrounding the death of Raymond McCord Junior and related matters. Belfast: Police Ombudsman's Office, 2007.
20. Irish Government's Houses of the Oireachtas Joint Committee on Justice, Equality, Defence and Women's Rights (2006) 'Final Report of the Independent Commission of Inquiry into the Bombing of Kay's Tavern Dundalk', Dublin: The Stationery Office, p. 61.
21. (01/02/05) http://www.sdlp.ie/prlewsleycommentsonvictims.shtm, accessed 24 August 2007.
22. (03/02/05) http://www.sdlp.ie/prdurkanmoreneededforvictims.shtm, accessed 24 August 2007.

23 Eolas, *Consultation Paper on Truth and Justice: A Discussion Document*, Belfast: Eolas, 2003.
24 Ibid., pp. 2–3.
25 An Phoblacht/Republican News: 13 October 2006.
26 Democratic Unionist Party (2003). A Voice for Victims, p. 8.
27 Ibid.
28 Ibid., pp. 8–9.
29 Democratic Unionist Party, 19 February 2004.
30 DUP Press Release, 22 February 2004.
31 Hansard, 1 April 2004, Column 1765.
32 Ibid.
33 Ulster Unionist Press Release, 14 April 2004.
34 Ibid.
35 Unionist Group, The (2006) 'Drawing a Line under the Past, the Unionist Group', Belfast, 16 March 2006.
36 Ibid.
37 Ibid.
38 Ibid.
39 DUP Press Release 28 March 2006.
40 Ibid.
41 Ibid.
42 UUP Press Release, 2 March 2005.
43 Irish News, 12 June 2006, p. 15.
44 Ibid.
45 Paul Murphy; Dealing with Past to Build a Better Future-Murphy; Friday 1 October 2004, http://www.nio.gov.uk/press/040527a.htm, accessed 24 August 2007.
46 EPIC (2004) *Truth Recovery: A Contribution for within Loyalism*, Belfast: EPIC.
47 Combined Loyalist Military Command Ceasefire statement; 1994 http://cain.ulst.ac.uk/events/peace/docs/clmc131094.htm, accessed 24 August 2007.
48 EPIC (2004) *Truth Recovery: A Contribution from Loyalism*, Belfast: EPIC, pp. 6–7.
49 Ibid., pp. 6–7.
50 Ibid., p. 7.
51 Ibid., p. 8.
52 Ibid., p. 8.
53 Ibid., p. 9.
54 Ibid., p. 9.
55 Ibid., p. 11.
56 Roy Garland, Irish News, 25 November 2004.
57 Farrington, Christopher, 'Unionism and the Peace Process in Northern Ireland'. *British Journal of Politics and International Relations*, 2006, 277–294.
58 Bruce, Steve, 'Turf War and Peace: Loyalist Paramilitaries since 1994', *Terrorism and Political Violence*, Autumn 2004, 16(3): 505.
59 Ibid., p. 509.
60 See Sieder, R. (2001) 'War, Peace and Memory Politics in Central America', in A. Barahona de Brito, C. Gonzaléz-Enríquez and P. Aguilar, *The Politics of Memory: Transitional Justice in Democratizing Societies*, Oxford: Oxford University Press, 2001, pp. 161–189.
61 Friday, 16 December 2005, BBC news.
62 Peter Biles, Monday, 1 May 2006, BBC interview with Desmond Tutu.
63 Hamber and Wilson, *Recognition and Reckoning: The Way Ahead on Victims Issues*, Belfast Democratic Dialogue, 2003, p. 8.
64 NIAC: 2005, Ev 193, Q 728.

Bibliography

Addams, J. (1912) 'Twenty Years at Hull-House; With Autobiographical Notes', New York: Macmillan. Online. Available HTTP: http://digital.library.upenn.edu/women/addams/hullhouse/hullhouse.html (accessed 11 March 2007).
Amnesty International (1994) *Political Killings in Northern Ireland*, London: Amnesty International.
Appleman, P. (1997) *New and Selected Poems 1956–1996*, Fayetteville, AR: Arkansas University Press.
Ardoyne Commemoration Project (2002) *Ardoyne: The Untold Truth*, Belfast: Beyond the Pale.
Arendt, H. (1967) 'Between Past and Future' The New Yorker, 25 February, 1967 reprinted in Baehr, P. (ed) *The Portable Hannah Arendt*, London: Penguin, 2000.
Arendt, H. (1978) *The Jew as Pariah* (ed.), Ron Feldman, New York: Grove Press.
Arendt, H. and McCarthy, M. (1995) 'Between Friends: The Correspondence of Hannah Arendt and Mary MacCarthy 1949–75', Carol Brightman (ed.) New York: Harcourt Brace.
Arendt, H. and Scholem, G. (1964) 'Eichman in Jerusalem: Exchange of Letters between Gershom Scholem and Hannah Arendt', *Encounter*, 22(1): 51–56.
Association of the Bar of the City of New York (ABCNY) (2004) 'Northern Ireland: A Report to the Association of the Bar of the City of New York from a Mission of the Committee on International Human Rights', New York: ABCNY.
Balkin, J. M. (1999) 'How Mass Media Simulate Political Transparency', *Cultural Values*, October, 3(4): 393–413.
Barahona De Brito, A., Gonzaléz Enríquez, C. and Aguilar, P. (eds) (2001) *The Politics of Memory: Transitional Justice in Democratizing Societies*, Oxford: Oxford University Press.
Batchelor, P. and Kigma, K. (2004) *Demilitarisation and Peace Building in Southern Africa: Vol 1 Concepts and Processes*, Aldershot: Ashgate.
BBC Television (2006) 'Facing Northern Ireland's Troubled Past', 3 March 2006.
Bell, C. (2000) *Peace Agreements and Human Rights*, Oxford: Oxford University Press.
Besley, A. C. (2002) 'Foucault and the Turn to Narrative Therapy', *British Journal of Guidance and Counselling*, 30(2): 125–143.
Biggar, N. (ed.) (2001) *Burying the Past: Making Peace and Doing Justice after Civil Conflict*, Washington, DC: Georgetown University Press.
Bloomfield, K. (1998) *We Will Remember Them: Report of the Northern Ireland Victims Commissioner, Sir Kenneth Bloomfield*, Belfast: HMSO, The Stationery Office.
Boraine, A. (2001) *A Country Unmasked: Inside South Africa's Truth and Reconciliation Commission*, Oxford: Oxford University Press.
Borer, A. (2003) 'A Taxonomy of Victims and Perpetrators: Human Rights and Reconciliation in South Africa', *Human Rights Quarterly* 25(4): 1088–1116.

Bouris, E. (2007) *Complex Political Victims*, Bloomfield, CT: Kumarian.
Braithwaite, J. (1989) *Crime, Shame and Reintegration*, Cambridge, UK: Cambridge University Press.
Braudy, L. (2003) *From Chivalry to Terrorism: War and Changing the Nature of Masculinity*, New York: Knopf.
Breen Smyth, M. (2005) 'Truth Recovery, and the Role of Victims' Voices: Observations from the Northern Ireland and South African experiences', occasional paper at the Centre for Democracy and Security, Euro-Balkan Institute, Skopje, 2005.
Brewer, J. (1998) *Anti-Catholicism in Northern Ireland 1600–1998*, London: Macmillan.
British Irish Rights Watch (1999) *Deadly Intelligence*, London: British Irish Rights Watch.
British Irish Rights Watch (2000) *Justice Delayed: Alleged State Collusion in the Murder of Patrick Finucane and Others*, London: British Irish Rights Watch. Online. Available http://www.birw.org/justice.html, accessed 24 August 2007.
Bromberg, N. and Small, V. (1983) *Hitler's Psychopathology*, New York: International Universities Press.
Bruce S. (1992) *The Red Hand; Protestant Paramilitaries in Northern Ireland*, Oxford: Oxford Paperbacks.
Bruce, S. (2004) 'Turf War and Peace: Loyalist Paramilitaries since 1994', *Terrorism and Political Violence*, 16(3): 501–521.
Bucholz, A. (1999) 'Militarism' in L. Kurtz (ed.), *Encyclopaedia of Peace and Conflict*, New York: Academic Press, Vol. 2, pp. 447–462.
Buruma, I. (1994) *The Wages of Guilt: Memories of War in Germany and Japan*, New York: Farrar Straus Giroux.
Butterfield, H. (1951) *History and Human Relations*, London: Collins.
Butterfield, H. (1953) *Christianity, Diplomacy and War*, London: Epworth Press.
Buzan, B. (1991) *People, States and Fear: An Agenda for International Security Studies in the Post-Cold War Era*, London, Harvester Wheatsheaf (2nd Edition).
Buzan, B. (1993) 'Societal Security, State Security and Internationalisation,' in O. Waever, B. Buzan, M. Kelstrup and P. Lemaitre, *Identity, Migration and the New Security Agenda in Europe*, London: Pinter, pp. 41–58.
Cadwallader, A. and Wilson, R. (1991) 'A Case of Any Catholic Will Do', *Fortnight: An Independent Review for Northern Ireland*, 6: 295.
Cairns, E. and Mícheál R. (eds) (2003) *The Role of Memory in Ethnic Conflict*. Basingstoke: Palgrave.
Carr, A., (December 1998) 'Michael White's Narrative Therapy', *Contemporary Family Therapy*, 20(4): 485–503.
Center for Civil and Human Rights (2006) 'Report of the Independent International Panel on Alleged Collusion in Sectarian Killings in Northern Ireland', Chicago, IL: Notre Dame Law School.
Chrisafis, A. 'Ulster truth commission planned' *The Guardian* (Tuesday, 6 April 2004) www.guardian.co.uk/Northern_Ireland/Story/0..1186520.00html, accessed 25 August 2007.
Cohen, D., Vandello, J. and Rantilla, A. K. (1998) 'The Sacred and the Social: Cultures of Honor and Violence', in Paul Gilbert and Bernice Andrews (eds), *Shame: Interpersonal Behaviour, Psychopathology and Culture*, New York: Oxford University Press, pp. 261–280.
Cohen, S. (1985) *Visions of Social Control: Crime, Punishment and Classification*, Cambridge: Polity Press.
Cohen, S. (2001) *States of Denial: Knowing about Atrocities and Suffering*, Cambridge: Polity.
Cooley, C. H. (1922) *Human Nature and Social Order*, New York: Scribner's.

194 Bibliography

Cory, P. (2004) *Cory Collusion Inquiry Report*, London: The Stationery Office, Online Available www.nio.gov.uk/index/nio-publication/nio-pubs-search-results.htm?category=Cory_Reports&keyword=&order=date&submitbutton.x=12&submitbutton.y=13, accessed 24 August 2007.

Crann, A. (2000) *Bear in Mind: Stories of the Troubles*, Belfast: Lagan Press.

Crocker, C. (1992) *High Noon in Southern Africa: Making Peace in a Rough Neighbourhood*, New York: W. W. Norton.

Crooke, E. (2001) 'Confronting a Troubled History: Which Past in Northern Ireland's Museums?' *International Journal of Heritage Studies*, 7(2): 119–136.

Darby, J. (2001) *The Effects of Violence on Peace Processes*, Washington, DC: United States Institute of Peace.

Darby, J. and McGinty, R. (2000) *The Management of Peace Processes*, Basingstoke: Macmillan.

Deane, S. (1996) *Reading in the Dark*, London: Vintage.

De Baroid, C. (1990) *Ballymurphy and the Irish War*, Belfast: Irish Books & Media.

Delgado, R. (1989) 'Storytelling for Oppositionists and Others: A Plea for Narrative', *Michigan Law Review*, 87(8): 2411–2441.

Democratic Unionist Party (2003) A Voice for Victims; The Democratic Unionist Party's policy on Innocent Victims of terrorism, Belfast: Democratic Unionist Party.

Democratic Unionist Party (19 February 2004) ' "Truth Commission and Amnesty the Last Thing Northern Ireland Needs" says Foster', Press Release, Democratic Unionist Party.

Democratic Unionist Party (22 February 2004) ' "Northern Ireland Doesn't Need or Want a Truth Commission" warns Ennis', Press Release: Democratic Unionist Party.

Democratic Unionist Party (14 April 2004) 'Government Must Address the Issue of Reconciliation', Belfast: DUP Press Release.

Democratic Unionist Party (28 March 2006) 'UUP Document "Utterly Vapid and Insulting to Victims" ', Belfast: DUP Press Release.

De Swaan, A. (1995) 'Widening Circles of Identification: Emotional Concerns in Sociogenetic Perspective', *Theory Culture Society*, 12: 25–39.

De Swaan, A. (1997) 'Widening Circles of Disidentification: On the Psycho- and Sociogenesis of the Hatred of Distant Strangers; Reflections on Rwanda', *Theory, Culture and Society*, 14(2): 105–122.

Dewey, J. (1927) *The Public and Its Problems*, New York: Henry Holt.

Edkins, J. (2003) *Trauma and the Memory of Politics*, Cambridge: Cambridge University Press.

Edmead, F. (1991) *Analysis and Prediction in International Mediation*, New York: UNITAR.

Elias, N. (1991) *The Society of Individuals*, edited by Michael Schröter, trans. Edmund Jephcott, Cambridge, MA: Basil Blackwell.

Elias, N. (1994) *The Civilising Process*, Oxford: Blackwell.

Emirbayer, M. and Goldberg, C. (2005) 'Pragmatism, Bourdieu, and Collective Emotions in Contentious Politics', *Theory and Society*, December, 34(5–6): 469–518(50).

Enloe, C. (2004) 'Margins, Silences and Bottom Rungs: How to Overcome the Underestimation of Power in the Study of International Relations', in C. Enloe, *The Curious Feminist: Searching for Women in a New Age of Empire*, Berkeley, CA: University of California Press, pp. 19–42.

Eolas Project/Relatives for Justice (2003) *Consultation Paper on Truth and Justice: A Discussion Document*, Belfast: Relatives for Justice.

EPIC (2004) *Truth Recovery: A Contribution from Within Loyalism*, Belfast: EPIC.
Ettin, M. F. (1988) 'By the Crowd They Have Been Broken, by the Crowd They Shall Be Healed: The Advent of Group Psychotherapy', *International Journal of Group Psychotherapy*, 38(2): 139–167.
European Court of Human Rights: Kelly v United Kingdom, App No 30054/96.
European Court of Human Rights: Jordan v 2001, United Kingdom, App No 24746/94.
European Court of Human Rights: Shanaghan v 2001, United Kingdom, App No 37715/97.
European Court of Human Rights: McKerr v United Kingdom, 34, Eur. Ct.H.R. 20, (2002).
European Court of Human Rights: McShane v United Kingdom, 35, Eur. Ct. H.R. 23, (2002).
European Court of Human Rights: Finucane, 2003, App No 2978/95.
Evans, G. and Duffy, M. (1997) 'Beyond the Sectarian Divide: The Social Bases and Political Consequences of Nationalist and Unionist Party Competition in Northern Ireland', *British Journal of Political Science*, 27: 47–81.
Farr, V. (2002) *Gendering Demilitarization as a Peacebuilding Tool*, Bonn: Bonn International Center for Conversion.
Farrington, C. (2006) 'Unionism and the Peace Process in Northern Ireland', *British Journal of Politics and International Relations*, 8: 277–294.
Fay, M. T., Morrissey, M. and Smyth, M. (1999) *Northern Ireland's Troubles: The Human Costs*, London: Pluto.
Feeney, B. (2002) *Sinn Féin: A Hundred Turbulent Years*, Dublin: O'Brien.
Feldman, A. (1991) *Formations of Violence: Narrative of the Body and Political Terror in Northern Ireland*, Chicago, IL: University of Chicago Press.
Finlayson, A. (1999) 'Loyalist Political Identity after Peace', *Capital and Class*, 69: 47–75.
Fischer, D. H. (1989) *Albion's Seed: British folkways in America*, New York: Oxford University Press.
Flackes, W. D. and Elliott, S. (1999 edn) *Northern Ireland: A Political Directory 1968–1988*, Belfast: Blackstaff.
Flanzbaum, H. (ed.) (1991) *The Americanization of the Holocaust*, Baltimore, MD: Johns Hopkins, Avon Books.
Frampton, M. (12 April 2005) 'Time for a Re-think?' *The Henry Jackson*, Online. Available http://zope06.v.servelocity.net/hjs/sections/northern_ireland/document.2005-04-21.8462124830 (accessed 11 March 2007).
Freedman, S. R. and Enright, R. D. (1996) 'Forgiveness as an Intervention Goal with Incest Survivors', *Journal of Consulting and Clinical Psychology*, 64: 983–992.
French, E. M. (1999) 'Democratization's Influence on CW Demilitarization: The Case of Russia', Paper to CWD99: The International CW Demil Conference, The Austria Centre, Vienna, Austria, 7–9 June 1999.
Freud, S. and Breuer, J. (1966) *Studies on Hysteria*, New York: Avon (originally published in 1895).
Gabriel, A. H. (1992) 'Grief and Rage: Collective Emotions in the Politics of Peace and the Politics of Gender in Israel' *Culture, Medicine and Psychiatry*, 16(3): 311–335.
George, A. L. (1979) 'Case Studies and Theory Development: The Method of Structured, Focused Comparison', in P. G. Lauren (ed.), *Diplomacy: New Approaches in History, Theory and Policy*, New York, Free Press, pp. 43–68.
Gill, G. (2000) *The Dynamics of Democratization: Elites, Civil Society and the Transition Process*, Basingstoke: Macmillan.

Bibliography

Gobodo-Madikizela, P. (2004) *A Human Being Died That Night: A South African Woman Confronts the Legacy of Apartheid*, Boston, MA: Mariner.

Goffman, I. (1959) *The Presentation of the Self in Everyday Life*, Harmondsworth: Penguin.

Goffman, I. (1963) *Stigma*, Englewood Cliffs, NJ: Prentice Hall.

Gormley-Heenan, C. (2005) 'Abdicated and Assumed Responsibilities? The Multiple Roles of Political Leadership during the Northern Ireland Peace Process', *Civil Wars*, 7(3): 195–218.

Haass, R. N. (1990) *Conflicts Unending; The United States and Regional Disputes*, New Haven, CT: Yale University Press.

Habermas, Jurgen (1980) 'Discourse Ethics: Notes on Philosophical Justification,' *Moral Consciousness and Communicative Action*, Trans. Christian Lenhart and Shierry Weber Nicholson, Cambridge, MA: MIT Press, pp. 43–115.

Habermas, J. (1990) *Moral Consciousness and Communicative Action*, Cambridge: Polity Press.

Hamber, B. (ed.) (1998) *Past Imperfect; Dealing with the Past in Northern Ireland and Societies in Transition*, Derry Londonderry: INCORE.

Hamber, B. (2004) 'Rights and Reasons: Challenges for Truth Recovery in South Africa and Northern Ireland', *Fordham International Law Journal*, 26(4): 1074–1094.

Hamber, B. and Wilson, R. (eds) (2003) *Recognition and Reckoning: The Way Ahead on Victims Issues*, Belfast Democratic Dialogue.

Hamber, B., Kulle, D. and Wilson, R. (eds) (2001) *Future Policies for the Past*, Belfast: Democratic Dialogue.

Hansard, 1 April 2004, Column 1765.

Harris, A. H., Luskin F., Norman S. B., Standard S., Bruning J., Evans S. and Thoresen C. E. (2006) 'Effects of a Group Forgiveness Intervention on Forgiveness, Perceived Stress and Trait-Anger', *Journal of Clinical Psychiatry*, 62(6): 715–733.

Hauswedell C. and Brown, K. (eds) (2002) *Burying the Hatchet: The Decommissioning of Paramilitary Arms in Northern Ireland*, Bonn: Bonn International Center for Conversion/Initiative on Conflict Resolution and Ethnicity.

Hayes, P. J. and Campbell, J. (2005) *Bloody Sunday: Trauma, Pain and Politics*, London: Pluto.

Hayner, P. (1994) 'Fifteen Truth Commissions – 1974–1994: A Comparative Study', *Human Rights Quarterly*, 16: 597–655.

Hayner, P. (2001) *Unspeakable Truths: Confronting State Terror and Atrocity, How Truth Commissions around the World Are Challenging the Past and Shaping the Future*, New York: Routledge.

Healing Through Remembering (2002) *The Report of the Healing Through Remembering Project*. Belfast: Healing Through Remembering.

Healing Through Remembering (2005) 'Storytelling' Audit; An Audit of Personal Story, Narrative and Testimony Initiatives Related to the Conflict in and about Northern Ireland, Belfast: Healing Through Remembering.

Healing Through Remembering (2006) *Making Peace with the Past: Options for Truth Recovery Regarding the Conflict in and about Northern Ireland*, Belfast: Healing Through Remembering.

Herz, J. (1951) *Political Realism and Political Idealism*, Chicago, IL: University of Chicago Press.

Hillyard, P. (1993) *Suspect Community*, London: Pluto.

Holbrooke, R. (1999) *To End a War*, New York: Random House.

Holland and McDonald (1994) *INLA: Deadly Divisions*, Dublin: Poolbeg Press.
Hoynes, W. (1994) *Public Television for Sale, Media, the Market and the Public Sphere*, Boulder: Westview Press.
Hunter, D. (1946) 'The Work of a Corps Psychiatrist in the Italian Campaign', *Journal of the Royal Army Medical Corps*, 86: 127–130.
Hutchinson, J. (1987) *The Dynamics of Cultural Nationalism: The Gaelic Revival and the Creation of the Irish Nation State*, London: Allen and Unwin.
Ignatieff, M, (1998) *The Warrior's Honour: Ethnic War and the Modern Consciousness*, New York: Henry Holt.
Irish Government's Houses of the Oireachtas Joint Committee on Justice, Equality, Defence and Women's Rights (2006) *Final Report of the Independent Commission of Inquiry into the Bombing of Kay's Tavern Dundalk*, Dublin: The Stationery Office.
Irish Information Partnership (1989) *Information Service on Northern Ireland Conflict and Anglo-Irish Affairs, Agenda*, London: Irish Information Partnership.
Irish News (Monday 12 June 2006) 'Reaching out to Loyalists in a Bid to Secure a Settled Future', Interview of Sir Reg Empey by Steven McCaffery, pp. 14–15.
Jenkins, R. (2003) 'Review: Ardoyne; The Untold Truth', *The Global Review of Ethnopolitics*, 3(1): 107–108.
Judt, T. (2001) 'America and the War', New York Review of Books, 15 November 2001, 4–6, in Leo Braudy, (2003) *From Chivalry to Terrorism: War and Changing the Nature of Masculinity*, New York: Knopf, p. 547.
Kitson, F. (1973) *Low Intensity Operations: Subversion, Insurgency and Peacekeeping*, London: Faber and Faber.
Kitson, F. (1977) *Bunch of Five*, London: Faber and Faber.
Kleiboer, M. (1994) 'Ripeness of Conflict: A Fruitful Notion?' *Journal of Peace Research*, 31(1): 109–116.
Knox, C. and Monaghan, R. (2002) *Informal Justice in Divided Societies: Northern Ireland and South Africa*, London: Palgrave Macmillan.
Knox, C. and Quirk, P (2000) *Peacebuilding in Northern Ireland, Israel and South Africa: Transition, Transformation and Reconciliation*, London: Macmillan.
Krog, A. (1999) *Country of My Skull*, London: Vintage.
Lamb, G. (2000) 'Reflections on Demilitarization: A Southern African Perspective', *International Peacekeeping*, 7(3): 118–125.
Lasch, C. (1984) *The Minimal Self*, New York: W. W. Norton.
Lasch, C. (1991) *The Culture of Narcissism*, New York: W. W. Norton.
Lebovic, J. H. and Voeten, E. (2006) 'The Politics of Shame: The Condemnation of Country Human Rights Practices in the UNHCR.' *International Studies Quarterly*, 50(4): December 2006, pp. 861–888.
Lederach, J. P. (1997) *Building Peace: Sustainable Reconciliation in Divided Societies*, Washington, DC: USIP Press.
Lederach, J. P. (2002) *Building Peace: Sustainable Reconciliation in Divided Societies*, Washington, DC: United States Institute of Peace.
Levi, P. (1989) 'Shame' in P. Levi, *The Drowned and the Saved*, London: Abacus, pp. 70–87.
Levi, P. (1996) *Survival in Auschwitz*, London: Pocket Books.
Lewis, B. (1999) *Fishers of Men*, London: Hodder and Stoughton.
Lindsay, K. (1981) *The British Intelligence Services in Action*, Ballyclare: Dundrod.
McAuley, J. (2003) 'Unionism's Last Stand? Contemporary Unionist Politics and Identity in Northern Ireland', *The Global Review of Ethnopolitics*, 3(1): 60–74.
McGarry, J. and O'Leary, B. (1995) *Explaining Northern Ireland*, Oxford: Blackwell.

McKittrick, D., Seamus, K., Feeney, B. and Thornton, C. (1999) *Lost Lives: The stories of the Men, Women and Children Who Died as a Result of the Northern Ireland Troubles*, London: Mainstream.

McWilliams, M. (1993) *Bringing It Out in the Open: Domestic Violence in Northern Ireland: A Study*, Belfast: HMSO.

Maguire, M. (1973) *To Take Arms: A Year in the Provisional IRA*, London: Macmillan.

Mearsheimer, J. (1990) 'Back to the Future: Instability in Europe after the Cold War', *International Security*, 15(1): 15–56.

Mearsheimer, J. (1992) 'Disorder Restored' in G. Allison and G.F. Treverton (eds), *Rethinking America's Security*, New York, WW Norton, pp. 213–237.

Meintjes, S. (2001) 'War and Post-War Shifts in Gender Relations' in S. Meintjes, A. Pillay, and M. Turshen, *The Aftermath: Women in Post-Conflict Transformation*, London: Zed, pp. 63–77.

Meyer, R. (2003) 'Paradigm Shift: The Essence of Successful Change', INCORE Working Paper, Derry Londonderry, INCORE, University of Ulster, January 2003.

Minow, M. (1998) *Between Vengeance and Forgiveness*, Boston, MA: Beacon Press.

Mitchell, C. (1995) 'The Right Moment: Notes on Four Models of "Ripeness"', *Paradigms*, 9(2): 35–52.

Mitchell, C. R. (1989) 'Conflict Resolution and Civil War; Reflections on the Sudanese Settlement of 1972', Institute for Conflict Analysis and Resolution, George Mason University Working Paper No 3, August 1989.

Moloney, E. Speech on the peace process, Presented at Court Case Victory Party, Rocky Sullivan's Pub, NY, Wednesday, 5 January 2000. Available www.rockysullivans.com/eventsarchive2.html (accessed 11 March 2007).

Moloney, E. (2002) *A Secret History of the IRA*, London: New York: Allen Lane/Penguin.

Moore, B. Jr (2000) *Moral Purity and Persecution in History*, Princeton, NJ: Princeton University Press.

Morrissey, M. and Smyth, M. (2001) 'Sectarian Deaths in Northern Ireland and Hate Crimes in the United States', *British/Irish Social Policy Association Annual Conference*, Belfast, June 2001.

Morrissey, M. and Smyth, M. (2002) *Northern Ireland after the Good Friday Agreement: Victims, Grievance and Blame*, London: Pluto.

Mowlam, M. (2002) *Momentum: The Struggle for Peace, Politics and the People*, London: Hodder and Stoughton.

Murray, R. (1998) *State Violence: Northern Ireland 1960–1997*, Cork and Dublin: Mercier.

Murtagh, B. (1994) 'Ethnic Space and the Challenge to Land Use Planning: A Study of Belfast's Peace Lines', Belfast: Centre for Policy Research, Paper 7.

Myre, G. (2003) 'Palestinians and Israelis Still Speaking in a Whisper', *New York Times* (4 November 2003), Late edition, Section A, p. 12. col. 6.

Ni Aoláin, F. (2000) *The Politics of Force*, Belfast: Blackstaff.

Nora, P. (1996) *Realms of Memory: Rethinking the French Past/Under the Direction of Pierre Nora*; foreword by Lawrence D. Kritzman; trans. Arthur Goldhammer, New York; Chichester: Columbia University Press.

Northern Ireland Affairs Committee, House of Commons, 'Ways of Dealing with Northern Ireland's Past: Interim Report – Victims and Survivors: Tenth Report of Session 2004–5 Volume I', London: The Stationery Office, 14 April 2005.

Northern Ireland Affairs Committee, House of Commons, 'Ways of Dealing with Northern Ireland's Past: Interim Report – Victims and Survivors: Tenth Report of Session 2004–5 Volume II Oral and Written evidence', London: The Stationery Office, 14 April 2005.

Northern Ireland Affairs Committee, House of Commons, 'Ways of Dealing with Northern Ireland's Past: Interim Report – Victims and Survivors: Government Response to the Committee's Tenth Report of the Session 2004–5. Sixth Special Report of Session 2005–6', London: The Stationery Office, 14 April 2005.

Northern Ireland Life and Times/ Patricia Lundy, 'Cautious Support for an Irish Truth Commission,' Coleraine: University of Ulster, press release, 11 July 2005. Online. Available HTTP: www.ulster.ac.uk/news/releases/2005/1776.html (accessed 20 May 2006)

Northern Ireland Office (NIO) (2003) Research and Statistical Series: No.7 – Who Are the Victims? Self-Assessed Victimhood and the Northern Irish conflict, Belfast: The Sationery Office.

Northern Ireland Statistics and Research Agency (1997) *Northern Ireland Annual Abstract of Statistics*, Belfast: The Stationery Office.

O'Connor, F. (1993) *In Search of a State: Catholics in Northern Ireland*, Belfast: Blackstaff.

O'Reilly D. and Stevenson, M. (2003) 'Selective Migration from Deprived Areas in Northern Ireland and the Spatial Distribution of Inequalities: Implications for Monitoring Health and Inequalities in Health', *Health, Social Science and Medicine*, 57(8): 1455–1462.

Paris, R. (2004) *At War's End: Building Peace after Civil Conflict*, Cambridge: Cambridge University Press.

Patočka, J. (1996) 'Heretical Essays in the Philosophy of History' trans. Erazim Kohák edited by James Dodd, Chicago, IL: Open Court.

Pattison, S. (2000) *Shame: Theory, Therapy and Theology*, Cambridge: Cambridge University Press.

Perry, B. (1997) 'Incubated in Terror: Neurodevelopmental Factors in the "Cycle of Violence"' in J. D. Osofsky, *Children in a Violent Society*, New York: Guildford, pp. 124–149.

An Phoblacht, Republican News, Thursday 31 January 2002. Online. Available at http://republican-news.org/archive/2002/November21/21new2.html (accessed 25 August 2007).

Police Ombudsman for Northern Ireland (2007) 'Statement by the Police Ombudsman for Northern Ireland on her investigation into the circumstances surrounding the death of Raymond McCord Junior and related matters', Belfast, Police Ombudsman's Office.

Poole, M. (1993) 'The Spatial Distribution of Political Violence in Northern Ireland: An Update to 1993' in A. O'Day, (ed.), *Terrorism's Laboratory: The Case of Northern Ireland*. Aldershot: Dartmouth, pp. 27–45.

Posen, B. R. (1993) 'The Security Dilemma and Ethnic Conflict' in M. E. Brown (ed) *Ethnic Conflict and International Security*. Princeton NJ: Princeton University Press.

Rolston, B. (2000) *Unfinished Business: State Killings and the Quest for Truth*, Belfast: Beyond the Pale.

Rothschild, M. (2000) 'Transforming Our Legacies: Heroic Journeys for Children of Holocaust Survivors and Nazi Perpetrators', *Journal of Humanistic Psychology*, 40(3): 43–55.

Roy, A. (1998) *The God of Small Things*, Flamingo.

Ruane, J. and Todd, J. (1996) *The Dynamics of the Conflict in Northern Ireland: Power, Conflict and Emancipation*, Cambridge: Cambridge University Press.

Sanders, J. (2006) *Apartheid's Friends: The Rise and Fall of South Africa's Secret Service*, London: John Murray.

Scheff, T. (1997) *Emotions, the Social Bond and Human Reality*, Cambridge: Cambridge University Press.

Scheff, T. J. (2003) 'Shame in Self and Society', *Symbolic Interaction*, 26(2): 239–262.
Scheff, T. J. (2004) 'Elias, Freud and Goffman: Shame as the Master Emotion', in S. Loyal and S. Quilley (eds), *The Sociology of Norbert Elias*, Cambridge: Cambridge University Press, pp. 229–244.
Sennett, R. (1993) *Authority*, London: Faber and Faber.
Shirlow, P. (2003) ' "Who Fears to Speak": Mobility and Ethno-sectarianism in the Two "Ardoynes" ', *The Global Review of Ethnopolitics*, 3(1): 76–91.
Shirlow, P. and McGovern, M. (1997) *Who are the People? Unionism, Protestantism and Loyalism in Northern Ireland*, London: Pluto.
Shirlow, P. and Murtagh, B. (2006) *Belfast: Segregation, Violence and the City*, London: Pluto.
Shorter, E. (1998) *A History of Psychiatry: From the Era of the Asylum to the Age of Prozac*, New York: John Wiley.
Showalter, E. (1987) *The Female Malady: Women, Madness and English Culture 1830–1980*, London: Virago.
Sieder, R. (2001) 'War, Peace and Memory Politics in Central America' in A. Barahona de Brito, C. Gonzaléz-Enríquez, and P. Aguilar, *The Politics of Memory: Transitional Justice in Democratizing Societies*, Oxford: Oxford University Press, pp. 161–189.
Smyth, G. and Graham, S. (2003) *Forgiveness, Reconciliation and Justice*, Belfast: Centre for Contemporary Christianity/ECONI.
Smyth, M. (1998) 'Remembering in Northern Ireland: Victims, Perpetrators and Hierarchies of Pain and Responsibility' in B. Hamber (ed.), *Past Imperfect: Dealing with the Past in Northern Ireland and Societies in Transition*, Derry Londonderry: INCORE, pp. 31–49.
Smyth, M. (1998) *Half the Battle: Understanding the Impact of the Troubles on Children and Young People*, Derry Londonderry, INCORE / the United Nations University and the University of Ulster.
Smyth, M. *Cost of the Troubles Study, Do You Know What's Happened? Personal Accounts and Images of the Troubles*, Touring exhibition, Opened November, 1998 by Secretary of State for NI, Dr Marjorie Mowlam, The Great Hall, Belfast City Hall; toured venues, including House of Commons, Westminster, Glasgow, Dublin.
Smyth, M. (1999) 'Working with the Aftermath of Violent Political Division' in H. Kelmshall, and J. Pritchard, *Good Practice in Working with Violence*, London: Jessica Kingsley, pp. 195–212.
Smyth, M. (2000) *The Cost of the Troubles Study/Northern Visions and then There Was Silence*, feature documentary/training video with accompanying training notes. 90 minutes. Northern Visions.
Smyth, M. (2000) 'The Role of Victims in the Northern Ireland Peace Process.' in A. Guelke and M. Cox, *A Farewell to Arms: From War to Peace in Northern Ireland*, Manchester University Press.
Smyth, M. (2001) 'The "Discovery" and Treatment of Trauma in Northern Ireland' in Democratic Dialogue *Future Policies for the Past*, Belfast: Democratic Dialogue, pp. 57–64.
Smyth, M. (2003) 'Burying the Past? Victims and Community Relations in Northern Ireland Since the Cease-fires', in N. Biggar, (ed.), *Burying the Past: Making Peace and Doing Justice after Civil Conflict*, Washington, DC: Georgetown University Press, pp. 125–154.
Smyth, M. (2004) 'The Process of Demilitarisation and the Reversibility of the Peace Process in Northern Ireland', *Terrorism and Political Violence*, Special issue on Northern Ireland 16(3): 1–23.

Smyth, Marie, (2004) *The Impact of Political Conflict on Children in Northern Ireland: A Report on the Community Conflict Impact on Children Study*, Belfast: Institute for Conflict Research.

Smyth, M. and Fay, M. T. (2000) *Personal Accounts of Northern Ireland's Troubles: Public Chaos, Private Loss*, London: Pluto.

Smyth, M. and Joy D., *Do You See What I See? Young People's Experience of the Troubles in Their Own Words and Photographs*. Opened May, 1998, by Assistant Secretary of State for NI, Adam Ingram in University of Ulster School of Art and Design, York Street, toured various venues in Northern Ireland, England and the Irish Republic.

Smyth, M. and Morrissey, M. (2002) *Northern Ireland after the Good Friday Agreement; Victims, Grievance and Blame*, London: Pluto.

Smyth, M., Fay, M. T., Morrissey, M. and Wong, T. (1999) *Report on the Northern Ireland Survey: The Experience and Impact of the Troubles*, Derry Londonderry, INCORE/the United Nations University and the University of Ulster.

Smyth, M., Hayes, E. and Hayes, P. (1994) 'Post Traumatic Stress and Victims of Violence in Northern Ireland: The case of the Families of the Bloody Sunday Victims', Centre for the Study of Conflict/N.I. Association for Mental Health Conference on Violence and Mental Health, Queen's University, September 1994.

Snyder, J. (1993) 'The New Nationalism: Realist Interpretations and Beyond', in Richard Rosencrance and Arthur A. Stein (eds), *The Domestic Bases of Grand Strategy*, Ithaca, NY: Cornell University Press.

Stedman, S. J. (1991) *Peacemaking in Civil War; International Mediation in Zimbabwe 1974–1980*, Boulder, CO: Lynne Reinner.

Stedman, S. J., Rothchild, D. and Cousens, E. (2002) *Ending Civil Wars: The Implementation of Peace Agreements*, London: Lynne Rienner.

Stevens, J. (2003) *The Stephens Inquiry*, Belfast; The Stationery Office. Online. Available at: www.serve.com/pfc/

Straker, G. (1987) 'The Continuous Traumatic Stress Syndrome – the Single Therapeutic Interview', *Psychology in Society*, 8: 8–79.

Suarez-Orozco, M. (1991) 'The Heritage of Enduring a Dirty War: Psychological Aspects of Terror in Argentian', *Jounral of Psychohistory*, 18(4): 469–505.

Sutton, M. (1994) *Bear in Mind These Dead...An Index of Deaths from the Conflict in Ireland 1969–1993*, Belfast: Beyond the Pale Publications.

Swap, W. L. D., Shields, M. and Abrams, L. (2001) 'Using Mentoring and Storytelling to Transfer Knowledge in the Workplace', *Journal of Management Information Systems* 18(1): 95–114.

Tangney, J. P. and Dearing, R. L. (2003) *Shame and Guilt*, New York: Guilford.

Taylor, P. (1999) *Loyalists*, London: Bloomsbury.

Teger, A. I. (1980) *Too Much Invested to Quit*, New York: Pergamon Press.

Thomas, L. M. (1999) 'Suffering as a Moral Beacon: Blacks and Jews', in H. Flanzbaum, (ed.) *The Americanization of the Holocaust*, Baltimore, MD: Johns Hopkins, pp. 198–210.

Tomlinson, M. (1995) 'Can Britain Leave Ireland? The Political Economy of War and Peace', *Race and Class*, 37(1): 1–22.

Turner, B. S. (2004) 'Weber and Elias on Religion and Violence: Warrior Charisma and the Civilising Process' in S. Loyal and S. Quilley, *The Sociology of Norbert Elias*, Cambridge, Cambridge University Press, pp. 245–264.

Tutu, D. (1999) *No Future without Forgiveness*, New York: Doubleday.

Ulster Unionist Party (14 April 2004) 'Truth Commission a Carvery for Republicans', Ulster Unionist Party Press Release.
Ulster Unionist Party (2 December 2005) 'Hermon: Victims Deserve Justice and Truth', Belfast, UUP Press release.
UN High Commission on Human Rights Report of the Special Rapporteur to the Commission on Human Rights at its fifty-fourth session on his mission to the United Kingdom, Geneva: United Nations High Commissioner for Human Rights in Geneva, 1998, (E/CN.4/1998/39/Add.4).
Unionist Group, The (2006) 'Drawing a Line under the Past, the Unionist Group', Belfast, 16 March 2006.
United Nations Human Rights Committee, 73rd Session, Concluding Observations of the Human Rights Committee: United Kingdom of Great Britain and Northern Ireland. CCPR/CO/73/UK;CCPR/CO/73/UKOT. Geneva: Office of the United Nations High Commissioner for Human Rights, 6 December 2001.
Wacquant, L. (2004) 'Decivilising and Demonizing; The Remaking of the Black American Ghetto' in S. Loyal and S. Quilley, *The Sociology of Norbert Elias*, Cambridge: Cambridge University Press, pp. 95–21.
Waever, O. (1994) 'Insecurity and Identity Unlimited.' COPRI Working Paper, no. 14: 19.
Walzer, M. (2000) *Just and Unjust Wars: a Moral Argument with Historical Illustrations* (third ed), New York: Basic Books.
Wilford, R. and Wilson, R. (2001) 'A Democratic Design? The political style of the Northern Ireland Assembly', Belfast: Democratic Dialogue.
Williams, B. (1994) *Shame and Necessity*, Berkeley, CA: University of California Press.
Williams, P. and Scharf, M. (2002) *Peace with Justice: War Crimes and Accountability in the Former Yugoslavia*, New York: Rowman and Littlefield.
Winer, S. (2003) 'South Africa, the High Price of Appeasement', ZNet. Online. Available at: www.zmag.org/content/showarticle.cfm?ItemID=2984 (accessed 28 January 2007).
Young, A. (1995) *The Harmony of Illusions: Inventing Post-Traumatic Stress Disorder*, Princeton, NJ: Princeton.
Zartman, I. W. (1985) *Ripe for Resolution: Conflict and Intervention in Africa*, New York: Oxford University Press.
Zartman, I. W. (1999) *Preventive Negotiation*, Washington, DC: Rowman and Littlehead.
Zeitlin, S. B., McNally, R. J., and Cassiday, K. L. (1993) 'Alexithymia in Victims of Sexual Assault: An Effect of Repeated Traumatization?', *American Journal of Psychiatry*, 150: 661–663.
Zussman, A. and Zussman, N. (2006) 'Assassinations: Evaluating the Effectives of Counterterrorism Using Stockmarket Data', *Journal of Economic Perspectives*, 20(2): 193–206.

Index

absolute truth 23–24; victims' desire for 28–30
acknowledgment 16, 133–134; collective 125; victims' need for 73
Adams, Gerry 112, 114
Allister, Jim 163
amnesty 13; qualifications for 79
An, Pham Xuan 36
Andrews, Esther (NIAC witness) 136
anger of victims 68–69
Apartheid: shame and 41–42; support for 41–42, 185 n.10; support for Apartheid following transition 41, 42
apologies 18; forgiveness and 87, 88; German 43; Loyalist 166; need for perpetrator's 136
Ardoyne Commemoration Project in Northern Belfast 28, 117
Arendt, Hannah: on victim/perpetrator status 82–84, 176
armed conflicts: fatal effects of 67–68; fatal effects of, in Northern Ireland 99–105; shame during 48–53, 57–62, 65; threat to life and 57–58
Armstrong, Billy 161
Association of the Bar of the City of New York (ABCNY), Committee on International Human Rights 148
Azanian People's Organisation (AZAPO) 13

BBC Northern Ireland: 'reality television' programmes 18
Beggs, Roy (NIAC member) 109, 110, 131
Belfast Agreement 4; Unionists' divergent attitudes to 167
Belinda, Lesley 18
Biko, Ntsiki 13
Biko, Steve 170

Bin Laden, Osama 55
Blair, Tony 54
blood money 73–74, 88, 133
Bloody Sunday 29, 156
Bloody Sunday Inquiry 92, 129; costs associated with 179; failure of British cooperation with 96; influence on public opinion on truth recovery 143–144; victims' need for acknowledgement and 73
Boal, Ann 129
Boeremag (Boer Force) (S. Africa) 41
Boraine, Alex: on forgiveness 17–18
Botha, P.W. 41, 169, 170; refusal to appear before TRC 34
Bradley, Denis 154, 160
British Army: fatalities in Northern Ireland conflict 100–104; killings by 112–113; warrior honour 55–56; *see also* Northern Ireland Veterans' Association
British government: attitude towards public inquiries into controversial killings 171; disposition to truth recovery 141–143, 144, 152–155, 170–171, 178; internal politics within 154–155; Nationalists lack of confidence 143; NIAC witnesses' concerns about government's role 127; SDLP and Sinn Féin's campaign against 157; UNHRC's observation of 147–148
Burnside, David 161
Bush, George 54, 97

Campbell, Gregory (NIAC member) 109, 137, 172
Christianity: absolutism vs. relativism 23–24
civilising process, Eliasian 7, 44, 61, 63, 175

civil society: role in truth recovery process 16–17
collective acknowledgement 125
collective emotions: role in social movements 68
collective forgiveness 19
collective responsibility 124–125, 179
Community Foundation 116, 124
community inquiries 27–28
Community Relations Council 118; reservations about timing of truth recovery process 120–121
confessions: truth recovery and 11
conflicts: effects of long term exposure to 30–31; human costs of 8–9; media's role during 11–12; in Northern Ireland 93, 96; silence associated with 26–27; truth and 30; *see also* armed conflicts
containment: truth recovery and 15–16
continuous traumatic stress syndrome 71
Cook, Robin 47
Cooper, Rosie (NIAC member) 109
Cory, Peter 154
Cory report 143, 154, 161
cross-community work 137–138
culture of silence 26–27, 33–34
'custom of violence' 62–63

damages: distribution of 9
Deane, Mrs. Barbara (NIAC witness) 136
deaths: British government's attitude towards public inquiries into 171; NIAC and 112–113; Northern Ireland conflict and 67–68, 99–105, 148–149; parties' burden of responsibility for 150; unsolved cases in Northern Ireland 13, 14, 95, 104–105, 148, 150
decivilisation process 59–60
degradation: shame and 50–51
Democratic Dialogue (NGO) 115
Democratic Unionist Party (DUP) 106, 160; Allister's attack on 164; Assembly elections 2007 165; rivalry between UUP and 168
denial: as coping mechanism 72, 86; potential for ending 6–8
dialogical truth 27–28, 175
Dickson, Brice (NIAC witness) 118–119, 127
Disabled Police Officers Association (DPOA) 116, 129, 135
discourses: access to discourses of "other" 8; of conflict 58; Habermas's rules of 10; inclusive history 9; incorporation of new material 10–11; of victimhood 78–79
disidentification: victimhood and 76–77
Donaldson, Denis 37, 143
Dover, Jo (NIAC witness): on timing of truth recovery process 119; on value of storytelling approach 118
Drawing a Line Under the Past 162–163
Dublin and Monagham bombings (1974) 156
Durkan, Mark 157
Du Toit, Andre 79

economic informalisation 60
Elias, Norbert 7; civilising process of 44, 61, 63, 175; notion of shame 44–45, 175
embarrassment 45
Empey, Reg 164, 168
enemy: objectification of 7
Ennis, Alderman George 160
Enticing Opportunity Model 145
Eolas 117, 134–135
Ervine, David 164, 167
ethnic identity: conflicts and 57–58
European Court of Human Rights 147
evil deeds: victimisation and 82–84
Ex-Prisoners Interpretative Centre (EPIC): members' evidence to NIAC 112, 121, 122; position on truth recovery process 164–167, 172

Families Achieving Change Together (FACT): members' evidence to NIAC 122, 130; rejection of truth recovery model 125–126
Families Acting for Innocent Relatives (FAIR) 20, 69, 76; memorandum to NIAC 130; remarriage after violent loss of partner and 74
Finucane, Pat 106, 148, 154, 156
Firinne 117, 140
forensic truth 25–26
forgiveness 17, 18–20, 86–87, 176; Christian approach to 88, 176; collective 19; functions of 19; S. African truth recovery process and 17–18, 86, 87, 169
Foster, Arlene 160
Frazer, William (NIAC witness) 20, 126, 172

Gallagher, Michael (NIAC witness) 129, 137
German identity: shame and 42–44
German pacifism: post war 43–44
Germany: truth recovery process 53–54
Gibson, Chris (NIAC witness) 118, 129
Good Friday Agreement (1998) 9, 89, 91, 92, 113; institutional change and 95; truth recovery and 143, 169; Unionists fears about impact of 97–98
Gourley, Celia (NIAC witness) 135
Grigg, Mrs. Gillian (NIAC witness) 135

Haass, Richard 97–98
Hackett, Sylvia 18
Hadden, Tom (NIAC witness) 114, 127
Halberstam, David 36
Haven Project 119
healing: collective dimension of 85–86; South African truth recovery process and 84
Healing Through Remembering project 3, 26, 115, 119, 120, 132, 141
healing truth *see* restorative truth
Hepburn, Stephen (NIAC member) 124
Hermon, Sylvia (NIAC member) 109
Hicks, Donna 18
Hillier, Meg (NIAC member) 109
Historical Clarification Commission (Comisión de Esclarectimiento Histórico) (Guatemala) 169
Holland, Tim (NIAC witness) 117
Holocaust: Arendt's approach to victim identity and 83; *see also* Levi, Primo
Homes United by Recurring Terror (HURT) 76
honour: violence and 56
humanitarian assistance 69; medical needs 70–73, 132
Hunter, Janet (NIAC witness) 122, 126, 130

identity: ethnic 57–58; German 42–44; societal security dilemma and 95; victims 67–69, 76–79
Imminent Mutual Catastrophe 144
impression management 45
impunity 12–14
Independent International Panel on Alleged Collusion in Sectarian Killings in Northern Ireland 148–149
Independent Monitoring Commission 116, 187 n.9

Inkatha Freedom Party (IFP) 41
insurgency: victimhood and association with 77
internecine violence 120, 180
Irish: as suspect community 25
Irish government: disposition on truth recovery process 155–156
Irish Republican Army (IRA) 63; Loyalists fear of intentions of 152–153; responsibility for fatalities 106; Unionists grievances against 92, 160–161

Jameson, Mr. William (NIAC witness) 131
justice: victims' need for 73

Khulamani 69, 185 n.10
Kilmurray, Avila: on goals of reconciliation 134; on Loyalist anxieties about truth recovery 124; on truth recovery model 125–126

Las Madres de Plaza de Mayo (Argentina) 20, 38, 69, 78; reparations and 73–74
law: truth and 24–25
Levi, Primo 19; account of shame 40, 83; caution about his memoir 32–33; feeling of degradation 50–51; on forgiveness 87; shame at inadequate efforts at resistance 49–50; shame at non-participation 49; shame at others deeds 51–53; on transition in Auschwitz camp 60–61
Lewsley, Patricia 156
Liberation Tigers of Tamil Eelam (LTTE) 55
life: threat to 57–58
Loyalists of Northern Ireland: anxieties about truth recovery process 123–126; external influences on 149; fatalities pattern 99–104; fatal rivalry between paramilitaries of 168; fear of IRA intentions 152; internal politics of 168–169; overall level of authority and responsibility 150–151; position on truth recovery process 164–167; relationship between security forces and 164–165; responsibility for killings 150, 187 n.9
Loyalist Ulster Defence Association 37
Ludlow, Seamus 155
Luke, Iain (NIAC member) 117, 141
Lundy, Patricia 153

McCartney, Robert 143
McClelland, Roy (NIAC witness) 116, 132
McCord, Raymond, Jr. 154, 160
McDonnell, Alasdair (NIAC member) 109
McGrady, Eddie (NIAC member) 109, 110
McGregor, Elizabeth 113
McGuinness, Martin 92
McMullan, Jackie 158–159
Mandela, Nelson 34, 41
masculinity: honour and 56
Mates, Michael (NIAC chair) 110–111, 112, 140; moral preoccupations of 113–114
meaning: Habermasian literal 10
media: role during conflict 11–12; role in contemporary western democracies 47
Mitchell, Marion 131, 136
moral superiority 14–15; victimhood and 74–75, 87, 176
Morris, John 156
Mowlam, Mo 78
Mtimkulu, Joyce 19
Murphy, Paul 126, 140–141, 164
Mxenge, Griffiths 170
Mxenge, Mbasa 13

narcissism: shame and 46
narrative truth 22, 26, 175
Nasiri, Omar 36
National Commissioner for Human Rights (Honduras) 169
National Guatemalan Revolutionary Unity (URNG) 169
Nationalists of Northern Ireland: on constitutional issue 97; grievances of 92, 96; internal politics of 159; lack of confidence on British government 143; NIAC's members approach to Nationalists witnesses 111–115; position on truth recovery process 156–157; representation in NIAC 109–110; support for truth recovery process 115–116, 117–118
National Unity and Reconciliation Act (S. Africa) 13
Nazis: denial of common humanity 53
Nelson, Brian 36, 37
Nelson, Rosemary 106, 148
New Lodge (Belfast) community inquiry 27–28

Northern Ireland: British-based victims 116, 130–132; cold case review 13, 14; continuation of conflict 93; fatal effects of conflict 67–68, 95; fatal effects of conflict, patterns of 99–105; fatal effects of conflict, responsibility for 105; 'innocent victims' portrayal of conflict in 95–96; predominant discourses in 95–97; public opinion on truth recovery process 143–144; societal security dilemma and 95; victim needs 86; victim status 79–80
Northern Ireland Affairs Committee (NIAC) 4–5, 91, 108–109, 177–178; approach to witnesses 111–115; composition of 109–111; concerns about government's role represented to 127–128; concerns about models of truth recovery represented to 125–127, 152; concerns about reconciliation represented to 127, 134–138; concerns about role of victims represented to 129–132; conclusions of 139–140, 143, 151–154, 171; deferment of truth recovery represented to 118–122; distribution of evidence by political affiliation/status 108–109, 110–111; evidence on reparations 132–133; members' concerns 129; opposition to truth recovery represented to 122–125, 171–173; support for truth recovery represented to 115–118
Northern Ireland Human Rights Commission: reservations about timing of truth recovery process 118–119; stress on truth and reconciliation 127
Northern Ireland Veterans' Association: reconciliation work with ex-prisoner groups 135; stand on truth recovery process 116, 117–118, 122; on timing of truth recovery process 121; views on trust in government's motivation in truth recovery 127–128

objectification of enemy 7
O'Connor, Paul (NIAC witness) 112, 117, 128, 131, 140
O'Loan, Nuala: report on Police Ombudsman 63–64
Omagh Support and Help Group 129, 130–131
One Small Step Campaign 129

Orde, Sir Hugh 63, 154
organised lying 35–38, 175; impact on one's personality 36–37

pacifism: post war Germany 43–44
Paisley, Ian 164
Parry, Colin (NIAC witness) 116
Pat Finucane Centre 112, 117, 131
peace process 2–3, 62, 174; role of victims 89–90
peace process, Northern Ireland 4, 91; since Belfast Agreement 91–97; destabilizing influences 143; differences in reparation 88; past grievances and 99; provision for reparations 88; readiness 5, 144; stalemate, 96, 97–99; *see also* Northern Ireland Affairs Committee
perception: violence and 30–31
perpetrators 4; acknowledgement of their role 73; amnesty for 13; Borer's conceptualisation of 79; claim to victimhood 80, 81; confessions of responsibility 11; shame of 53–54
personal danger: armed conflicts and 57
personal truth *see* narrative truth
Pirabakaran, Velupillai 55
Police Ombudsman for Northern Ireland Report 34–35, 63–64, 154–155, 160
Police Service of Northern Ireland (PSNI) 14
political leadership: Northern Ireland 97–98
political stability: impact of truth recovery process on 5
politics: de-legitimisation of violence 62–63; public opinion and 32; shame and 46–48; truth and 31–33
post traumatic stress disorder (PTSD): diagnostic category of 70–72
Potter, Michael (NIAC witness) 132
Pound, Stephen 130
Prevention of Terrorism Act (UK) 25
principle of job 75–76
Progressive Unionist Party 164, 167, 168
propaganda war: victimisation and 78–79
psychotropic drugs: distress associated with trauma and 72; for management of unhappiness 70
public education: media and 11–12
public opinion: in Northern Ireland on truth recovery process 143–144, 153; politics and 32; truth and 32, 84
Purvis, Dawn 167

Queen's University, Human Rights Centre: members' evidence to NIAC 115–116, 127

Rawding, Andrew, Reverend (NIAC witness): concerns about government's motivation for truth recovery 127–128; on reconciliation 135; on value of truth recovery process 117–118, 122
Rea, Desmond 154, 160
readiness/ripeness for truth recovery 5, 144–146, 178–179
readiness/ripeness for truth recovery, Northern Ireland's 144, 178; indicators 146–147; internal politics and position of the parties 150; parties' overall level of authority and responsibility 150–151; third party intervention and 147–150
reconciliation: NIAC's witnesses concerns about 127, 134–138; South African TRC and 138–139; truth recovery and 176–177
Red Hand Commando 112, 155
Reilly, Clara (NIAC witness) 112
Relatives for Justice (RFJ) 125; concerns about government motivation to truth recovery 128; memoranda to NIAC 117
religion: truth and 23–24
reparations 16, 89; evidence to NIAC on 132; qualifications for 79, 88; refusal to accept 73–74, 88
Republicans of Northern Ireland: allegations of spying by 143; attitude towards Unionist grievances 96–97; external influences on 149; fatalities pattern 100–104; grievances of 92; internal politics of 159; position on truth recovery process 156–159; responsibility for killings 150; suffering 106; support for truth recovery process 116–117
resistance: shame at inadequate efforts at 49–50
responsibility: collective 124–125, 179; IRA's responsibility for fatalities 106; Loyalists responsibility for killings 150, 187 n.9; Northern Ireland parties' responsibility for deaths 105, 150; perpetrators confessions 11
restorative justice 28, 180
restorative truth 28
retaliation: rule of 56
retributive justice 2, 56, 175, 179–180

Ribeiro, Chris 13
Ribiero, Fabian 171
Ringland, Trevor (NIAC witness) 125, 129
ripeness for truth recovery *see* readiness/ripeness for truth recovery
Ritchie, Mike (NIAC witness) 117, 134–135
Rivers, W.H.R. 71, 72
Roberts, Tom (NIAC witness) 112; on collective responsibility 124–125; on distrust of Republicans motives in supporting truth recovery 123; on past involvement in UVF 113–114; on timing of truth recovery process 121; on value of truth recovery to Loyalists 124
Robinson, Andrew (NIAC witness) 119
Rwanda: Hutu organised lying 35–36

Sachs, Albie 138–139
Saville Inquiry *see* Bloody Sunday Inquiry
Scappaticci, Alfredo 36
Schroeder, Gerhard: apology for Warsaw uprising 43
Scott Report: into 'Arms-to-Iraq' affair 47
security dilemma 94
shame 4, 40–41; Apartheid and 41–42; contemporary significance 46; Cooley on 45; degradation and 50–51; efforts to encourage 64–65; Eliasian 44–45, 61, 175; German identity and 42–44; honour and 54–57; naming and shaming 47–48; at non-participation 49; notion of 44–46; origins of 45; at others' deeds 51–53; perpetrators' 53–54; in post-conflict period 62–64; in public domain 46–48; role in transformation process 61; in social domain 62; truth recovery and 65–66; during war and armed conflict 48–53, 57–62, 65
Sharpeville massacre (S. Africa) 29
Shot at Dawn Campaign (UK) 55
silence 26–27, 33–34
Sinn Féin 35, 92, 116, 137, 172; position on truth recovery process 156–159; rivalry between SDLP and 159
Smith, William (NIAC witness) 112, 121, 123
Smyth, Martin (NIAC member) 109, 110, 112

social control: shame's role in 64–65
social dedifferentiation 60
Social Democratic and Labour Party (SDLP): position on truth recovery process 156–157; rivalry between Sinn Féin and 159
societal security dilemma 93–95
South Africa: continuation of violence 120; transitional society 41
South African Defence Force (SADF): organised lying 36
South African Truth and Reconciliation Commission (TRC): FAIR's views on 130; forgiveness and 17–18, 176; healing and 84; provision for reparations 88; resistance to participation and 170–171; a restorative process 28; rituals of reconciliation 138–139; typology of truth and 22, 25–26, 27–28; victim/perpetrator identification 79; victims' need for acknowledgement and 73
Spratt, Jimmy 63–64
Stephens report 143
stereotype victims 74–76, 176; deconstruction of 80–81
Stobie, William 143
Stone, Michael 18
storytelling 26, 129, 133; value in truth recovery process 118, 120
suffering: Northern Ireland and 85, 99–106; victim status and 75–76
suspect communities 25
Swift, Bernice (NIAC witness) 140

Tami, Mark (NIAC member) 124
Thompson, Mark (NIAC witness) 112–113, 125, 128
threat to life: conflicts and 57–58
Tim Parry/Jonathan Ball Trust 118, 119
Touchstone Group 77
Training for Women Network 131
traitors 50
transitional justice 1–2; retributive forms of 2
transitional societies 7–8; South Africa 41
trauma 69; polarised views of 71–72; war-related 70
truth: conflicts and 30; dialogical 27–28, 175; forensic 25–26; legal concept of 24; narrative 26, 175; nature of 22–23; notion of 4, 175; philosophical concept of 22–23; in political domain 31–33;

power of 38–39; public opinion and 32, 84; religious concept of 23–24; restorative 28; shame and 65–66; victims' desire for 28–30
truth recovery 1–2, 3–4, 174–175; civil society's role in 16–17; confessions and 11; damage distribution and 9; discourses and 8, 9–11; forgiveness and 17–20, 176; functions of 4, 6, 20–21; hindsight and 33–34; impact on political stability 5; impunity and 12–14; learning from the past and 15; potential disincentives to violence and 8–9; potential for ending denial and 6–8; readiness/ripeness for 144–146, 178; reparations and 16; resistance to 34, 35; societal reconciliation and 176–177; victim's role in 4, 16, 20
Truth Recovery: A Contribution From Loyalism 164–167
truth recovery process 6–7, 177; proliferation of 174; state-sponsored 3; timing and 34–35
truth recovery process, German 53–54
truth recovery process, Guatemalan 169
truth recovery process, Honduran 169
truth recovery process, Northern Ireland 4–5, 107, 177–178, 180–181; British government position on 140–142, 144, 151–155; concerns about models of 125–127, 152, 179; deferment of 118–122, 171; healing and 85; impact on relationships 5; inclusivity 128–129; internal politics and position of parties 150–151; Irish government position on 155–156; Loyalist opposition to 122–125; Loyalist position on 164–167; Nationalist support for 115–116, 117–118; provision for reparations 88; readiness/ripeness for 5; readiness/ripeness indicators for 146–147, 178; relative benefits and costs 129; Republican position on 156–159; Republican support for 117, 123; resistance to 169, 171–173, 178; role of victims and victim centredness 129–132; third party intervention and 147–150; Unionist opposition to 115, 118–122; Unionist position on 159–164
truth recovery process, South African: forgiveness and 17–18, 86, 87; healing and 84; provision for reparations 88

Tullyvallen Community Association 136
Tutu, Desmond 34, 169; role in promotion of Christian forgiveness 17, 18, 87

Ulster Unionist Party (UUP) 106; Allister's attack on 163; Assembly elections 2007 164; rivalry between DUP and 167–168; Unionist Group 162–163
Ulster Volunteer Force 55
Unionists of Northern Ireland: attitude to paramilitary groups 168; decommissioning of IRA weapons and 63, 92, 96; divergent attitudes to Belfast Agreement 167; fears about Good Friday Agreement 97–98; fears about IRA 152, 160; grievances and fears of 92, 97–98; largest volume of evidence to NIAC 110; opposition to truth recovery process 115, 118–122; position on truth recovery process 159–164; suffering 105–106
United Nations Commission on Human Rights (UNHRC): on British government's responsibility in Northern Ireland 147–148; naming and shaming 47–48
United Nations Special Rapporteur on Summary and Arbitrary Executions 147
United States: Northern Ireland situation and 147, 149

victim(s) 67; anger of 68–69; association with insurgency and 77; British-based victims of Northern Ireland 116, 131–132; construction of complex victim 82–84; cultures of victimhood 79–80; deconstruction of stereotypes of 80–81; desire for truth 28–30; identity 67–69, 77–78; identity complexities 79–80, 81–82; legitimacy 76–79; moral superiority and 74–75, 87, 176; portrayal of conflict in Northern Ireland 95–96; in 'reality television' programmes 18; reparations, refusal to accept 73–74, 88; reparations and 73–74; role in any settlement and in post-conflict developments 89–90; role in truth recovery processes 4, 16, 20, 176; status 75–76; stereotypical conceptualisations 74–76, 176
victim blaming 81
victim discourses 78–79

victim needs 84–85, 176; categories of 69; medical 70–73, 132; need for acknowledgement 73; need for justice 73; in Northern Ireland 86
Victims Liaison Unit 77
victims voluntary groups, Northern Ireland 76–77; support for truth recovery process 115–116, 117
violence: continuation in South Africa 120; creation of potential disincentives to 8–9; 'custom of violence' 62–63; de-legitimisation of political 62–63; distribution of 9; effects of 68; facilitation of 7, 58; honour-related 56; influence on personal life 58–59; methods of dealing with 7; NIAC's stand on 113–114; in Northern Ireland conflict 4, 99–106; perception and 30–31; shame as deterrent to 4; spatial concentration of political 68; victimhood and legitimisation of 80
voluntary groups: for victims in Northern Ireland 76–77, 115–116, 117
Vorster, Thomas 41

warrior honour 4; shame and 54–57, 175; WWI British soldiers 55–56
WAVE: members' evidence to NIAC 111, 126, 130, 131
Wilkinson, Oliver (NIAC witness) 119
Wilson, Gordon 19
Wilson, Robin (NIAC witness) 122
Wilson, Sammy (NIAC member) 109

Yealland, Leonard 71, 72

eBooks – at www.eBookstore.tandf.co.uk

A library at your fingertips!

eBooks are electronic versions of printed books. You can store them on your PC/laptop or browse them online.

They have advantages for anyone needing rapid access to a wide variety of published, copyright information.

eBooks can help your research by enabling you to bookmark chapters, annotate text and use instant searches to find specific words or phrases. Several eBook files would fit on even a small laptop or PDA.

NEW: Save money by eSubscribing: cheap, online access to any eBook for as long as you need it.

Annual subscription packages

We now offer special low-cost bulk subscriptions to packages of eBooks in certain subject areas. These are available to libraries or to individuals.

For more information please contact webmaster.ebooks@tandf.co.uk

We're continually developing the eBook concept, so keep up to date by visiting the website.

www.eBookstore.tandf.co.uk